GARRETT HONGO's
VOLCANO

"Passionate, wrought, often inspired . . . Hongo's book of origins is a work of beauty and consolation."
—*Los Angeles Times Book Review*

"Garrett Hongo's *Volcano* is a memoir of his homecoming to a place that was never home, a natural and human history of extraordinary visual acuity." —*The New Yorker*

"Rich, varied. . . . Hongo takes his cue from the volcano itself, the flows that fold in on themselves, creating new forms by building on the old." —*Chicago Tribune*

"Hongo writes with equal skill about the lush beauty of Hawaii and the rage and emptiness with which he struggled for most of his life. . . . The prose is so rich that one feels, hears and sees what is described: the imagery of the rain forest, the vivid dreams Hongo recounts." —*San Jose Mercury News*

"A strikingly elegant family history, shot through with a poet's appreciation of Hawaiian geology. . . . Lyrical and aching in all the right measures, a finely crafted piece of work distilled to its essence." —*Kirkus Reviews*

ALSO BY GARRETT HONGO

POETRY

The River of Heaven
Yellow Light

ANTHOLOGIES

The Open Boat: Poems from Asian America
Songs My Mother Taught Me: Stories, Memoir, and Plays by Wakako Yamauchi

GARRETT HONGO

*V*OLCANO

Garrett Hongo attended Pomona College, the
University of Michigan, and the University of
California at Irvine, where he received a Master of
Fine Arts degree in English. He is a professor at
the University of Oregon, where he was Director
of the Program in Creative Writing from 1989 to
1993. He is the author of two books of poetry,
Yellow Light and *The River of Heaven*. He lives in
Eugene, Oregon.

VOLCANO

A Memoir of Hawai'i

GARRETT HONGO

VINTAGE DEPARTURES

Vintage Books

A Division of Random House, Inc.

New York

for *Alexander* and *Hudson,*
and to the memory of my father,
Albert Kazuyoshi Hongo

He mana'o he aloha, ea. . . .

All rights reserved under International and Pan-American Copyright Conventions. Published in the
United States by Vintage Books, a division of Random House, Inc., New York, and simultaneously
in Canada by Random House of Canada Limited, Toronto. Originally published in the United
States in hardcover by Alfred A. Knopf, Inc., New York, in 1995.

"Kubota" was originally published in a slightly different form in *Ploughshares* in 1990.

Grateful acknowledgment is made to the following for permission to reprint previously published
material:

Clayton Eshleman: Excerpt of poem from *Human Poems* by César Vallejo, translated by Clayton
Eshleman (Grove Press, 1968). Reprinted by permission of Clayton Eshleman.

Alfred A. Knopf, Inc: Excerpt from *The River of Heaven* by Garrett Hongo, copyright © 1981, 1983,
1985, 1986, 1987, 1988 by Garrett Hongo. Reprinted courtesy of Alfred A. Knopf, Inc.

The Library of Congress has cataloged the Knopf edition as follows:
Hongo, Garrett Kaoru, [date]
Volcano : a memoir of Hawai'i / by Garrett Hongo.
p. cm.
ISBN 0-394-57167-3
1. Hongo, Garrett Kaoru, [date]. 2. Volcano (Hawaii)—Social life and customs. 3. Volcano
(Hawaii)—Biography. 4. Japanese Americans—Hawaii—Volcano—Biography. I. Title.
DU628.V65H66 1995
996.9'04'092—dc20
[B] 95-8183 CIP
Vintage ISBN: 679-76748-7

Random House Web address: http://www.randomhouse.com/

Printed in the United States of America

CONTENTS

PROLOGUE:
'AUANA AND KAHIKO

*I WAS SIX, living with my parents and younger brother in an apart-
ment house in midtown Los Angeles. There were other Japanese
families from Hawai'i and I had cousins around, aunts and uncles, who
came mostly from plantation towns that neighbored ours on O'ahu—
Waialua, Wahiawā, Sunset Beach, Hale'iwa, and Lā'ie. King Sugar
had died in Hawai'i and his subjects had all dispersed—some to town
in Honolulu, some to the military, some to the Mainland seeking new
jobs, new ways of life. Our shacks were gone, so we found stuccoed
apartment buildings in Los Angeles.*

*Around us, in other buildings nearby, in small houses and large
houses divided up into multiplexes, there were families from Mexico,
Korea, Hong Kong, and Mississippi. We were on a bus route to down-*

town. We were a few blocks from my school. We were under palm and eucalyptus and jacaranda trees, bracketed among crowned asphalt streets and alleyways crowded with bins of fetid trash. At night, I could hear the neighbor televisions bursting with the whistling flight of super-heroes. Grease spattered alive in a skillet on a stove in another kitchen I could hear through the screen of our kitchen door, and on our window-sill, a wooden bar aflame with the light from outside shining upon it, I counted out a row of several avocado seeds germinating in a set of teacups and jelly jars. When we went to the market, we got Green Stamps. My "home job" was to paste them into books. My "outside job" was to do well in school. My mother helped me by teaching me "Mainland English," the mother dialect of the Hawaiian pidgin (a creole) that I grew up speaking.

We are seated at the kitchen table by the humming refrigerator, next to the tiered coffee cart that housed a toaster, an automatic rice cooker, and a lazy Susan filled with sugar cubes, tea bags, a bramble of toothpicks, and packets of Kool-Aid. She teaches me fricatives, gives me exercises, shows me where to place my tongue against my teeth. I say there, there, there, constructing a calisthenic phalanx of enuncia-tions. I say earth. I say with. She teaches me to flatten the melody of my speaking, taking the lilt of Portuguese from my sentences, the singsong of Canton Chinese. I extract the hard, clipped vowel-oriented syllables of Hawaiian, saying poor, not pu-a. I have to soften my tongue to shape it around the new way of saying words, to make it shape itself in my mouth more quickly so that I can make more sounds, smaller sounds, faster sounds in a sentence that has to flutter the way a mullet swims, almost surreptitiously, through lagoons of syntax rather than churning through the blunt reef of my thinking like ulua, a jack crevalle that hunts, like speaking pidgin.

Mainland English is more like 'auana, my mother says, like the swaying breeze-through-the-trees of wandering hula danced to a wavy *melodic song. Hawaiian English is like* kahiko, *the ancient dance, the* kanaka *dance of tradition, she says, harsh moves, slaps, and full of pounding force. So, in* English, *I say, "I'm going to school now," flattening the music, softening the cadence, shallowing the explosiveness of the vowels. I would say, "I go* scuuul *now" in pidgin, "I go* Main'lan', *I go* ahhs-sighde," *running out to play in the afternoon rain shower.*

She was taught by a schoolmarm from Illinois who came to the plantation town where my mother grew up. The teacher was a tall, handsome woman who became principal of the plantation school, and she took on my mother, a tomboy in the fourth grade. My mother played coconut baseball, a game that combined the action of lawn bowling with the rules, competitive object, distribution of players, and playing field of the national sport. She rolled a brown coconut, stripped of its husk, by her sisters occupying the infield, by the other boys and girls scattered around the rest of the diamond, and skipped it by the sand patches around shortstop into the short grass of the outfield. She shouted I make heet! I make heet! and ran the bases, scoring ahead of the coconut, rolling back from the edge of tall canes out in left field. Her teacher found her, took her out of those games, got her books and into social clubs, took her for trips into Honolulu, taught her to enunciate r's and l's, coached her on accent and grammar, on a way of speaking with the elongated syntax of standard American English. My mother would graduate high school, she said. She would perhaps go to college. *Proper English was the key.*

"No pidgin!" my mother would say, turning from the pot of nishime on the stove and back to me at the kitchen table. She held up her forefinger and waggled it like a frond of bamboo. She smiled with encouragement, staring me down.

I said a short sentence—The teevee is on. *I said,* Rain falls the same here as it falls in Hawai'i. *A long sentence,* kahiko *out of my voice.*

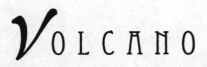

VOLCANO

ŪGETSU

I WAS BORN in the village of Volcano, in the back room of the kitchen of a general store my grandfather built on Volcano Road, twenty-nine miles from Hilo on the Big Island of Hawai'i, the newest in the mid-Pacific chain its first human settlers called *Hava-iti,* a name which means, in their ritualized language, "the Realm of the Dead" or, more simply, "Paradise." Volcano is a settlement in the fern and *'ōhi'a* rain forests bordering two active volcanoes—Kīlauea, a huge caldera and chain of craters leading eastward to the sea, and Mauna Loa, a magnificent earthen shield that places the entire landscape under its shadow, gathering its republic of rain clouds by midafternoon every day, and, at thirteen thousand feet above sea level, the largest volcanic mass in the world. I could have grown up here, in this natural garden and amphitheater for fire, fountains and rain, except that there was some family quarrel which made my parents leave with me when I was eight months old. We ran off first to Oʻahu and my mother's fam, ily, and then, finally, to Los Angeles in California, with its foreign culture and ways of anonymity. I'd grown up there, ci, pherously, a child of immigrants to the Mainland, and, for half a lifetime, I knew nothing of the family history or the volca, noes I was born under. I was past thirty when I first returned, and the place astonished me.

Volcano is a big chunk of the sublime I'd been born to— the craters and ancient firepit and huge black seas of hardened lava, the rain forest lush with all varieties of ferns, orchids, ex, otic gingers, and wild lilies, the constant rain and sun,showers all dazzled me, exalted me. And, at nearly four thousand feet, its climate was strangely *cool,* the sweltering tropics several cli, matic zones below, so that temperatures stayed in the high six, ties during the day, sometimes dropping to the low forties by early morning. While outdoors, the villagers all wore flannels and sweatshirts and corduroy trousers—mountaineering clothes. During that first visit, Volcano seemed to me an exotic and slightly miraculous place that I associated with the Macondo of García Márquez, the Macchu Picchu of Pablo Neruda. There was something magical about it—a purgatorial mount in the middle of the southern ocean—and there was something of it native to me, an insinuation of secret and violent origins and an aboriginal past.

My first trip back was a pilgrimage, an exploration, and a reunion. I'd come from Honolulu the evening before, after fly, ing in from Los Angeles, where I was teaching, and stayed in

Hilo on the Big Island for a day. The next night, I gave a poetry reading in the local courthouse, a strange venue that
matched the strangeness of my being there over thirty years since
its clerk had registered my birth. It stormed while I read, and
my words felt sad and ineffectual under the sizzle of rain.
Cousins came, adults who'd grown up completely differently
than I and were as unknown to me as I must have been to
them. And my father's two sisters were there, women as different in their beauty as orchid and ginger flowers. This was the
first time I'd met these relatives, yet I felt accepted by them.
They had known me as an infant, and I wondered if they'd attended my birth.

They were bright, handsome people with the gracious island manners I remembered from my childhood. My uncle had
met me at the airport and, though he was over seventy, had insisted on carrying my bags to the car. I could have stayed at a
hotel—the university would have paid—but he brought me to
his home and fed me a fine dinner, inviting all his children,
each grown and with their own families. I was nearly over-
whelmed by all the attention and the respect I felt it meant for
my father.

The next day, my aunt and uncle chauffeured me the
twenty-nine miles upslope from Hilo through the intervening
villages to Volcano. I felt as if I were stepping back in time.
We drove through a misty rain past canefields and open scars
of dark, volcanic soil by the roadside, harvest vehicles idle along
the gravel shoulders. Along the way, passing clusters of plantation huts, Quonset barracks, and the few Japanese-style
houses bordering the road, I thought back to the stories I'd
heard all through my childhood, to my father's life, and then
forward into my own. So many things I was seeing and hear-

ing seemed like relics—either from a distant, almost mytholog⁄
ical past or else from my own dreams. I felt as if I were enter⁄
ing a book about my own life.

In the middle of a vacant field by the modern airport was
a swaybacked palomino hitched to a Chevy's rear axle. Down
a dirt road through a canefield was a single shack under its tin
roof shaded by banana and papaya trees. Above us all, the huge
sky was azure at one end over the sea, but at its other, by the
mountain, it was crowded with a parade of lavender rain
clouds, tufted welts like an elaborate garland of purple orchids.
Working at my desk by the beach in L.A., it took all I had to
bring pictures like these up from memory, "cracking my
brains," as W. B. Yeats might say. But here, all I needed was
to look around, and the past—historical or familial—and my
own childhood were tangible as the mirror⁄beads of rain streak⁄
ing against the car window.

I wiped the fog from the glass and saw through to the
plantation past and the residue of all the years of immigration
and settlement. Architecture, it seemed, followed history.
Houses looked either vaguely Oriental—a garden out front with
its stone lantern and small, decorative thicket of bamboo, a shel⁄
tered porch and upswept eaves to a roof somehow too large and
highly peaked, as if an oversized medieval Japanese warrior's
helmet had been placed over flimsy walls—or else plantation⁄
influenced, with low windows and a boxlike construction re⁄
sembling an elongated shotgun or a compressed Grange hall. I
thought about my great⁄grandfathers, second sons and dispos⁄
sessed, overtaxed farmers coming over from Hiroshima and
Fukuoka to work here as laborers on the sugar plantations of
Castle and Cooke, C. Brewer, and the Campbell Estate. I
imagined rows of workers in khakis, hands wrapped in gauze,

stooping over the land, hoeing the earth into furrows and chanting work songs about coal mines, hauling nets, or ferrying the
souls of the dead out to a burial at sea. I thought of calligraphy
on a passport, of destinations and points of origin recorded on
a labor contract, and dual citizenships noted on a birth certificate. On the line designated for such things, my own certificate
listed "29 Miles, Volcano Highway"—the surveyed distance
between Hilo and the Hongo Store—in block capital letters as
my place of birth. Now, I was going back there.

At Glenwood, a crossroads where a light concentration of
farmhouses and the wayside of a general store and gas station
lined the highway, the climate suddenly became much cooler.
The highway vegetation was much more dense as well—the
cleared canelands and pasture lined with short stands of brushy
eucalyptus lower down gave way to a section shaded by a
canopy of gigantic *koa* trees interspersed with myrtle and eucalyptus growing almost as tall. At about twenty-five hundred
feet, Glenwood marked the first zone on the trip upslope that
had little of the tropical in it and much more of the rainy mountain. The fogs here were much more dense, as if we'd driven
into the cloudline, that band of foul weather which almost constantly surrounded the volcano. Glenwood was its main catch.

The highway was cut through a magical wood. What I
saw then I'd see repeated in the rain and cloud forest everywhere
from this transitional elevation up to the summit at four thousand feet. It was a visual sonata, lavish and detailed as any jungle fantasy painted by Henri Rousseau. The forest had three
distinct layers—the upper canopy of high trees (sometimes *koa*
and eucalyptus, more commonly *'ōhi'a,* the native myrtle with
leaves like green doubloons and trunkskins, stripped of their
bark, which were smooth and sensuous as eucalyptus and sil-

very white) thirty feet or more above the ground; then, ten to fifteen feet high, the mid-canopy of broad-leaved tree ferns called
hāpu'u, each of their boughs stark and individual as a green
eagle's wing; and, finally, the diverse understory of low-lying
natives and exotics, grasses and emerald mosses and bamboo
orchids with the fleshy white-and-purple flowers that looked
like tiny Korean wedding gowns. Here in Glenwood, the understory was made of dense bamboo thickets and Brazilian
lasiandra bushes flowering with its peacock's-eyes of violet blossoms. This was a special microzone of climate and vegetation,
the thick brakes of feathery-leaved, sallow-stalked bamboo re-
minding me of woodblocks of Chinese forests, pandas and
tigers posed against a backdrop of intricately carved underbrush.
The richest color, though, came from the green fronds of ginger plants growing by the side of the road. Their flowers were
either sparse and an almost pure white, looking like delicate
origami cranes, or else yellow and full of splendor, blossoming
in huge chandeliers of ray and petal, torchlike over the green
sleeves of the forest.

I was nervous. In spite of all the beauty I was seeing—
the dense mists, that sublime promise of a volcano up ahead—
I had a growing sense of unease about the place. I felt I'd be
dispersed somehow, separated into molecules, rushing to meet
some shadow of myself like Shelley's Alastor, that symbol of
the poet's pure spirit encountering its own demonic incubus. I
was going through an initiation of some kind, and I wasn't
quite ready. Everything was such a surprise and revelation and
yet so familiar as well, as if I were recalling something I didn't
know—a premonition or an event foretold.

I thought about a couple of photographs I'd seen once.
Years ago, while we still lived in the apartment house on

Olympic in Los Angeles, my father had shown me a dozen or so small prints like slips of glossy paper or large metallic stamps. They were cut from a proof sheet of 35-mm film shot on an old Leica he'd brought back from Germany after the war. There was a shot of me, only months old and naked, being dunked into a river or pool by my mother, who was dressed in some kind of one-piece bathing suit in a style made popular by Esther Williams. It was just a few months after she'd given birth, but she looked as petite as in her high school pictures. I always thought this took place at Rainbow Falls, but this couldn't be true since I knew it would have been impossible to wade in the deep and rough waters of the Wailuku River there. Rainbow Falls was the cascade the river made as it fell from one layer of an old lava bed to another, thirty feet or more below. Water ran across the hollow of an old lava tube and then down to a murky pool which frothed and swirled strenuously before it gave way to its main course toward the sea. It must have been a joke of my father's, naming some local creek after the grander stream.

Another photograph was of my father and me in front of the Hongo Store, which was started in Volcano by my grand-father Torau Hongo before the war and run, at the time the pic-ture was taken, by my mother and father. My father held me, a naked newborn clasped between the side of his head and an up-raised arm, sitting on his shoulder. He had the incredible grin on his face I somehow always associated with his being from Hawai'i, it was so unabashed. I called it his "Lucky Come" smile after that phrase I used to hear around the house some-times—"Lucky *come* Hawai'i!"—as if the islands were the Buddha's Western Paradise, a pure land of imminent enlight-enment and salvation. Perhaps it was. My father's face sure made it seem so, benign and completely unself-conscious. A toothpick dangled from his lower lip like a Bogart cigarette. And I grinned too—or my mouth made a grin. My eyes were startled, astonished, as a newborn's often look. Perplexed. "In the still cave of the witch Poesy," as romantic Shelley described the dissociation of the poet's consciousness, the fracturing of identity in a dreamscape—everything a new and bewildering experience. Behind us there are gas pumps with their cranks and dials and rubber hoses. The "7" half of the oil company 76 peeked out over my father's other shoulder. And the whole shot was framed by the two stone pillars that supported the front and the overhang roof of the store. These were beach-smoothed lava rocks and mortar shaped into tall, quadrilateral pyramids under the beams of the store's entryway. They'd been there awhile and would be for a while longer.

In the mid-seventies, while I was living in Seattle and trying to survive running a theater group, a friend of mine from the troupe had visited Hongo Store—it became a famous stopping-place along Volcano Road between Hilo and the crater. The store was a hangout for idlers of all sorts and the tour buses stopped there for snacks and beverages. The local post office was there too. My grandfather had sold liquor and prepared food (mostly Japanese things like beef *teriyaki* and shrimp *tempura*) as well as groceries and dry goods, so a clientele of tourists, on-leave military, and village malingerers had built up as the day trade over the years. It had acquired a reputation through the islands as the one stop you could make before you reached the volcano. My friend had visited, poked around the shelves a little, talked to the gruff man who owned it then and held position behind the counter, and then stepped outside to snap off a couple of shots on his camera. What he brought back to me were photographs of the Coca-Cola sign under the new awning that had been put up over the store's old façade. It obscured and placed under shadow what was once, as you cruised by it and rubbernecked from the highway, the locally famous legend that said HONGO STORE.

In the thirties, when my grandfather had started his business, Coke would press out or paint on a sign for any storekeeper in the world whatever they wanted so long as that storekeeper stocked its cola. My grandfather, being cheap and expeditious when it came to business, took the company up on its offer and got one of those signs. On one end was an apple-cheeked brunette seeming to accept the outsized bottle of Coke from a crew-cut blond gentleman in a tan suit. He smiled cheerfully, almost rakishly—a little like the Hirschfeld cartoon of a suave Gilbert Roland—raising the soda skyward in a grand gesture of a toast. At the other end was the famous red shield and white speed-lettering that was the Coca-Cola logo, and, between them—the handsome Caucasian couple and the well-known trademark—were the black pyramid letters and green highlighting that read HONGO STORE. It was this picture from the seventies that I carried in my mind as I rode uphill.

Soon enough, I found myself stepping into that picture. We'd driven nearly the entire distance, climbing slowly from sea level to nearly four thousand feet, following the well-repaired road as it cut through canelands and rain forests, traversing old lavas from both Mauna Loa and Kīlauea. My uncle turned off the highway and onto another road that paralleled it—"old" Volcano Road, he said, bypassed in the sixties. We passed a few ramshackle homes, one with a greenhouse in the front yard and all of them seeming to be crumbling under the weight of several decades of steady rain. Parked in the graveled drive of another place was the rusting pickup that seemed the obligatory lawn toy in these parts. My uncle pulled over slowly after a few hundred yards of this and cruised his Oldsmobile to a stop on the asphalt lot beside the building where I was born.

I got out, crossing the parking lot in a few steps, breathing deeply of the cool mountain air, and walked around to the front of the store. I saw the gas pumps, new ones now and not the glassdomed ones I remembered from the photograph, but they were in the places where I expected them to be. And the lava rock pillars were there, painted over with a yellow spray paint, but still there. And the sign. I looked up above the broad entrance door and I saw the sign, its paint flecked and its surface decorated with blossoms of rust but still there, still with our name on it. I felt a rush of feeling, and I almost bowed as I crossed the threshold, recalling the gesture of *gasshō,* a simple handstogether genuflection I learned when I lived in the temple back in Japan my first year after college. But I didn't bow. I entered the store simply, without ceremony, and I felt as if I were going back in time.

I saw low shelves painted a light green and stocked with canned goods and bins for grains and flour. I moved through the aisles and glanced over the hardware—batteries, small hand axes, flashlights, mousetraps, saws and hammers and boxes of nails, screwdrivers and wrenches and garden gloves, tins of allpurpose oil and tubs of hand cleanser. There were gas mantle lanterns painted green and red, familiar to me from summer camping trips, and a portable stove, cans of lighter fluid and white gas. I picked out something—a dozen boxes of wooden matches wrapped together in a gray paper with a seal that had the profile of a medieval knight as its emblem. I took them from the shelf, wanting something from the place that had always meant my name, took them up to the counter, and paid the sixty-five cents plus tax that they cost. It was to be a token of mine through the next few years, a relic from the old store, a crude incense to an abandoned shrine.

The cashier, a woman with long brown hair who was approaching middle age, rang up my purchase on an electric machine. I imagined my grandfather would have had a large black register of cast-iron housing and with round keys on long metal prongs hard to push down. Or would he have used a *soroban*—an abacus of hard, enameled wood? I looked through the door propped open with a cardboard box filled with newspapers by the side of the counter and on through to the back room of the store. It was a kitchen with a badly worn and stained linoleum floor that was peeling loose and rotten with mildew at the corners and edges. An old refrigerator, rounded and domed like a fifties jukebox, stood against one wall. There was a wooden table, shaped like a butcher block, and a chair or two all painted that same light, high-luster green of all the shelves in the store. And beyond these was a concrete double-sink like that of a laundry room under the rusty screened windows in the far wall. I saw all of this in a glance, wondering if I might have been born there, in that room, on the green butcher-block table.

I moved through the aisles and saw tiny cans of corned beef and lunch meat, Norwegian sardines and Hawaiian tuna. There was a cooler at the front by the counter full of hams, briskets, and a large uncut rib roast. It seemed a little like a Mainland deli, except its contents were sparser and more exotic—the light, chocolate-colored paste pounded from taro root called *poi* set alongside the macaroni salad in plastic bags. There was a Pepsi logo sign at the back of the counter on the far wall.

It had the names and prices of sandwiches marked on it in movable, lunch-stand lettering.

When my father managed the store, he made a run into Hilo every day, stocking up on his canned goods and produce, but also picking up fresh *tōfu* and *tempura,* cold bean curd in ten-gallon, galvanized cans and deep-fried shrimps already cleaned and butterflied which he cooked in sweet yellow skins of batter. There was *sushi* too, though not the kind in current fashion. These were made up in large rolls of black seaweed stuffed with the vinegared rice that itself held a varicolored core of pink shrimp powder, tiny slices of carrot and watercress, marinated eel meat, and a long yellow spine of fried egg sweetened with sugar and the distilled spirits of millet. My mother would slice small circular cakes out of the long black rolls of *sushi,* revealing the tiny blossoms of color in their mantle and core, arranging them as ziggurats on brown lunch-stand plates for the policemen and farmers and other villagers who'd drop in. By the looks of this deli counter, I guessed that folks must still come by and that the store had somehow kept the goodwill of the village.

I left the store with my purchase—that talismanic set of kitchen matches—and walked around its outside. I looked for the window that had cracked once, and found none as large as the one in the picture in my mind. These windows were smaller and in different positions. Bins of produce and a table covered with cut lilies, anthuriums, and orchids in baskets and two-gallon mayonnaise jars crowded the sidewalk outside the front of the store. I looked across the street to the cedar trees and the undergrowth of bramble and thought about what it might have been like to have grown up here.

My aunt, who had been busying herself looking through the flowers, noticed I'd come out of the store. She pointed across the asphalt of the parking lot ponded with rain puddles to the thicket of flowering green bramble crowding over the chain-link fence at the property line.

"That's the flower we had here when I was a girl," she said. "We called it *mi-no-sabi* because we didn't know its name."

I looked across the lot to the deeply violet, morning-glory-like flowers sprouting from herbaceous stalks of green. We walked across the lot together, and I stepped to the fence to pick one of the blossoms. It had four petals that were truly indigo and symmetrically arranged around a yellow center. There were fine reddish-shading-to-purple stamens at its core, almost hairs, in postures that suggested Arabic script. I held it to my nose, but noticed no fragrance.

"No smell, yeah?" my aunt said, her voice lilting in the pattern of gracious island speech. "Such a pretty flower and yet no scent."

"What's its common name?" I asked, still holding on to it, turning it over in my hands.

"I don't know!" she answered. "We just called it that— *mi-no-sabi*—broken Spanish for 'I don't know'!" and she laughed a little at the old joke.

I laughed with her, but another idea had already begun to insinuate itself into my thinking. In Japanese, *mi-no-sabi* had a meaning too—"the sadness of beauty," or perhaps the "poverty" of it.

I looked down the cinder road that ran alongside the chain-link fence. It disappeared behind a dilapidated garage and storage shed brown with its own rot, its wood turning into sponge under the continual soakings of rain. I remembered my mother had told me several times how, when we were all in

Volcano, the three of us had lived in a house in back of the store, a house built on the old farmland next to a low bog where my grandfather had once tried to raise strawberries. And I knew that his widow, sole inheritor of the family property, my grandfather's third wife and stepmother to my father, still lived back there. I started walking down the cinder drive to where it led.

I rounded the bend down the short road. I saw a small Japanese-style house painted the same light green as the counter shelves in the store. There was my first home. It stood on the gray cinder soil under galvanized sheet-metal roofs with aluminum flumes off its eaves running to three water cisterns sided with cedar shakes. And on the rain-puddled grounds, except for the asphalt drive bisecting the property, was a runaway field of thousands of calla lilies in bloom, floral swans roosting among the bright green stalks that seemed to cover every inch of land around the house. 'Ōhi'a trees grew arroyo-like on the back property line and a thick surf of lasiandra bushes, their violet blossoms like iridescent baitfish boiling in the green face of the wave, seemed to crest in from the rain forest and tumble over the hurricane fence put up to keep it out. A warm mist, blue and then, losing its cerulean hue, shading out to gray, gauze-like in the afternoon light, rolled over all of this. I could tell at once it was a place "of moonlight and rain," as they say in Japan, *ūgetsu,* a world of faery and imagination where the dead might dance in the right light, where the milky river of stars and the swallow-bridge of heaven might set down and be a passageway between this and the afterlife.

There were fogs and fingers of cloud, steam released from the lava-heated earth and rock below, creations of weather and thermal caprice, insubstantial and without outline, forms with no form carried on the wind. I saw ghosts curling in the mists drifting toward me from a grove of cedars downslope and across the field of lilies. It was a gathering in the mists, a past briefly and surreptitiously glimpsed, and they were shades from the realm of the dead I wanted to speak to and have tell me their stories.

This was my father's failed family, apparitions who, for a reason I didn't thoroughly understand, could not become those he'd finally keep as our household gods. They took shape in drifts of light-falling rain moving upslope over rain forests to the volcano. They gambled, playing their cards, tossing quarters and half-dollars back and forth across a lacquered table, taunt-ing each other, squabbling about rules and the accuracy of the tote sheet. They sat on *zabuton*, Japanese floor cushions of batik-dyed cotton and tasseled satin cloth. They sipped tea laced with bourbon and played *hanafuda*—a rummy game of flower-print cards in suits of chrysanthemums, irises, peonies, and fall-colored maple leaves. A gust of wind swept up the cards and then the ghosts too, trailing a line of mist and blossoms of light into the store. Someone began to count up the stock and some-one else complained about the ethics of selling spoiled food at the meat counter.

A plume of cloud, slender but billowing like smoke from a lit cigar, broke off from the rest and took shape—a squat-legged woman dressed in a worn housecoat, a yellow sweater, and a red knit cap. And she wore woolen leggings too, mak-ing her look, with the flat features of her face and a taut swarthi-ness of skin, a little like a Tibetan lama. Her glance was beatific, stupefied as she drifted under the Pepsi sign of the store's deli. She found a rotting ham, its fat gone already green, and began to eat, like a dog, tearing off chunks of it with her

teeth, imploring the others to do the same. My grandfather got
up from his card game, wiping his hands on the lapels of his
light summer gown, and went over to join her. He rose slowly,
stooping up from his cross-legged sitting position to a crouch
and then pushing off with his hands on his knees to achieve
his full height—nearly six feet and extraordinary for a Japanese.
All of this left a young couple alone at the table for an instant,
a man in a T-shirt and dungarees and the woman with bobbed
hair and wearing a housedress. They soon got up too and
drifted toward the forests, mists disappearing in mist.

I wanted to walk after them and into the rain, become
ghost and vapor and haunt the land as the moon and starlight
must, making things luminous and known even in evanescence.
In the rain-drizzled half-acre plush with thousands of calla
lilies, I felt a dreamy clairvoyance that was more than I knew
of any poetry in the mind. When sunlight broke through a fault
line in the clouds, I felt as if a river of stars had showered down
through the living air.

An old story, deep in my memory, had emerged out of the
fogs and into the light. I must have heard it dozens of times
during my childhood. My mother would speak it like a myth
or a fable—one about losses and disappointments—with a
moral that the blood bonds within families are supremely faith-
less and too easily mislead into trusts that are inevitably betrayed. And it is about land, as it is always about land.

It was 1949, and Torau Hongo, my grandfather, had
owned the store for more than twenty years when he found out
he had become ill with throat cancer and would die within a
year's time. He needed help running the business. He called on
my father, at the time a bachelor in Honolulu back from the
war and going to night school on the GI Bill. My father was

working days in an agricultural lab at the University of Hawaii, not making much money. The proposal was that my father would move to Volcano and take over the day-to-day operations of the Hongo Store. In exchange, he would inherit the business and the property around it after his father died. On that promise, my father proposed marriage to my mother. They had met at night school in Honolulu, dated awhile, and slowly begun thinking of a future together. It seemed to make sense. My mother's father was a village storekeeper as well, and every-one liked the Volcano idea.

My parents married in April of 1950 and moved to help run the Hongo Store very soon after that. But Torau had be-come impatient meanwhile, waiting for my father to come, and had hurried to get married himself—to his stock clerk, a woman named only as "Eveline" in the family lore. Eveline was country all the way, a poor woman from a small plantation town on the northern point of Hawai'i. For about six months, my mother and father lived with this older couple, sharing meals, cooking, and cleaning. My mother became pregnant, and, perhaps using the excuse that her body had become more delicate and burdened with a new weight, she stopped helping out around the store. Eveline, the tough, up-country mother-in-law, now my father's stepmother, may have thus begun to resent my parents. All that while, by Eveline's shrewd ac-counting, they had been mounting a secret debt, billed for rent and expenses in her private ledger. Then, only a few months before I was born, Torau Hongo died, leaving behind a will, written in Japanese, that said half his property was to go to his wife and the other half to his son, my father.

But Eveline, as I have always been told, had been waiting with a plan. She had hired a lawyer and an accountant and they contested the will, arguing that, as the surviving widow, she was already due half of the Hongo family property. Tōrau, therefore, could only will half of his share to my father, in effect granting my father a fourth of the entire estate—less than an acre of land and a quarter of the family business. Family lore had it that Eveline then produced the ledger containing the secret debt accrued by my parents during the time they had lived at the Hongo Store—a time spanning just over two years. This secret debt all but wiped out the cash value of my father's share of the property. Eveline claimed that, in fact, my father owed her a few hundred dollars—a debt she would forgive if he promised not to countersue. My parents, bewildered and inexperienced, afraid of lawyers and courts and entanglements, were thus bluffed out of any patrimony. They packed up and left, cutting their losses, leaving the store and a complicated past behind. They took me, born in Volcano just a few months before, off with them to Oʻahu and a new start there among my mother's people. It was Eveline who stayed in Volcano. And, I knew, she was *still* there, living in the house behind the store.

After my aunt, uncle, and I drove away from the Hongo Store, it was this old family story that kept running through my mind as I looked through all the fogs, sun-showers, and blazes of exotic flowers throughout my tour of Volcano. So much had turned dreamlike and was caught up with the past, both in my mind and in the "out there" of the supposedly real world, that I thought how different I had suddenly become to myself, how transported and given back to time, to a place. We drove next to the National Park, out to the high bluff overlooking Kīlauea caldera, and my mind turned, finally, away from reflection to take in the new, earthly things.

I REMEMBER the sky had clouded over, though not quite enough to obscure the grand view. Clouds hovered over the crater, bunched and tufty as they often are around the Golden Gate Bridge in San Francisco. Fogs broke themselves loose and a low bank had settled over the crater and sunk its tendrils like a system of aerial roots in drifting bundles to the crater floor. Tourists trickled in from the parking lot and over to the look⁄out on the ledge of Uwēkahuna Bluff.

Out past the viewpoint, I could see three brown lava ledges scarred by erosion lines giving way to a brown⁄gray floor of rock wider than the eye could see in a single glance. Kīlauea was an immense bowl of old lavas, oxidized brown in huge patches over the years. Its expanse suggested an ocean that had been drained of its water, a biblical scene cut from both Gen⁄esis and the Apocalypse.

A sign attached to the rock wall running alongside the cliff explained that Halemaʻumaʻu—the tremendous sink blotched with sulphurous yellow patches within the caldera it⁄self—had once housed an active, bubbling lake of lava during most of the nineteenth century and on into the early part of the twentieth as well. Mark Twain had come and seen it, describ⁄ing it for readers of the *Sacramento Union* as a "crimson caul⁄dron." Halemaʻumaʻu, a word in Hawaiian that might mean either "House of Ferns" or "House of Fire," seemed an im⁄posing remnant, exactly like an omphalos linking the world and its visceral center to the heavens which were its origin. The cloudbank overhead and small plumes of steam escaping from the crater's cliffsides appeared to confirm the celestial connection.

Kīlauea was an almost pure nothingness—a blankness of scene so complete, its nominal shades of gray, black, and brown all served to heighten the overall effect of its *absence* of genuine, living colors. Here was the sublime in front of me, some huge place of the dead almost three miles long and nearly two miles wide. And Ka'ū Desert, the lava plain stretching out in the western distance beyond the caldera, added its own expanse to make this view seem infinite. I could imagine Joseph Turner trying to capture the tones of black and gray in the seas of lava and the fogs that obscured them. I could also imagine Sesshū, that fourteenth-century Japanese master of the austere, Zen-influenced monochrome style of ink-painting, brushing in the line of spatter ramparts to the south in one long, squiggling sweep of his hand, suggesting the fogs hazing over the broad, tinctured wash. It was obvious to me that here was both inspiration and difficulty brought together in a relentlessly spectacular landscape.

The overcast began to drizzle down lightly, and we piled back into the car to continue along Crater Rim Drive to what would be our last stop circumnavigating the volcano. We pulled into the lookout at Kīlauea Iki, the small crater adjacent to the huge summit caldera of Kīlauea itself. Rain swept in light sheets against the cliffside opposite the parking lot, and as I stepped out of the car and up to the railing along the steep ledge, I felt a cool onrush of air rising from the crater floor. There were scrubby 'ōhi'a hanging over the cliff edge, their flowers like the red crests on a rare crane. They rocked and bobbed in the strong updraft from the crater floor, counterpunching against the stiff shots of the wind. I let the rain spatter against my face, beading my glasses. It swept my hair up in a plume, and, no matter which way I turned, the rain seemed to come

from all directions now, even from below me in sly uppercuts
along the cliffside, droplets blown upward by the wind.
The caldera seemed to create its own weather. Steam from
the vents along the smooth black lava of its surface rose in
straight vertical banners from the floor, flattening into the fist-
and-anvil shapes of thunderheads only as they reached the level
of the crater rim. The rain looked as if it might even be passing
completely over this spot, repulsed by its tricky wind currents.
I wasn't altogether wrong. Rain did fall, if lightly, on the
caldera floor. And though the steam plumes rising upward were
true signals of the air currents there, the slanting, curtain-like
pattern of the gray rain moving laterally like an impromptu
frieze of hooded Franciscans against the far cliffside was not an
illusion. My aunt told me that Kīlauea Iki, like Kīlauea itself,
created its own minisystem of wind currents that affected its
weather. On clear days, it was obvious its black surface created
a strong thermal updraft that reached hundreds of feet into the
air above it. Sometimes, if the weather was especially good, she
said one could see the 'io, a small reddish-brown hawk native
to Hawai'i, circling lazily over any of the craters from here
down the East Rift Zone about twenty miles to Kalapana,
where the lava sometimes spilled into the sea. Or, one might
see pairs of koa'e-kea, white tropicbirds conspicuous for their
long tail streamers, climbing in the updrafts in gradually widening gyres. Light clouds tended to slip around Kīlauea, fog-
banks evaporated, and even whole cumulus layers sometimes
opened up to let a sun-shower through as they passed overhead.
Today, the light rain swept along the inside of the crater,
falling straight near and around its center, then spinning around
in stiff currents as if cornered along the crater rim. A column
of rain could fall in a light cascade over the steam plumes while,

at the clifftops, the stubby trees had to roll with the punches of billowing air and spinning raindrops.

At Kīlauea Iki, the lookout was a small wooden plat-form built out over an uneven ledge that seemed to crumble away a little as I stepped onto it. I could see an impressive black pool of hardened lava, smooth for the most part, bro-ken here and there by pressure mounds and ridge-cracks where the magma might have built up and spumed through a previously hardened surface. Or, the mounds might have been chunks of fallen-in caldera all swept up in the new lavas and partially melted down, slumping as the entire pool cooled. It was hard to tell the actual geopathology, especially for a novice like me. Steam devils, slightly sulphurous, lifted them-selves in lazy helixes over the pond, vapor produced by the still molten lens of cooling lava only forty feet or so below the surface, heating the solidified rock and groundwater around it. The mist flowing across my sight line, like an ink wash of a Chinese painting, gave the caldera a feeling of great depth, the buff-colored mountain of ash that rose up beside me an added air of dread.

From the posters on the information kiosk by the parking lot, I learned that Kīlauea Iki had last erupted in 1959, provid-ing the most spectacular display of recent volcanic activity in the United States until the explosive eruption of Mount St. Helens in 1980. Lavas here had built a small lake swirling over the sur-face of the old flow, and fountains had gone from a swarm of outbreaks to coalesce into a single red geyser of molten rock nearly two thousand feet high. The devastation surrounding me seemed evidence of the earth's grand and catastrophic powers, a monument to the outbreak of a sweet light from great, hellish depths.

I looked east from the spatter rampart which loomed up and then gave way to a talus slide below me. A babble of voices drifted upward along the cliffs, sometimes clear and then fad-ing intermittently, brought along by the inconstant currents of the wind. It sounded like the ocean, almost cheerful, but faint, as if I were standing along an inland channel somewhere and the thrash of waves and choiring of shorebirds reached me only on the onrush of the tide. The drizzling rain had subsided by now, and I could see a troop of about thirty or forty school-children, dressed in yellow slickers, walking in single file across the black caldera floor. The fresh sunlight breaking through cloud cover glistened on the pearly residue the rain had left on their coats and on the shining black lavas. There must have been a teacher or two, one leading the way and another trailing the pack, making sure that they all kept off the lightly worn footpath over the lava bed. These were schoolchildren out on a field trip. They carried lunch pails in wonderful plastic colors swinging from their clenched hands—semaphore rectangles of blues, reds, and yellows against the dark field of lava. And they were singing a song that I myself had sung in my own child-hood—I remembered a hand-clapping game went along with it and its lyric was about the blossoming of orange flowers. It was about a road which led you away and another, somehow more crowded, which led you home. I left the railing and turned back, opening my jacket to the wind. We drove away through the ferns and ʻōhiʻa of the rain forest and under their dappled shade. For the first time in years, it seemed, I saw what my labor might be and I looked forward to it.

YEATS SAYS in his *Autobiography* that for a poet to write a last-ing work, he must first find metaphors in the natural figures of his native landscape. It's an idea so romantic that it stuck with me, though I didn't immediately see how I could apply it. But, back on the Mainland, a friend showed me something tangible of what Yeats might have meant. A college professor on leave, this friend had spent a year in England and Ireland, working up an essay on *A Vision,* Yeats's book of the occult that out, lined the soul's progress toward a splendid consciousness. Among other things—one of them an artfully drawn mandala that was a complicated chart of incarnate states derived from Yeats's theories and speculations—my friend brought back a color slide of Ben Bulben. I had never seen a picture of it be, fore, and now that I had, I thought I understood Yeats and his assertion. The fan of the borrowed slide projector whirred in the dark and seemed to billow the grand image of a barren moun, tain rising out of a wide green heath onto the off,white sheet taped to my living room wall. Ben Bulben was a blue and slate, gray behemoth of rock weathered by wind and rain, forbidding and issuing a simple challenge—"Be equal to me."

Something like that had spoken to me too, in my own life, when I finally saw my own birthplace, a sentient adult called by my own mountain. I suddenly wanted to be *better* than I had been, more a part of the earth I was born to, its rock and gar, land of ferns, more a part of the history which had been kept from me out of some mysterious shame, and more a part of my own poetic mind, an elusive and beleaguered thing, almost out of keeping with our own time.

I thought I might turn my family losses around—the store that had passed out of our care, the broken promise of its in, heritance, the life we'd been sundered from—by becoming as familiar with this extraordinary place and its various histories as a Hasid is with his chosen text, as a Buddhist monk might be with his puzzling *kōan* and regimen of meditation. Because I did not grow up here. Because I did not understand my fa- ther—so much *of* Hawai'i and another time—though I loved him. I wanted to know the place and I wanted to tie my name to it, to deliver out of the contact a kind of sacred book—a book of origins.

DRAGON

My father died in a poor Los Angeles hospital, gasping for breath, his heart already stopped. He was getting tucked into his remade bed in intensive care, telling the cheery Filipino nurse, who had just told him the mini-chronicle of her move from Manila, that he was a wanderer too, when his heart, which had been racing all day without steadiness, which had suffered some inconsolable damage, simply quit on him in mid-sentence. One instant he was saying, quietly, with deliberation and in the normal rhythms of exchange, that he was from Hawai'i, and in the immediate next, with no prefatory remark or transition, he was panicked, saying that he couldn't breathe. Death had slipped itself into his body that swiftly. Within seconds he passed—the heart monitor had already beeped—and everything else went into flatline. A doctor came and administered the drill, sustaining it for nearly twenty minutes, but my father was gone.

He'd been ill for nearly a week. He came home from his night-shift job in Santa Monica with intense pains in his chest, falling through the front door of his house, calling out loud for my mother, who was far back in the bedroom of the tract home, sleeping. She told me he was sitting down on the gray carpet by the entryway, breathing hard, pumping his arm, balling his fist again and again, already rising, trying to stand. She thought he was drunk and had passed out on the floor. She worried he would vomit. She argued with him, spewing out rebukes, until she realized how serious things were and called the paramedics. They too thought he was just drunk—and he had been, downing a huge dose of Yukon Jack while he sat in his car in the parking lot of his working place before driving home around midnight.

He'd been fighting with his bosses, arguing about the way to do things, about the way he'd done things years before on some instruments he'd built for a helicopter control panel. The unit had come back on guarantee, and no one in the factory could fix it except my father. The boards under the dials didn't conform to specs, so it fell to my father, a senior troubleshooter, to devise how to repair it. But there were no plans, no handbook or electronic blueprints to work from. He'd have to improvise, do lots of checking, take time and do shitwork in order to get it done. He was being punished for screwing up. He had been given work that was obviously humiliating, and the bosses had rebuked him for objecting. In front of everyone. Someone had laughed. Most were silenced by the public dressing-down, embarrassed for him, an "old-timer" with the company, helplessly waiting out his pension. My father had gotten angry, and stalked off, fuming in Hawaiian pidgin English—his only language. Hard-of-hearing since childhood, language and speech came with difficulty to him, so he befriended others who also spoke differently. But even his cohorts on the job—nonunionized Chicanos, southern blacks, Thais and Cambodians, a Native American who asked him deer-hunting every year—had ignored or mocked him, ostracizing him further, fearful of being allied, of being marked for firing, as he certainly was.

He was only five years from retirement, maybe two if he'd decided to take it early, and the company was probably trying to force him out, make him quit early and save a little on the payments, encouraging him to move out before the big payday. They wanted him out—that seemed certain—and they chose to bust him down in front of the boys in order to motivate him to make a move. With executives, companies act high-minded and give them a golden handshake. With factory workers, they parcel out scorn and ridicule, layoffs and dismissals. So, my father got angry one night after a meeting with his boss and stalked away, grabbing up the little red pack of his shirt-pocket tool kit, walking across the factory floor, kicking a plastic trash can, scraping the legs of his metal stool across the concrete floor when he sat down and hunkered over his drafting table, awakened to his own expendability.

Was he being fired? I never found out. My mother drew a silence down on all of it. It was another secret she drew over his life, like the huge one over our beginnings.

If ever I asked her about any of these—about the death of my father, about our lives in Hawai'i, about my Hongo grandparents—I'd get evasive or silly answers, a switch in subject. I wasn't to know. During childhood and adolescence, it was no hard thing to silence questions and stifle curiosity with small bits of fact—"Your Hongo grandfather was a tall man . . ." "Your dad used to work construction for the military . . ." "Your relatives on the Big Island grow orchids . . ." "Your Uncle Torakiyo lost all his property in a tidal wave . . ." But if I probed deeper, if I wanted the telling to continue, I was cut off with impatience, with mocking, or with anger. Her sister and my uncle, who lived near us in Los Angeles, who shared holidays with us, would shush me too. My mother was bothered by these things. She would not let me know but the barest sketches of the past. Until I was past thirty, I was allowed nothing of simple family knowledge. And, for over thirty years, little curiosity had risen within me. But after the funeral, after I had buried my father who had come from such faint and unknown beginnings, I felt the deepest shame that would not be buried with his

*ashes. After my father's death, family secrets, evasions, and my own ig-
norance fed an anger and a desire to know that would not abate.*

*I remember paging furiously through the newspaper the day after
he died, looking for the weather report, needing to prepare some dis-
tracting fragment of information to give to his sisters in Hawai'i when
I called them. At the end of the Sports section, on the page where regional and national temperatures are printed, where the barometric lows
and highs ran, where the moon phases and tidal charts were given, was
a satellite picture of the Los Angeles basin on the day before. There
had been a terrible Santa Ana storm—desert winds blowing in from
the east and across the mountains—a day in which the normal onshore
patterns were powerfully reversed. A merciless continuum of hot, des-
iccating, blasting air had scoured through from the canyons down across
the flatlands and out toward sea. I remember the news reports of gusts
up to eighty miles per hour in the Anaheim Hills. Dust and trash
kicked up, Dumpsters clanged and banged their lids, eucalyptus and
jacaranda trees had their limbs sheared off, and streetlights suspended
over traffic bounced and dandled like panicky moths caught struggling in
deadly, electric webs over the intersections of the city. People got surly
and turned inward. I had shielded my eyes from the dry, stinging heat
slapping at me all that day. A visiting instructor at a university, I had
taught my classes, driving to school in the heavy winds, feeling my tiny
car bounce and swerve a little on the freeway as I drove to campus and
then with my wife Cynthia to the hospital later that evening. The aerial photo showed all of this in a huge swirl of clouds over the L.A.
basin. Between San Bernardino and Santa Monica, between the eastern
mountains and the large bay to the west, was the white serpentine of a
dragon spiraling out from my father's deathbed.*

NATAL

Cottage and Daidokoro

SO, WE WENT BACK to Volcano three years later—my wife, our nine-month-old boy, and I. When we arrived, it was late afternoon and, though the air was thick with humidity, everything around us seemed freshened with my own expectations. The red blooms of the coral tree spreading its huge canopy of feathery green boughs alongside the airport's circle drive seemed like small flotillas of canoes aflame with fleshy red sails as we passed under it in our rent-a-car shuttle van.

But for the world and time, Cynthia and I could have been the love-suicide romantics of an eighteenth-century Japanese puppet drama—a *sake* salesman and the daughter of a flower merchant who, betrothed to others (a cousin whose father jobbed and sold wagon wheels or a soldier stationed in the capital), were trying to flee their karma and sought sanctuary in their own passion for each other and the idea that they might find a haven in another province, amidst the folk of the coun´try, among strangers. Cynthia is the daughter of Mennonites and Quakers, farmers in Manitoba and North Dakota who lost their lands in the drought and hardships of the Depression. And my people—the dispossessed who came from Fukuoka and Hiroshima in Japan to work the new sugar plantations of Hawai'i at the end of the last century—were only half known to me. The Shigemitsu and Kubota on my mother's side were southern Japanese peasant farmers displaced from their ancestral lands and so impoverished that years of unspeakably tough, all´but´forced labor in Hawaiian canefields seemed a good way to make a new start on another life.

At the rental car agency, we could gaze toward the lower, grove´stubbled slopes of Mauna Kea like van Gogh's French hillsides. I spoke pidgin and bantered with the clerks, signed papers for an air´conditioned Nissan Sentra. We strapped our baby into his safety seat and started up the highway to Volcano. Along the way, there were the intermittent villages of remnant plantation shanties and Japanese´style homes with their hedges of cedar and tree ferns I remembered from my first return trip upslope when my aunt and uncle had driven me three years be´fore. That afternoon, I drove nearly twenty´nine miles along the same road my father and grandfather drove every day the years they ran the store, hearing the hiss of rainwater on the car's tires, feeling the fog and chill of the Hawaiian mountain clouding the air of our ascent.

Just below the fault line and the summit, where the old highway divided off and led into the old village, we drove off the highway into a grid of asphalt roads carved into a thin forest of *ʻōhiʻa,* the native trees that can colonize fresh lava flows within months of their cooling. A mile in, I noticed a lonely street sign beside a huge gray scar in the earth, a lot freshly bulldozed and scraped bare of its greenery of ferns. Left down a lane narrowing into *ʻōhiʻa* and ferns, we passed two or three small, jerrybuilt homes of the selfreliant. Right down a gap in the forest, an even smaller lane carved through the plants and scraped over its bed of black and gray lavas shining in the rain. There was just room enough for the tiny compact car to maneuver, but the green ferns crowded in against the doors and windows like a forest of aboveground kelp. I had the feeling I was in a kind of Nautilus cruising under Nemo's rich sea.

Our retreat home was a tiny cottage tucked under the dripping canopy, plastic flumes and pipes from its galvanized roofing running audibly with the rushing rain that filled an aluminumsided standing swimming pool that was its companionable water tank. The instructions said to get the key on the left of the porch, "under clay mask." I found the thing, squat and goblinlike, a replica of the fourteenthcentury Japanese Noh masks of demons who guarded minor temples and wayside shrines scattered in the country. There were eyeholes, a piglike nose, and a huge, toothy grimace in the shape of a figure eight lying on its side. I found the key, a common brass thing, and shoved it in the deadbolt lock of the cottage door. When it swung open, the forest silence and the drizzling night seemed suddenly swollen with all my senses and, in the briefest instant, before I knew I had thought anything at all, it shut around us like the huge eye of an African flower closing its sexual petals down at dusk around its male colonies, erect purple anthers dusted yellow with a sleepy pollen.

THE COTTAGE WAS a kind of weekend hideaway—no more than an A-frame, really—owned by a Honolulu attorney but rented to a poet I knew who offered to sublet to us while she went back to New Hampshire. She planned to be gone about nine months or so and we'd care for the place for the duration. "Two hundred fifty dollars a month, regular plumbing, a sauna, two outdoor cats, a loft, bedroom, and library," she'd said over the phone. When I hesitated, just slightly, the poet offered it to us for a thousand dollars cash, in advance, and, though low on funds, we jumped at it sight unseen.

It was an artist's shack made up of struts, plywood, planking, and fanciful design. It stood on stilts over a small drop-off of ground that I later learned was the side of an old lava tube or lava bank that the forest had grown over. Though basically rectangular, its builder had smartly sectioned off different quadrants into a small bedroom, a rear sitting room and library with a child's bed built in under the bookshelves, a largish *tatami*-mat living room, and a sleeping loft extending partway over it. By far its most distinctive and intriguing feature, though, was its kitchen—an old-fashioned Japanese-style *daidokoro*—a banner-shaped room the width of the house that dropped off three feet or so from the mats of the living room down to the traditional dirt floor of a lower level, which then opened to the outdoors through rear and front entrances. At one end, by the rear entrance, was a propane stove you lit with matches. Near the front door, there were sinks and the water faucets, which were driven by a water pump I was instructed to attach to my car battery. The toilet flushed, but was off on its own, detached from the cottage in an outhouse under a shed built onto a small rear deck that ran alongside the cottage's back wall. There were stacks of *Smithsonian* magazines in there and a skylight of flat window glass high above the seat. There was a tiny sauna, built on the other side of the shed; to fire it, you stoked a tiny woodstove the size of a piece of hand luggage. Our shower was outdoors, built on a rampway that ran along the opposite side of the toilet. Someone had planted red and white impatiens in the forest beside the runway, so that, when you washed, pie-pan blooms and the intermingled veil of shower spray and the rain forest's constant drizzle became your curtain. Hedonistic yet efficient, everything seemed designed for a weekend idyll.

However things had been designed by its attorney-owner, our absent poet-host had made them over so that the ambience of the interior had an unsettling charm that was at once austere and yet alive to potentials for splendor. She was a Buddhist, and one of the more ancient Tibetan sects. There were small brass incense bowls scattered around the house on dressers and bureaus and desks. On the walls, there were a few double-sided satin hangings, yellow backed with red. On them were mandalas—stylized cosmic fires encircling images of squatting black Bodhisattva with wild, lavishly curling scarlet tongues. And upstairs in the sleeping loft, I found meditation pillows—the large, square, and oversized *zabuton* for a floor mat and then the bulging, circular rump pad, both upholstered in a thick red-and-black cotton cloth. Had they been Japanese and Zen-style, the cloth would have been a brown or some other subdued color. Tibetans, I recalled, seemed to favor the garish, with its reminder of the sexual and the sublime.

Over in a corner of the loft was another pillow, an LP-sized red square one with a deep impression sunken into it. The quilted padding rose up like a sponge cake around its inner bowl. I'd seen pillows like this before. This was a bell pillow, made so that a meditation bell shaped like a salad bowl carved out of a single piece of wood could be placed on it. They came in different sizes—small as ice cream dishes, middle-sized like cereal bowls, then large as tubs for the Haida potlatch. I'd seen them in Japanese temples and I'd rung a few of them myself. You sat on the *tatami* with your legs tucked formally under you. You bowed a deep, forehead-touching-the-floor bow before them and murmured the phrase of a prayer or you were stoically silent, depending on the instructions and protocols of the sect. You picked up a thick, hammer-handle-sized stick lying on the mat next to it, a plain and smoothly rounded thing the charac-ter and heft of one of a pair of rhythm sticks, and you began your chant, sharply striking the farthest edge of the bowl as if it were a bass drum. It rang a deep, reverberating peal full of overtones and undertones, suggesting the mind's depth and the infinity of the cosmos, suggesting perfection and clarity, sug-gesting nothingness. You hit it and you chanted, bell to soul. You hit it and your voice droned its sutra and the bell shim-mied out its concentric circles of wisdom.

The bell bowl was pushed into the corner under a verti-cal wall hanging. Long as a bedroom-door mirror and strangely out of place, the hanging was Japanese, not Tibetan—an ink-painting of a cliffside waterfall. A contemporary imitation of the fourteenth-century scholarly style, I thought. It had dry, tense brushstrokes and a suggestion of the macabre. The Buddhahead sublime. But the bell bowl under it was Tibetan enough, made of brass and unpolished, thin on its sides. Mortar and pestle, its stick rested on an angle inside it. Both were lighter, more delicate than the ringing paraphernalia I had been introduced to in monasteries in Japan.

On my knees, I took up the stick and bell. I scooted over
to the pillow and put the bell in it. It fit. And everything looked
right—brass bell, red pillow accepting it like an opened hand
its opposing fist, no tassels, the hardwood stick in my hand. I
took a breath, closed my eyes, and tried to think of *Mu,* the classic *kōan-*puzzle and meditation-target for the Zen mind. *Mu*
could not be hit with mere thought.

Mu is one of the *kōan* studies of Rinzai Zen. A *kōan* is
a phrase or a word or a verbal conundrum that is supposed
to block the mind from running on its mundane, rational
tracks and derail it so the chance for irrational, radiant enlightenment will be made easier and the event of its attainment
a mental cataclysm. Students spend months and years working on a *kōan.* "What is the sound of one hand clapping,
dude?" Or, "What is a cart without its wheels, without its
axles?" It can break not only the mind but the body in two.
Bodhidharma, the sixth-century Indian patriarch of Zen who
brought its practices from northern India to southern China,
is said to have meditated so hard and so long in the lotus position that his legs not only grew stiff and numb but putrefied
and completely fell away from his body. He tossed them aside.
Without legs, he could sit all the more easily. The *kōan* he is
reputed to have been working on was a version of *Mu.* "Mu"
is the Japanese word for "Nothingness," pure metaphysical
vacancy, perhaps Maya unveiled. It is written with an elaborate, eighteen-stroke ideogram that looks like a Polynesian hut
on four crumpling stilts. There are vertical bars, horizontal
bars, a kind of scripted cap above them that looks like a
thatched roof, a few squibs, and then the little shortened tent-
poles calligraphed deftly under the whole thing. This is
"Nothing"—and a hard character to draw.

In the temples, the acolytes suffer from emptiness and a chronic lack of sleep. They have empty stomachs, empty minds, empty hearts, and empty pocketbooks. They get up at 3 a.m. and bow and meditate and chant and meditate some more and then go out and clean up the temple or start cooking noodles or gathering firewood or conniving a way into town for a lapsing binge back into the worldliness of cheap road-stand Chinese food, cigarettes, puerile adult cartoon books, and *pachinko*. They find a ride back, clean up, chant some more, slaver down a quick bowl of noodles or rice and salty yellow pickles for dinner, and meditate in the detached outdoor temple, mosquitoes or no, sometimes past midnight. They bow to every doorway, at the entrance to every room, they talk not at all or in brief, declarative bursts of reverential shouting. I learned to yell that way, mimicking their vigorous piety, became practiced at bringing my voice up from the tensed diaphragm, my body in its martial posture, ferocity on my face like Bodhidharma's scowl of determination. But I let it go—shouting, rigor, reverence, and all—once I left the temple and came back to my American mind.

In the sleeping loft, I took in another breath and tried for Nothing again, this deep, Buddhist mystery of *Mu*. I raised the stick up near my ear and rapped it briskly against the waist of the bell. The bell clanked. This surprised me. I hit it with the stick again. Again the bell clanked. I tapped it, softly this time. Again it clanked, a soft clank. I picked it up and looked under it and then inside. There was Tibetan script embossed on its base and it was empty inside, as my heart/mind should have been. There was nothing else to notice. The bell seemed perfectly fine, if a little thin in gauge, much thinner than the Japanese bells I thought I knew. Maybe its thinness had something to do with its recalcitrance to ring, my failure to inspire a peal.

But it was too much and I too little. I put everything away and stopped experimenting. *Facsimile* is the word I thought of, this representation of natural splendor. An illusion. I walked back down the stepladder to the rooms below.

Our first night there was chilly and magical. A foggy rain trellised down outside. Then things went so dark, it seemed we could have been at sea on a boat for the nothingness that surrounded us. No streetlights or passing cars, no neighbors nearby. And, except for the gurgling of rainwater through the gutters along the roof, the forest and the house around us were completely silent. There wasn't even the domestic hum of refrigerator noise because the little thing was placed outside on the back deck. We had electricity, but it seemed almost obscene to use it. We'd found some votive candles and backpacker's lanterns in the kitchen that day; romantically, we lit them and moved around the cabin in small, luminous pools accompanied by Halloween shadows until bedtime. We settled Alexander down in his cot under the library shelves and fell asleep ourselves in our host's bedroom on the *futon,* under cold, damp quilts, heavy and thick and covered in a sturdy brown cloth I guessed had something to do with a Tibetan lesson in humility.

Natal Morning

Our baby woke us early and the world outside seemed to break quietly into yellow streaks of flame, first on the dark ferns and mosses covering the ground, then blazing up the mottled black and silver-gray trunks of the *'ōhi'a* trees that made up the forest

around us. Sunlight shone in on the cabin from the lower windows and from huge panels of skylights built into the ceiling
and one entire wall. We could see the small white shreds of
clouds racing just over the tree line beside the cabin. It was a
new world we'd fallen into.

I woke, dressed, and made tea on the propane stove—
ban-cha—Japanese tea I scooped from a tubular tin I found
tucked behind a curtained shelf stocked with the plenty of
canned goods and handsome jars of assorted grains. I boiled the
water in a kettle, then poured it steaming onto the little aluminum bathysphere of tea drowning in a glazed ceramic pot. I
found dark brown teacups, oddly shaped, arranged them at the
little breakfast table on the ground near the steps to the living
room floor, and poured tea, breathing in the fragrance, admir-
ing the clear amber of the liquid.

I remembered the fragment of a story that my grandmother,
Tsuruko Kubota, had told me. She is my mother's mother and
the woman who raised me—both in Hawai'i and in California, where she came to live with us for five years between the
time I was ten and fifteen. It could have been after I'd grown
up and finished college and graduate school and while I was
driving her somewhere—to an airport, probably, where she and
I seemed always to be going whenever we saw each other these
days, the last few before I lose her. I remember she spoke then
with disdain for the mere recollection of my grandfather whom
I'd never known. Tsuruko said that he had once practiced and
taught the tea ceremony to a small club of young women from
the village, high school girls sent by their countryish parents to
learn a nicety of civilization and femininity before marriage.

"Another way to milk money from the neighbors," Tsuruko said, her mouth tightening into a frown, but her wrinkled

cheeks and eyes blazing with mirth. "He was rascal, him," she said. "He know how for pick pocket without use his hand!"

One of my aunts, his daughter, had confirmed this to me, saying, "My father was a dreamer but he could also see where money was to be made." And if it could be done with some style, with the prestige of traditional culture attached to it, so much the better. "He didn't sell encyclopedias," she said, "but he was always looking for something aesthetic he could sell lessons for. Tea, calligraphy, even flower arrangement. He didn't care. All those womanly things! If anyone made fun, he could cut off their credit or just let them have a mouthful because he was the best talker and the biggest man, you know." Torau, my grandfather, stood more than a head taller than most any other Japanese man in Volcano Village.

I called to my wife, who woke and draped herself in a light cotton *yukata*. Cynthia and I drank the tea, clasping our cups in both hands, sipping it slowly, gazing out from the cabin at the world around us that was suddenly made both old and new at once. A rooster crowed, wandering away from our neighbor's lot an acre away and through the underbrush, its calls rising and diminishing, an inconstant tide in the botanical eddies of the rain forest. I rolled up a cloth diaper and tied Alexander to the back of one of the dining chairs. We fed him milk, raisins, and crackers and made plans to explore. I turned a faucet to fill a glass, and the water pump chugged on like a bus engine. I thought of our little red rental car and the heavy-duty orange cable that I ran to the house from its small battery, an electric charge running in over chicken shit, *'ōhi'a* roots, and mossy lava to the water pump beneath the planks of the floor. "Thighbone connected to . . ." I sang silently, thinking that all here seemed hooked to its immediate cause, even, finally, myself as well. I laughed out loud.

WE WENT to get groceries. We drove back to the new high-way near the 26-mile marker and then in from it onto a cross-road that was an access turnoff to the old highway and down that another quarter mile past some old lots marked off in the twenties and thirties and their old-growths of windbreak *'ōhi'a* and eucalyptus. The houses on them were the familiar rectan-gular, Japanese *minka*-roof designs built on shallow posts set in concrete up over the wet ground. Where a garage or front lawn might be, a few had bentwood-frame hothouses covered with old sheets and rotting plastic tarps, crammed with plank tables and a few meager rows of potted orchids. Everything was under a midday drizzle.

We passed a large, craftsman-style building painted yellow and set back from the road. It had a circular driveway, rock pillars at its entrance, and a fabulous lawn hedged with well-tended hydrangea bushes. There was a modest stand of Japa-nese cedars in the lot's corner. I guessed the summer residence of a grower or else the retreat headquarters of an O'ahu church—something rich and "off-island."

We passed the Hongo Store, glancing past the gas pumps and under its eaves, trying to glimpse the old sign, its paint peel-ing but the letters still there, we knew, though it was invisible from the highway. I'd pass by the store maybe a hundred more times before I could give up looking to see the name, before I could stop thinking back on the year I was born, my father's earnestness, and my grandfather's foolish betrayal of it. It looked empty and desolate now, and I could see black pools of rain ponding in the asphalt of its tiny parking lot, empty of cars and delivery trucks as we drove by.

We went to the store at the next crossing at Haunani Road—a larger and newer store, bustling with customers and its little apron of a parking lot crammed full with the new and sparkling Japanese rental cars of tourists parked alongside the rusting Chevrolet and Ford heaps of the locals. This store had a set of new gas pumps at one end of it and a long porch run/ ning along its raised front that provided space for a flower shop and a lunch counter busy with tourists writing postcards and or/ dering up fries and Cokes for their kids. Bored locals with their cups of coffee sat on stools and benches, talking story about a local election, the death of a relative, or the future of geothermal energy. In the past, it would have been my grandfather's store that was the center of this kind of cheerful prodigality.

Cynthia and I walked in and split up, scavenging around its narrow aisles for what we needed. I strolled through the sec/ tions, Alexander asleep in my arms for his noontime nap. I languished at the open bins of island fruit and vegetables, cata/ loguing each item and checking it off in my storehouse of natal memories. As if to weave a spell, I waved a cupped hand over the stumpy and hairy warts of Japanese potatoes and recalled them, peeled and gray in a plain stew they made at every New Year's feast. I gazed at the brown paste of Hawaiian *poi* wrapped in plastic bags and stacked like bread in their own section and recognized their red/and/yellow labels from my childhood.

I wheeled the wire carousels and felt the wrappings on the dried Chinese plums and slices of island mangoes, glutinous and wrinkled and red under hard cellophane. Li Hing Mui, the moist pink ones were; Salt Seed, the dry white ones. You used the first for "kid soup," a sweet/and/sour tea a child could make at home alone. And you could pop a whole one in your mouth, peel the flesh from the pit with your tongue and teeth, and not feel anything but the skin on the roof of your mouth turn tight and gelatinous like the skin of a red frog. The second, salty one no one but an adult uncle could eat whole, and then only with teacupsful of whiskey. Children bit off small pieces of its sandy flesh, and when it went down, it stung and purged your throat clean as a mouthful of dry, foamy surf. You ate it when you were sick with a cold or flu. Yick Lung was the brand name, a yellow-and-red label shaped like a trowel above the dried plum poultices, Chinese and full of sensible usages. When I was a kid, any package of them could be had for a dime.

Going through that store, I was returning to an archive: tea was an afternoon service to the dead my grandfather conducted in front of his home shrine, a lacquered box inlaid with the fig- ures of temples and dragons and phoenixes dancing on the streaming flames of red-and-silver clouds carved from glass and mother-of-pearl. A package of yellow Japanese cookies made from spices and sugar and rice flour was a Fourth of July pic- nic at the beach when it rained and a cloudburst cooled the air, petaling the frosting of a cake left out in the drizzle. A can of tinned beef or deviled ham might be the year of prosperity and surfeit when an uncle once filled an entire wall of our garage with the stacked boxes of canned goods in repayment of a mys- terious moral debt he owed my father. Nothing was without its meaning or its memories. I could not buy sausage without think- ing of the sweet and zesty gifts from the Azores brought to the palate of my childhood and the lilt of affection in every half- sentence of speech uttered in these islands since the late nine- teenth century. "I geeve you, brah. No need pay," someone said over thirty years ago, offering a rice sack, and my father put on his rubber slippers and walked out of the man's house with half a tuna or a slab of sweetened coconut milk gelatinized with taro.

The names of items, the brand names, and even the shapes they came in were like talismans I'd once relinquished which now rushed back to my hands, still faintly magical and powdered with the gauzy sheen of a generation lost to time and the move my family made away from this place. I walked, vaguely supplicant, through the aisles and from shelf to shelf, weighing memory against need, and felt nothing but exhilaration as I paced over the wooden floors. I saw and then recalled many things: *kinako,* a Japanese soy powder one used to flavor sweet rice cakes at New Year's; *panko,* another powder one used to flavor the batter for *tempura,* the deepfry for shrimp and sliced vegetables; Botan and Fukusuke and Shirakiku and Hakutsuru were the brand names of the fifty and hundredpound paper sacks of rice that went for an amount less than what you paid for a sixpack of beer. A red peony blossom, a white chrysanthemum, and a crane were pictured on their labels. In canned goods, there were items like bean curd, sweet black beans, bamboo shoots, and sliced lotus root—a starch shaped like the inexorable wheels of Buddhist law, which you ate in a bowl of stewed carrots mixed with seaweed and long white radishes cut down from roots shaped like the thighs of fat infants. A universe of associations came rushing back to me as I put item after item into the little wire basket I carried. It grew heavier to carry than my sleeping child.

I met Cynthia at the counter, Formicatopped and crammed with boxes of candies, matches, plastic spoons, forks, and wooden chopsticks. There was a bulletin board hanging above the register covered with business cards and community flyers. A wire rack beside the counter was stocked with girlie, surf, survivalist, and bodybuilding mags. Liquor fifths filled the shelves behind them. The woman at the register was dark-skinned and slight, Japanese and stoical. The supplies we'd gathered came to about sixty-four dollars—almost a fortune for a country store. A local would have bought only a few things, or else stocked up from a supermarket down in Hilo, but my excitement had overridden any prudence.

From down the counter a bit, a stocky, youngish man in a thick blue T-shirt, jeans, and rubber slippers came up beside the woman at the register and asked, modestly, glancing briefly at my face and then looking quickly away, if my name was Hongo. I was surprised, but said yes, and the man told me to wait, then turned away and walked off toward the back storage room of the store. He came back a minute later with a large box of files I had sent ahead from Missouri. "Diss yours, eh?" he said, unshouldering it, and plunked the carton down on the wooden floor.

I loaded the groceries and came back for the box, lifting it from the damp, unswept floor, and carried it down the steps and to the trunk of the car.

"Was there something funny about the way the guy at the store spoke to me?" I asked. Cynthia nodded and turned to look at the road ahead.

Kazumasa Okamoto

It happened again, almost right away, when we stopped at the Volcano Post Office to pick up mail I'd had forwarded from the Mainland. People recognized me even before I'd introduced myself.

"Are you Mistah Hongo?" the postman asked, stone-faced.

He had the air of a mortician—a Nisei man of about fifty-five or sixty, I guessed, dressed in an aloha shirt with a sub-dued pattern of island flowers. His face was tanned, lined with age, and though the expression on it was impassive, the flesh and skin turned down into deep frown lines around his mouth. His face was clean-shaven, its main feature the small flock of brown, Oriental moles dispersed across the shallow hollows of his cheeks.

"Was Albert your faddah?" he said, his face as expres-sionless as before. It was a strange interrogation. He'd caught me off guard. What I had taken for a sullen inscrutability had been a mask used to study me.

"How did you know?" I blurted, without eloquence or ceremony.

"Your face dah same as your faddah's, ass why," the man said, using the thick pidgin I recognized was of the country and of an entire generation ago, explosive and heavily stressed. "You look like your faddah."

"Oh," I said, nodding. People had said that about me since childhood. But who was *he*? "Did you know him?"

"Yesh, I did," the clerk said, his face still stone. "Your faddah ol' days wass running dah stoah, eh?—*Hongo* Stoah—dah one down below. . . ." His voice trailed off and he ges-tured with his chin and a pursing of his lips in a downslope direction. "You know dah wann, eh?" he asked, his face show-ing puzzlement, suddenly supposing I might *not* know my own origins.

"Oh, yeah," I answered, slipping into pidgin myself. Then I felt obliged to sketch out a piece of the story. "Hongo Stoah my grannfaddah he wen' built 'em, eh? Ann my faddah he run 'em for couple years, yeah?" I wanted to establish my connection to the place, and speaking a bit of the story seemed to be a way to do it, to persuade another that I belonged to it too.

"Yeah," the postman said, nodding. "So what? You come back for search your roots or somet'ing?" His face broke then, nearly grinning in that bemused and intimate, derisive way of island Japanese. He guessed my secret, his wise smile showing the flecks of gold backing on his teeth. He was teasing me and I accepted it.

"Who are *you*?" I shot back, trying to make my own face stone this time.

"Okamoto," the postman answered, bowing, placing his hands stiffly at his sides and bending from the waist. His head bobbed down, then quickly up again. "Kazumasa Okamoto from Volcano." He had the pose and formality of the old days, I thought, part of the generation that, deep in their bones, knew the stance and rhythm and feeling of Japan. His shirt was green and made of acrylic, like a body sheath of vermilion. The hair on his head was close-cropped and shining with an old-fashioned oil, the kind men used in movies from the fifties. I'd stepped back in time yet again.

I shook his hand and walked back to the parking lot, where Cynthia and the baby waited in the car. I told her that the postman recognized me, said that I looked like my father.

"I guess I'm home," I said romantically, and wanted it to be so.

We drove off for the National Park, a little stunned at the discovery that, without foreknowledge, I'd fit into an identity

here apart from anything I'd done in my own life, independent
of all its facts except for the one that had me born here, the son
of Albert and grandson of the old man who'd built the general
store nearly sixty years before. Even my face had a meaning.

I steered up past a row of silver-trunked *'ōhi'a,* banked
gently right by the curve of the old highway, and accelerated up
into a thick cloudbank of fog drowning the rich greens of roadside ginger plants that lined the road toward Kīlauea Summit.
Though we were slowly climbing, gaining a few feet in altitude
as we drove, I still felt the weight of a feeling I guessed to be
nothing if it wasn't pure descent.

THE HONGO STORE

Onsen: *Torau and Yukiko,
from Charlotte Watching It Rain*

THIS WAS BEFORE my father died. It was raining hard in
Hilo. I'd heard it pounding on the courthouse roof earlier
while I read my poems there, its wind buffeting through the
large, open windows, small, explosive puffs splashing over the
sills. I'd circled around to where I was born, finally, over thirty
years since my parents left with me when I was an infant. A
poet with one book to my name, I'd given a stiff reading to a
stiff audience and three of us—my aunt, uncle, and I—were returning to my aunt's home higher along the hillscape behind
the town.

The land rose slowly along a stately *accelerando* march of
rock that climbed another thirteen thousand feet to the peak of

Mauna Loa, miles in the distance, an invisible presence through the rain and the night. My little audience of relatives and amateur poets had dispersed—the *haiku* club of Hilo, the little klatch of community college wits and *haole* hippies, the Japanese schoolteachers, all my aunt's children and grandchildren, and my father's other sister and her husband. Once in his own house, my uncle went off to bed, saying he had an early golf date in the morning. Seventy-three, and he played golf three times weekly.

In the kitchen, my aunt made some tea, put pink and green rice cakes on a plate and poured some shining bronze crackers in a bowl, motioned me out to the living room, and we took seats there opposite each other. With no other preface than that, she began a long monologue that was a generation's worth of the family story. Some of the facts I already knew, and I nodded and tried to add things at first. But it was clear to me that a saga was being imparted and I was to quiet myself. My silence let her find a rhythm to her own telling, find the right tone of voice, the delicate colors of emotion and recollection. She was giving me a dimension to things which had been both veiled and excised from consciousness and curiosity almost since my own birth. She told me who I was.

Torau Hongo, my grandfather, her father, was the youngest son of an impoverished *samurai* family. His name is written with the ideograms for "Tiger" and "the Way"—the same ideogram for "the way" of Taoism—and his name means, of course, "the Way of the Tiger." The family name is written with the ideograms for "Home" and "Place." Hongo, then, means "Homeland." Torau Hongo came from Kumamoto Prefecture in Japan during the early part of this century—sometime after the Gentlemen's Agreement between the Japanese government and the

United States administration under Theodore Roosevelt. One of the stipulations was that, in order for America to allow plain laborers from Japan to immigrate, Japan had to send along a few members of the educated class too. So Japan started encouraging educated people to come to Hawai'i—sons of *samurai* and merchants, teachers and a few professionals.

An older brother, Torakiyo (his name means "Purity of the Tiger"), had already emigrated—to Hilo—and started an insurance business in the Japanese community there. This brother started working to build a church too—a Christian church, the Church of Christ. It was slightly progressive for a Japanese to be Christian. Torakiyo and others like him could initiate things—business and community ventures—because they came educated in mathematics, in Japanese writing, in some of the arts. They knew how communities ran, and therefore acquired a little stature. Japanese banks would lend them money to build small businesses, schools, churches, even to buy property. And it was a natural thing for a family member to sponsor another member of the family in coming over. So, Torakiyo backed Torau, my grandfather.

But, like their names, they were the difference between innocence and experience. Their parents had divorced or separated—unusual for that time in Japan—and Torakiyo had gone with his father and had a hard, struggling life in a small town. Torau had gone with his mother to the city where her parents lived and was raised by his grandparents, secure and prosperous in a provincial capital. Torakiyo came to Hawai'i first, then my grandfather Torau followed, running, it was said, from gambling debts.

If Torakiyo was frugal and prudent, if he was respected in the community and set the tone for progress, then Torau

Hongo was profligate—a drinker, a gentleman gambler, loving the ladies and the floating world of the teahouses. But he dressed well and his back was straight. People said he looked good in a suit, rare for a Japanese to wear in those days. Only a few even knew how to put one on. He was educated too, but he used his arts for entertainment and persuasion rather than progress. He recited poetry and made people remember Japan, weakening them at evening parties with *sake* and nostalgia. By day he was a salesman, and went door-to-door with Fuller brushes, gadgets, and home remedies. Later, he sold ladies' *kimono* and very nice ones made of the best silk and brocade. The commission was very high for a *kimono,* which would be worth thousands today. Torau was a great talker and could convince people of nearly anything. But he ran through money like it was dirty rice. Hilo was too slow, and even the territory of the Big Island wasn't enough for him. Another story has it that he found a man in Kona who sponsored his sales, who had three daughters, the youngest a beauty who succumbed to him, and gave him a bastard child.

Torau fled—from debts, from his lover and new child—and he took the interisland steamship to Honolulu, trying to get himself lost in the milling throngs of new immigrants from Japan, driving cabs for a while, hustling in Chinatown, and looking again for a job selling. Soon, he landed in a portside showroom for automobiles, about a mile from downtown, dressing up in his suits, making a fine picture with his oiled hair raked back and a gleaming Chevrolet or Buick beside him. He based his look on ads and fashion layouts from American men's magazines that came his way. From a book an army officer left behind one day, he chose "Princeton" as his style and looked for the right tie, spats, and closely woven gabardines for his suits. A gifted impostor, he found he could almost change societies by changing clothes.

Somehow he managed to put enough money together and gather some backers to buy into a teahouse in Nu'uanu, a lit/ tle valley just outside of Honolulu where a stream ran down from the *pali* cliffs through many trees and a little grove of bam/ boo. The air was cooler there and the spirits of weary men were made lighter at night. He married. He had a child, a girl, my aunt, who was telling me this story. But then he fell in love with a younger woman, a dancer, a *maiko* named Yukiko, "Child of Innocence," trained in the classical repertoire in Japan.

Her family name was Kiriu, and she was born in Kaua'i to a plantation storekeeper's family, who gave her up for adop/ tion and training in the arts in Japan. She apprenticed in Nagoya, where she was transformed into a dancer. She returned to make a living in Hawai'i once her training was completed, found a place in the Nu'uanu *onsen* owned by my grandfather, and impressed him. He sent his first wife away and married the dancer. He had to pay her teacher's family in Japan and her family on Kaua'i too in order to marry her. She was consid/ ered a talented property one could make money from, so Torau had to buy them out.

He took on the *onsen,* the teahouse, but then things started to go wrong. He fathered three more children—another girl, then two boys, the elder my father. There was trouble with money. There was trouble with the customers. Torau was vain. He didn't like his wife flattering the men who were their cus/ tomers. She was raised gently, with a *geisha*'s manners, with ex/ pectations that her wardrobe would be maintained, that her husband would find her young women to train as her students in dance. When he did neither, she found a customer who was willing to add a fan or a sash to her collection, who could introduce her to a family who had a teenage daughter who needed training in *Nihon-buyō,* the classical dance. She bowed to him, and Torau, incensed, beat his wife. She beat my aunt, the oldest girl, her stepdaughter, who was raising the others. One daughter was starting school, the other was in kindergarten, my father was two, and the youngest boy was an infant when their mother, the dancer, ran off, *ha'alele hana,* with another man, who was a foreman at the 'Aiea sugar plantation.

It was an evening when the air in Nu'uanu was particularly cold and misty, *ūgetsu,* the Japanese say, a moon veiled with mist, and Yukiko ordered the oldest girl, the helpmate, the stepdaughter, to sweep the dirt floor of the kitchen, the *daidokoro,* and to fire up the cookstove and the *hibachi.* The boys were sick with fevers from a flu. They were fed salty rice gruel and pickled plums. The baby nursed on Pet milk. Yukiko, the dancer, went through her closets, sorting, throwing things out, packing. The plantation foreman came to the door of the house behind the teahouse, his hair slick and shining. He had just come from the barbershop. His face was dark, deeply tanned; he worked in the fields, yet he wore a suit and freshly polished shoes. The children were forbidden to answer his knock at the door. Instead, the dancer grabbed up her things—a few boxes and her chest of *odori* costumes—the fancy *kimono* and gilt fans, the brocade slippers—and, like a longshoreman leaning to shove a pallet of shipped goods along the docks, she pushed them slowly into the living room. She picked up a cardboard suitcase tied together with string. He helped her load her things into the car that was waiting, and they went, a scent of hair oil and talcum lingering briefly in the air of the household behind them.

That was it. She didn't see her children again until after they were grown up. Her new husband, a man named Katayama, never allowed her to get in touch in any way, to write, or to exchange gifts. Once, in high school, the daughters got together and sent her something, hoping for word. The gift was returned, unopened, the postal wrap and the department store wrap inside still intact. Katayama had intercepted the package and sent it back. He must have been afraid that the old life would pull her back. He wanted no contact, no tatter of emotion connecting her to her children. Once he got her to flee from Torau, Katayama wanted her to have no bridge back to him. It was the tough, Japanese way—an irrevocable break, almost as complete as death.

If I consider her life for a moment, I see that it was already a sequence of breaches and exiles, sunderings. Given up for adoption during childhood, she would have left the love of her parents and the squalor of a plantation camp in the middle of sugarcane or pineapple fields. Imagine the scene—her mother tying belongings into a bag—a comb, a piece of cloth, a ring and an amulet, perhaps a photograph already turning brown on its stiff commercial mounting. Her father leads her off, through the dirt mule-track down the middle of her village to the railway, where they pick up a ride in the open bed of an empty cane car for the trip to the docks in Līhu'e or Princeville, where a go-between meets them, gives the father a roll of bills, and then leads the girl up a rampway to a steamship bound for Yokohama. Yukiko cannot cry, she cannot write, she cannot pine for the love of parents or home. She swelters in her tiny cabin, making up a song to soothe what heart she maintains. She thinks of a story she'd been told about the splendor that awaits her, about a kingdom of riches and

delight. She feels as if she were the fisherwoman who, diving
for pearls, is led by a handsome merman to the Shangri-la at
the bottom of the sea where she will find her new life—a destiny like no other. She dives no more, she fishes no more. Her
food is no longer plain, but filigrees of ambrosia. She grows
and becomes a woman, learns the way of elegant dress and the
movement of the body to music, and the tune from a zither dis-
places the clapping of oars as the music that gives rhythm to
her life. She dances rather than weaves rushes into baskets. She
sings rather than twists her hands around the knobby, bar-
nacled shells of oysters. She abandons memory for imagined
pleasure and distinction. Yukiko relinquishes herself to her
karma, forlorn but full of promise. She has been stolen, and if
she returns, that former world will have disappeared from her
soul, her parents aged, and whatever might have been love
transformed into the cake of dust she will use to whiten her face,
her neck, and her gentle hands fluttering over the lacquered kit
of her makeup case and ebony stand of her toilette. She will
move from Kaua'i to Japan, from a cane worker's family to a
dormitory for young girls in training as entertainers. She will
move back again, a kind of debutante for the teahouses, a piece
of fancy moistening for the dry lives of Japanese men.

   To what can she belong, hold absolutely as her own—a
child, her mother, the silken, umbilical thread of semen to her
lover and the shacks and canefields she left as a child? Can she
grasp, as parental, the iron ship that sent her back and forth between Hawai'i and Japan? Then what was the little floating
world that was the site of her apprenticeship?

   Of what importance is the *onsen*, my grandfather no lover
but an incarnation of the dragon of ten thousand years, a piece

of lightning sent by heaven to leap upon her until she blazed into extinction? Her children, coughing in the night, crying to be fed like cranes swooping out from the sandy shore of an old poem—what could they be but imperfect accompaniments to a song already fading to memory? To what could she be loyal? What pain could there have been without love?

There are dimensions to this story that I cannot imagine. There are reasons for flight, for theft, for abandonment that will transform their tellings into quests for freedom and sagas of pure survival. What can womanhood have been for her? This story, half imagined, only gives its silhouette.

When I first heard these things, my aunt telling the stories through a stormy night, I felt flickers of rage and little smudges of pity ruin my heart. My father's mother, my "grandmother" I'd heard nothing about. I searched back into the little grab bag of family stories and realized that there was nothing there about this woman. As a child, I'd heard that she'd died soon after Bobby, the last child, was born. I asked when she'd died and was astonished when Charlotte answered that she was still alive. She lives in Honolulu and teaches dance, my aunt said. "Here," Charlotte said, getting up, "I have her address in the bedroom." She got up and came back a moment later, hand/ing me a slip of paper with a name on it, an address, and a telephone number. "You should call on her when you get to town," Charlotte said. "You should see your own grandmother while you're in Hawai'i."

A dragon's tail knotted and unwound itself in my body. I felt its scales rubbing against my ribs from my inner torso. I felt a flame from its opening jaws unfurling and reaching the body of my father, clad in pajamas, sleeping in his Los Ange/

les bed. There was a woman being gathered up by the dragon's
tail, and she danced like a golden moth in the twist of its grasp.

M c C u l l y

Charlotte, my father's *half*-sister, had to care for the three other
children. She washed the clothes, fed them, changed diapers,
wiped their noses when they were sick. Their mother had mis-
treated them, but their father was almost completely neglectful.
There wasn't enough rice to eat. Once, for nearly an entire
week, Torau stayed away and the children were home on their
own. They stayed indoors and did not go to school. Torau had
gone off to Hilo again to see his brother. He was begging
Torakiyo for yet another loan, another chance. Torakiyo could
not do it—not for the *onsen*—and he sent Torau back to Honolulu empty-handed. In a year, the *onsen* was failing—nobody
came anymore. Yukiko had been the attraction, singing and
dancing, all of grace in a savage world. Torau once again took
up selling, going isle to isle with his *kimono* for women. He
brought enough money in to hire a housekeeper to watch the
children, to cook and clean. Though he still quartered his children in the house behind the *onsen*, he had no money to buy
liquor or to hire another dancer. He could pay no staff. The
sliding doors and paper windows stuck in their guttering, and
they cracked and broke through. He boarded them up, unable
to afford repapering. Heavily in debt, he was losing the property. He sent his oldest daughter to Hilo for a summer, to
Torakiyo, who had a daughter too, just a little older.

They got on, and Charlotte, her household duties light-ened, grew less resolute and more gentle. Inspired by sur-roundings of kindness, she adopted her uncle's religion. Torakiyo softened a little, and got an idea from the Japanese truck farmers up in a little village by the volcano. They needed a local store up there because it was so remote, away from Hilo by nearly thirty miles, and they couldn't afford to go down to town all the time to get their supplies, foodstuffs and utensils and luxuries like cigarettes and liquor. They needed a store and a storekeeper. A regular Japanese store. Wouldn't Torau be in-terested in that? He could get out of the expense of the teahouse, stabilize his life, and pay his debts.

Whatever Torau was thinking—always a schemer, he may have accepted the offer simply to get more money out of Torakiyo—the brothers made a new agreement. Torau bor-rowed from Torakiyo to buy the plot of land up near Kīlauea, the volcano. There was only an old shack up on short stilts there and a strawberry patch behind it, but Torau made the shack into a store and built a kitchen on it and added little bed-rooms like berths on a steamship.

Apart from the Japanese, who had been busy acquiring free acreage through a federal act, the people up there were landowners with names like Morse, Dillingham, Shipman, and Webb—Scotch and English who were the growers and plan-tation bosses called *luna*. The Japanese had farms, but the whites had summer homes in Volcano. Customers enough for a business. The two older girls came to live with Torau. He could use them to help, clean and cook, start the business for the local farmers up there. The farmers grew vegetables, came in with muddy boots and dirty gloves. Rough hands. Torau put in gas pumps out front, stocked canned goods, tools, and sacks of beans and rice. Nails came in kegs and the large cuts of meats came up from Hilo on slabs of ice. Ice itself came in blocks Torau chopped with a hammer and a pick. Charlotte and his younger daughter Lily grew up country girls in Volcano, but he left his two sons behind. It was the Depression. A family was a luxury for those times.

My father Albert and his younger brother Bobby grew up in Honolulu, cared for by a housekeeper, the cleaning woman Torau had hired to watch them while he made his trips interisland. He left a little money and said he'd send more from time to time. The cleaning woman had a little house in McCully and the boys moved there with her. My father called her *ba-chan*—"grandmother." They grew up city boys, the relatives say, flashy and a little tough, going to shows and reading books and playing lots of sports at "Tokyo High," McKinley High School near downtown Honolulu, which was so dominated by Japanese they honored it with a name that mixed derision and recognition. My father worked shining shoes on McCully Street to bring in extra cash. He had a box and he had brushes. He worked with a little troop of local boys, and they kept a running stream of jabber going about music, sports, and Saturday nights. On one of those nights, Albert saw Hugh McElhenny, the halfback from Washington who played for the San Francisco 49ers, run for a touchdown in an off-season All-Star game at Honolulu Stadium. Albert played halfback himself, running for "Tokyo High" with teammates nicknamed "Itchy" and "Bighead," the quiet and intellectual center who would say, if asked, that he worried about injuring his hands. He wanted to be a surgeon. My father was fast and athletic and he had change in his pockets from the shoeshine job.

And what did he do with the money he made besides buy
a ticket to a Pro-Bowl game? He bought *bonsai,* dwarf pines and
miniatures of ornamental pear and plum trees. He found them
beautiful, their knobby limbs and gnarled trunks seemed to gentle and heighten themselves into a special language of incarnation.
He discovered them on McCully Street one day, in a flower-shop
window. He had money. He bought one, a little jewel of pine
needles twisted into an organic dance over its mossy bed of potted earth. He discovered more of them in a display at a summer
festival. He began to collect them—a cherry, a little cactus, some
acacias and jacarandas—and imagined entire scenes of them like
backdrops to a movie set, orchards of them and painted deserts
and a petrified forest sprung up in the radiance of musings inspired by his tiny saguaro. His mind traveled oceans and seas and
made for him worlds of his own imagining. A dreaminess came
over his life, and he fell deeply into its intricacies, hurrying home
after school, skipping a football practice perhaps, rushing to the
little patch behind the cleaning woman's home on the McCully
alleyway, dallying over the spray of water misting each of his
plants as if he himself were the afternoon weathers gathering
themselves around each in a string of mid-Pacific islands. He
mooned over them with a vague sexual want that his younger
brother recognized. Bobby laughed derisively and named the ornamental peach "Lana Turner" and the plum blossom "Rita
Hayworth." Albert sprinkled him with water.

But the other guys laughed at him too, puzzled and put off
by their halfback's dreaminess. The fullback called him an "ass"
once, then twice, then yet again at practice in front of the whole
squad, shaming my father, and the dreaminess ended, as did the
friendship. Albert gave up watering and tending his dream-plants
and they shriveled and died. Whatever wasn't dead in a week or

two he demolished, wrenching them from their pots, dashing their roots against the stone and plank walkway. It was savage. Seeing the wreckage, Bobby, the younger brother, questioned my father, wondering why what had been so loved was destroyed.

Bobby slammed a locker door into the bully's face the next day. He stepped on the guy's hand and broke some of the spongy inner bones of the palm. The fullback had crumpled, but when he rose he raged, his mouth opening in a shout. It was an opportunity, and Bobby, trained as a boxer, took a straight shot with a right lead at the upper line of the back's teeth, knocking a few of them out, the blood spattering and Bobby's fist cut from the blow. The revenge was public and instantly acknowledged. The brothers would not now lose the respect jeopardized by Albert's frailty.

While the brothers were still small children, a little money had come in from Torau, but then nothing came for a long time. Time and the distance—now a couple of islands—made connections easy to slip. The cleaning woman kept both of the boys nonetheless—the promise to care for them was to herself now—but asked her brother to move in with them. The boys called him "Uncle," in English. He worked as a delivery man for local Japanese businesses, then as a gardener for the wealthy around the St. Louis Heights neighborhood of Honolulu.

There is a photograph I saw of the two of them once. An old, withered woman in a plain sack dress, holding a handbag with a long strap dandling past her abdomen against her knees, her face drawn and set in a flat frown that seemed perpetual, stands beside a younger, shorter man, his head tilted upward, his round-rimmed glasses half-lit with the sun, obscuring his eyes. He wears heavy cotton worker's pants and, surprisingly for Hawai'i, a cardigan sweater buttoned over a collarless shirt.

They are standing on the seashore, on a rock slick with spray, and he wears dark socks inside of open-toed leather sandals. With a calm and inquisitive face, "Uncle" looks a little like the emperor Hirohito. He wears a biologist's demeanor of gentle curiosity, holding one rim of his glasses between a thumb and forefinger, adjusting his glasses against the slant of sun.

It must have been my teenage father who snapped the photo, the three of them out for the day to Koko Head and the Blowhole there. They must have driven there in "Uncle's" car. They might have been saying goodbye a day before my father was to ship out for boot camp and the army. Hawai'i boys were called up just before the end of things, just in time for campaigns through Anzio and the stubborn fortifications at Monte Cassino. My father stood on a ledge of lava rock a little above *ba-chan* and "Uncle." He must've called to them. My father snapped the photo, pressing down on the periscope of the trigger, the shutter making its little, pneumatic crank of a sound, and the lens opened like the pupil of a fish's eye, and sucked in whatever light was left in the day, arranging flecks of dark mineral on a smear of film, and the picture was made. This is all that speaks to me of that family, whether stoic or tender, only a generation ago. What were their names? Where are their graves? Who can tell me now that my father himself is gone?

The Hongo Store

In Volcano, Charlotte and Lily ran the store for their father. By wartime, though, Charlotte had gotten more than tired of the routine. Although assigning blame wasn't her way, she must have begun to understand that her father was taking advantage of her, and she looked for a way out. Weekends, she drifted down the mountain and spent time with Torakiyo's family in Hilo.

"We all grew up separated those hard times. Gran'pa always meant to send for the boys, but he never did. I know he wanted to, but he ended up just sending money when he could from time to time, not keeping in touch, but holding back, trying to make a go of it. My sister and I grew up Volcano girls! Country girls! Whereas your father and uncle grew up big town city boys! That's a difference! It's sad when I think of it sometimes, but our lives weren't easy in those days, and we all did the best we could. It was the Depression when all this happened.

"I had it rough as the oldest, responsible for all the cooking and cleaning and even minding the store and the gas station in Volcano. You had to crank that old gas pump! It took strength! Your father grew up reading books and going to shows—the movies—whereas my sister and I learned bookkeeping and wholesale and profit. And your uncle learned gambling! The bright lights. Downtown city boys!

"After a while, I just couldn't stand it. I was older, in high school, and more and more, I went away for weekends and a few weeks during the summers to live with my aunt and uncle down in Hilo Town. Things were always right there. They were prosperous, but it wasn't only that. They were kind. They were Christians and took me to church and I met a lot of nice people that way. I learned that there was another side of life! People could live in good spirits, they could have fun! They could care about each other! I decided then that I would live that kind of life, that trust sometimes was more important than profit. Others sacrificed for me. I was eighteen or thereabouts. I met my husband and left home and we started our own family down in Hilo. My sister stayed in Volcano for a while, but, pretty soon, she moved out too. She lived in Volcano, but she got married and found her own house.

"Well, my father was at a loss! He couldn't run the store himself. All that produce, the canned goods, the sacks of rice to carry and meats to cut and refrigerate. He couldn't even chop ice! He was a playboy like I said! He never could keep money.

"About this time—this was already after the war—your father started writing us. Oh, his penmanship was so impressive! And the postmarks and stamps on the letters. He was in the service on guard duty in Germany—at Nuremberg, where those trials were—and he wrote such elegant letters! Even now I can still remember them—the language, the fancy writing, the stamps and the names of places. My father wrote him back, just short notes he dictated to us in Japanese. We were instructed to translate, I remember—*Hello, how are you? Do you have enough to eat?* and like that. But he didn't send money. Your father sent money! His soldier's pay! They never had written before. It must have been strange for them both.

"But then my father got sick. He got *cancer*. From all that smoking and drinking and carrying on. Coughing so bad, he couldn't even get out of bed. In those days, there wasn't anything to do but try to stay comfortable. No therapies. I heard about it down in Hilo, but I was already married and had children to care for! And so did my sister. And he was worrying about passing things along, I suppose. That's how my father got the idea to ask your father to come to Volcano. Albert had come back from the war, writing us all the while—from Italy, from Nuremberg, where he was a guard, then Hamburg—and the next thing we knew he was in New York and Chicago, San Francisco. Oh, he was a whirlwind! And then, wouldn't you know it, he was finally back in Honolulu, a returning veteran. Your grandfather was so proud to speak of him then. He suddenly had a grown son he could talk to the villagers about—a veteran of the war. I thought it was a little strange, but . . . Albert had jobs—in agriculture, in a lab at the university. Then, eventually he told us that he had found a nice girl, your mother, and that he was going to marry her. Well, my father had to do something after all that talking, so he gave them a big party down in Hilo—at a teahouse of all things!

"My father wasn't too lonely, but he thought he needed help with the store. There were lotsa plantation girls running around loose in those days—no money, no prospects, no likely man. All the young ones were off in Europe fighting. Or else they were *too* young—in high school. When you went to the Bon dances, ohh, there the girls would be, all in their twenties, and then the boys all still in high school with their pants too tight and shoes untied. So the girls couldn't find anyone.

"But my father needed someone. There was a stock girl working parttime. Pretty soon she knew everything. I don't know exactly how he found her—an ad in the paper. Whether it was for a wife or a stock girl, I don't know. But some say there was a matchmaker involved—you know, just informally, an older woman in town who has a cousin or someone she knows who knows someone from another town. At first we thought she was just a cleaning lady or stock clerk he'd hired to tide himself over until he could figure things. Well, pretty soon, he must have realized he could save money by simply marrying her! He wouldn't have to pay her anything and she could run the store, do all those hard physical labor kinds of things he didn't like to do. All he had to do was get married. So he did. He married Eveline, a woman from Hāwī—a plantation town up Kohala way. North. Where Kamehameha is from. Where there are lotsa valleys. You can look from there across the channel to Maui, purple mountain.

"The next thing you know, Albert was here! My longlost younger brother. We were so excited. And he worked *hard*! He pumped the gas, went every morning to town to pick up supplies, stocked the shelves, priced everything, worked on the books. He was eager. He wanted to prove himself to his father, I think. Ohh, I remember him moving *fast* around the store in his crisp khaki pants—he pressed them himself, you know—and aloha shirt. You could just *feel* his energy. Everyone in the town was impressed. Such a young man and working so hard. Japanese like that. They like to see effort. So it was because your dad came to Volcano to run the store and your mother along with him. That's how come you were born here—the only Hongo from Volcano. Your father Albert was running the store!"

When my aunt fell silent, this last bit of the long family story over, the rain falling outside filled the silence I would not. It came down in gray fingers brushing damp the screens across the windows, shredding the jouncing leaves of the banana tree I could see being buffeted near the back door, its porch lit with the yellow light spilling out from the kitchen. I imagined the flaglike sleeves of a weighted green gown, torn and raveled by a terrible angel. Illusion had worn the gown and now stepped from it naked as a dancer shedding a costume skin of satin and brocade. I was not who I had thought myself to be, the nothing sprung from a nothing without history. I'd been born to an amazingly twisted line, to a dancer and a libertine, equally prodigal, and to a filial but orphaned father, each of us a de-scendant of shame, inheritors of no tangible patrimony. I had sailed back, but no tie but this ripped and jagged story bound me to the place. Outside, I saw banana leaves bouncing in the wind and rain, tearing themselves into sheets and strips of vivid, tropical life.

HOUSE OF FERNS/
HOUSE OF FIRE

Hāpu'u

IN VOLCANO, it was an amazing thing just to step outside the little cabin. During the days, I set about trying to inform my ignorance about things biological, sorting through and try‑ ing to remember the shapes and characteristic features of each of the strange plants that surrounded the little house. There was a giant tree fern called, in Hawaiian, *hāpu'u*, that made up the mid‑level of the forest, the second canopy under the tall *'ōhi'a* trees. I'd heard them referred to as "lantern ferns," and imag‑ ined their huge, dolphinfish‑sized fronds as emerald lamps within the shadows of the forest, pitching with the roll of the wind and constant light rains. There were books on the shelves that told me a little about them, but I learned more from tak‑

ing short walks through the understory where I'd come upon an old pig⁄trail that led me through the dripping green curtain of the forest and over lava⁄hummocked earth.

Hāpuʻu grows from a small plant low in the shadows (like the ground fern you'd buy in a local nursery) to a gigantic and imposing tree of fifteen to twenty⁄five feet with a lavish crown of fanlike green fronds large as the spiral brushes of a commer⁄ cial car wash. "Big enough to obscure a meedjum land mam⁄ mal," my biologist friend Jim Jacobi once said. As it grows, its lower fronds sag and dry up, nearly breaking off but not quite, collapsing to the ground yet still joined to the tree, a spray of them radiating from the trunk like ribs from a broken um⁄ brella. The *hāpuʻu* gets heavier and heavier as it grows, taking on more and more water weight and plant material, putting on its thick canopy of luxurious foliage, stressing its fragile, root⁄ less base in the earth. It can fall horizontally and begin grow⁄ ing again from the top end, the old bole acting as both a counterweight and a new, outsized root system. I've seen num⁄ bers of them fallen in this way, pushed over by pigs or brought down by their own weight, their broken columns jointed at near right angles on one end, the new trees growing from the col⁄ lapsed forms of the old, the plumes of fronds making the com⁄ bination look as if a colony of giant tube worms had taken up residence in the forest's understory.

For the *hāpuʻu* has no "roots." Its stump is its root, a thick bundle of matlike fibers that take on sustenance from the rains. The standing trunk is actually a bundle of fibrous stalks, radi⁄ ating upward in successive growth⁄rays around a phloemlike core surrounded by an absorbent, spongy matting that knits everything together. This matting is, in actuality, a system of in⁄ tertwined aerial roots that can look black to bronze⁄colored, de⁄

pending on the amount of water it holds and the intensity of light shining through the canopy. The villagers here in Volcano know that you must water *hāpu'u* from the *top* of its trunk, not at its base. Its roots are *adventitious,* bundled into a communal shape like a stovepipe in air rather than groping through the ash and loam and crumbling lava like an underground bole. The *hāpu'u* grows, then, like a gigantic mushroom in the rain forest, its at-tachment to earth a fine and fragile thing, the step of an angel.

A huge, newborn stalk of one of these trees, curled and filigreed with budding fronds, emerges out of this natal bundle looking like the fiddlehead of a bass violin made of a soft green wood but bronzed with *pulu*—the protective feathering of silky hair that clothes it as it arrives into the world. As you walk through a stand of them, you can imagine hearing the fronds thump and snacker with the bass thrummings of birth, a silent jazz and a uteral rending going on both at once. People often steal these plants from the forest and plant property lines and fringe front lawns in ludicrous straight rows of *hāpu'u* as mon-uments and paeans to space conquered from wilderness.

Foraging pigs, feral hybrid descendants of the domestic stock and the breed brought by the Polynesians, like to knock over the trees and grind through the stalks and aerial roots to gouge out and devour the starchy cores. Back before World War II, *hāpu'u* was a delicacy the Japanese farmers made by cutting into a tree or two and, like the pigs, stripping out the cores, shaving and slicing them down into bite-sized grayish pickles cured in a spicy brine. My aunt remembers eating *hāpu'u,* receiving jars of them as gifts from neighbors, somehow associating them with the poverty of her childhood. But there are those who covet them, especially now in these nostalgic and trendy times, as a garnish, in salads, or otherwise employing them as a delicacy something like artichoke hearts only more imposing.

Through town gossip, I heard about a naïve or oppor-tunistic Filipino woman (it was never clear which), a school-teacher married to the director of the community center, who cut down an entire row of young *hāpu'u* used as a border on her neighbor's property line. She wanted them for the tender *hāpu'u* hearts. She used a resolute combination of a handsaw, a machete, and a Swedish filleting knife to do the job. It took the morning and most of the afternoon, but by *pau hana* (quitting) time, she had gone through over a hundred feet of *hāpu'u* trees spaced one every seven feet or so—about fifteen healthy plants and enough to have provided five gluttonous wild pigs with their weekly portion of necessary carbohydrates. She sliced them and pickled them in jars, "putting them up." When her Japanese neighbor returned from his work as an electrician, he wept to see the demise of his plants. Then he got angry when he realized that his neighbor had done it. He complained, trying to confront her as best he could in the mixed English and Hawaiian pidgin he possessed. He wanted to go after the woman, whom he thought a criminal, with a machete himself, but, polite Japanese male chauvinist that he was, he yelled at the woman's husband, who should have known better than to allow his wife to do such a thing.

The husband was Caucasian and a personnel manager, the director of a small business, and would not be pushed around, particularly not by a hysterical Japanese electrician, however indignant and righteous in his belief. The manager argued that the tree ferns were mostly on *his* side of the property line and that those that weren't were *on* the property line and therefore a fair or arguable crop for his wife to harvest as she chose. The Japanese neighbor stalked off to his garage, picked up a roll of white twine from his toolbox, marched down through the back of his lot, crashing through ginger plants and *uluhe* underbrush until he found what he wanted. He tied on to a rusty corner stake driven into lava during a survey he ordered when he'd bought the property thirty years before. He walked the property line then, defining the boundary along his angry march, threading the twine through the shredded stumps of *hāpu'u*. Near where their graveled driveways came to a conflu- ence, he rummaged around until he found the other corner stake, rusting and bent at the top, but still solidly sunken into its concrete, tied twine to it, and broke off the roll. He pointed along the demarcation he'd just made—a somewhat jagged line mostly *beside* the row of decapitated trees, clearly demonstrating that they had been on *his* property.

"Now don't be going *technical* on me," the manager began to say, slipping into his Georgia accent. But the Japanese elec- trician, moved by his own incontrovertible evidence, wanting to inspire consensus, proceeded to give just testimony about how he had raised each tree from its shoot like a baby, like a litter of puppies from one mother, how he had watered and cared for them, how he had given them plant food and boosts of nitrogen from time to time, how he had gleaned them of epiphytes and zoological parasites, how each plant almost had a personality for him, how, once into their adolescence (*hāpu'u* grow to be thirty to forty years old at full maturity, and these were twelve- to fifteen-year-old plants), he even thought they should be given *names*—Hawaiian names, Japanese names, American names. It was a long, rambling appeal to sentiment, tenderness, and po- etic understanding, little of which his defensive neighbor pos- sessed or was inclined even to fake, as he might have if the appeal had been made publicly at the local Lions Club annual fund-raiser for the Program for Literacy Among Hawaiian Schoolchildren. The Japanese had spoken in an incomprehensible but melodic mix of Japanese, Hawaiian, and broken English—completely unfathomable though intimidating to his neighbor, who only recognized key phrases like "good neighbor" and "bad wife" and *kuleana* (Hawaiian for "responsibility"). Instead of a creole soliloquy, the manager heard a polyglot harangue. He stalked over to his own garage, picked out a shovel, went over to the one *hāpu'u* still left untouched, and began to try to dig it out of the ground from its base up. A fight ensued, the Japanese tackling his neighbor, the man from Georgia flinging the shovel aside and throwing wild good-ol'-boy Sunday punches, the fight ending with a *jūdō* throw, ground-wrestling, and amateurish hammerlocks, broken up by the screaming schoolteacher, who hit at them both, beating them each about the shoulders and ears with the flat side of the abandoned shovel. They cleaned themselves up, each thought about going to court, but instead settled on waging a durable campaign of gossip and mutual boycotts against each other that attempted to pull in the entire community. Most folks simply avoided becoming involved, but everyone enjoyed telling the tale eventually known as "*Hāpu'u* Wars" throughout the village of Volcano.

American principle: *The natural world is a crop.*

I read about early-twentieth-century entrepreneurs harvesting *hāpu'u,* trying to capitalize on its commercial value as a source of starch for laundry. They'd saw or knock down the trees, rip open the bundles to the soft cores, and scoop out the piths, boiling them down in huge iron vats once they'd collected enough. Shirts starched in *hāpu'u* must have borne a damp, rain-forest stiffness reminiscent of daylong drizzles. When you sweated, the shirt must have clung like an epiphyte around your neck.

Pulu—like a fuzzy vernix around the new stalks emerging from the trunk—was harvested too, thousands of trees cut for the bronze hairs, tried as a stuffing for pillows and mattresses during the last century. Hiking along the East Rift Zone from Mauna Ulu (a largish spatter cone piled up from the Kīlauea eruption from 1976 to 1982) to Nāpau Crater, I suddenly came upon the ruins of one of these *hāpuʻu* factories. They were nine-teenth-century mud brick walls in a clearing canopied by *ʻōhiʻa* and a healthy stand of the tree ferns, nodding guardians over the unsettled bones of Hawaiian Fordism. *Pulu* factory work-ers, wearing cowboy bandannas over their noses and mouths, stripped the stalks of the usable fibers and bundled them into sackcloth and burlap bags, which then went on muleback a few miles across an ancient trail through the rain forest and over the cliffs to the flat lava plains near the eastern shore of the island. Packtrains carried tons of the fluff from the Nāpau factory to a landing off the surf-pounding sea cliffs near where a clipper ship bound for San Francisco had anchored itself on its way back from taking on stores in Lahaina on Maui. Sailors used skiffs to make the transfer of goods, since there was no harbor, and over the course of fifteen years, from 1867 to 1881 (the very year my great-grandfathers are said to have made their immi-gration crossings from Kumamoto, Hiroshima, and Fukuoka to Honolulu, Hilo, and Waialua), transported more than four million pounds of the fibers from Hawaiʻi to the continental United States. That would mean tree ferns enough to reforest an entirely new emerald island somewhere. It also means that we nearly lost the island of ferns we have today.

Jim Jacobi, my biologist friend, told me that the *hāpuʻu* is *an immortal tree.* "It's almost magic, really," he said as we traipsed through ʻŌlaʻa Tract about a thousand feet below

Kīlauea Summit, a few miles from Volcano Village. He was trying to show me a lobelia specimen he'd identified the year be⁄fore, a rare one though not particularly endangered. We came upon an older part of the forest where the *'ōhi'a* had died off and been replaced by a grove of *hāpu'u* as the upper canopy. He pointed out how wet and swampy the soil had become, how many trees had fallen over and grown back again.

"The *hāpu'u* gets to a certain point when it's too old or too heavy to support its crown—about thirty or forty years. Then it collapses, and you'd think it'd die, but it just sends up an⁄other shoot and makes a joint back from the fallen trunk up to the canopy again and lives for another thirty or forty years until it collapses another time and sends up a new bundle of roots and fronds. A tree can fall a bunch of times, make a series of joints like you see around here, and send up a new crown every time. From under the canopy, the old trunks look like jointed pink plastic snakes you get at the ringtoss for prizes at the county fair. They're amazing. Who knows how long they can live? Or how old any given plant is. If you measure a single life from stalk to crown to tree collapse, you get maybe thirty years. But if you count all the times a tree's collapsed and sent up a *new* crown, then crown after crown, who *knows* how old the plant is? It's *immortal!*"

I'd seen them strewn about that way, the old trunks mossed over and stinking. Some trees might have two or three old trunks, others more, zigzag elbows of reeking, lichened rot on the forest floor.

For me, *hāpu'u* became part of Hawai'i's and the world's most primitive splendor. Walking through the rain forest, I once had the thought that any of them could be the tree of W. H. Hudson's *Green Mansions,* the slender, elflike girl of spir⁄

itual fantasy tucked inside her sparkling gown of spiderwebs and the moist, bronze-bearded trunk of the *hāpu'u*. Or a stand of them, isolated and a little desolate under a high covering canopy of *'ōhi'a,* might be the Grove of Suicides of Dante's *Inferno,* confessing their sins and mistaken passions to the moths and faint wind fluttering through the forest shadows. Yet, they seem more purgatorial than hellish to me, plants that might have been part of the promising beginnings of all things rather than their eternal ends in damnation. These are ferns, gigantic and prehistoric and numerous as beads on an immense abacus, counting me back more than the scant generation of family history I missed not growing up here, counting years past all of human history back through Holocene time to the Upper Cretaceous or Paleocene when man was born as one with the beasts.

Hāpu'u shook me out of my own mind, its pettinesses, its inglorious memories of quotidiana and notions of identity and the personal, and joined me to something else, not quite beyond time but anciently a part of it—a *via negativa* I glimpsed in the presence of the most chthonic, intimate piece of botanical creation I've ever seen.

Uluhe

On another hike, I came upon a line of steam vents girdled with the singed bramble of another fern, called *uluhe* in Hawaiian, commonly known as false staghorn fern—this is a vine that could hug the ground closely or bridge a tiny chasm between cracks in the earth. They'd take over the ground places where a fire had burned a clearing or stripped down the upper canopy of 'ōhi'a. They'd also take over ground that had been freshly bulldozed and, I'd heard, where cattle had been allowed to overgraze. I'd find them mounding up in bogs or little sinks where the earth might have collapsed from a quaking in the vol-cano. On hikes, I'd find snarls of *uluhe* winding themselves slowly around and up along the trunks and boles of trees like a flow of lava itself making fiery, pythonlike pirouettes through a grove of 'ōhi'a.

Uluhe is a major part of the ground cover in the rain for-est. Its yellow-green fronds grow out from a tough central stem that branches into separate, wiry leaf stalks bobbing over the wet ground. Latin name *Dicranopteris linearis, uluhe* grows into thick bunches and mats that cover areas of the forest that might have been opened up by a burn or a bulldozer or a recent lava flow, or else it bundles up around steaming gulches or cascades down slip-faulted cliffsides of the volcano. Vinelike, it makes a swirling, light green tangle that can look like a leafy surf, three to four feet high, foaming over a line of understory exposed by highway cuts or else the low crest of a fault scarp it has over-grown. At times, it climbs and twists like liana up a tree, but it never becomes an epiphyte, those miraculously parasitic worts and lobelias and ferns that grow with roots driven into the boughs and crotches of a host tree. *Uluhe,* however much it climbs from the floor of the forest and garlands the 'ōhi'a, has its own roots in the earth, forming multiple trails of interlacing stems sticking fast to the ground.

Near one of the craters, I came upon a dense web of them that served me as a kind of rope-bridge across a small chasm in the earth. I saw there was a crack in the earth underneath me that ran about twenty feet uphill from where I was standing and another twenty downslope. The divide might have been two feet or it might have been six feet—there was no telling. And I had no choice, could do nothing but keep going, as I'd already stepped onto the little bridge of *uluhe* quivering under me before I realized what I'd done. The fronds and stems made a woven matting and overlapping latticework tough enough to bear my weight as I stepped cautiously through the bramble. As I picked my way across, I remembered a story of some other people, rangers or biologists in the National Park, who had fallen through a mat of *uluhe* while they were on the trail of some wild pigs. I didn't recall how they'd gotten out. It also crossed my mind that there might be lava tubes below the bushes, a huge cave someplace with its ceiling broken through and *uluhe* grown over it like the patching on a roof. You'd step there and then fall through to a black and root-entangled world of eyeless albino spiders, blind native bats, and the ancient spirits of the dead whose bones and petroglyphs might have been deposited there before the coming of Captain Cook. Who would ever find you? I pieced my way through that day and came back without telling anyone.

Another time, I came upon a thickened wharf of *uluhe* growing up as a matted fringe around a crack in the ground where steam was escaping. Around the loamy edges of the crevice were fronds browned from the heat. There was a fringe of dead, gray plants that showed how the vapor spilling into the air from the split earth was a killing one, sulphurous and noxious. I wondered what a full-on eruption would do, what drilling this earth would do, as some were planning on a wide scale on this island. I saw devastation, a blank, basaltic desert as on the moon, a resolute plain of craters and ash and pumice that drank in all light and water and returned nothing. "The sterile back of Leviathan," I said aloud to the vapors swirling around me, to the pythons of *uluhe* wrapping themselves up the trunks of the *'ōhi'a* a clearing away. Pele—the fearsome Hawaiian goddess of volcanoes. From a fanciful painting, I remembered a face wreathed in fire, her long hair a plume of erupting lava. The bridge trembled under me.

E x c u r s i o n s

With Alexander, Cynthia and I took a few tourist trips around the volcano and forest. I had a guidebook that mentioned a huge lava tube in the fern forest near Kīlauea Iki, the little caldera next to Kīlauea where I'd seen the schoolchildren marching and singing. We went there, parking our car in a lot filled with buses and ambling tourists dressed in polyesters. We entered the tube through a tear in the lip of a crater that had been filled in with a small forest of tree ferns. Circling downward along an asphalt pathway from above that dense growth, it seemed like the bottom of the world had opened up a hatchway for vegetation of another, lusher time to grow sheltered inside a little sunken bubble on the face of the earth. I carried Alexander in a Gerry pack, fitted snug against my back, and he lolled and napped, and banged at my head with his pacifier as we trekked downward, entering a dank world of dripping things, epiphytes, and aerial roots. I'd heard of a blind albino spider that tracked a blind albino cricket into the cave made by the lava tubes about twenty-five thousand years ago. They made a genetic tango exiting out of the light and entering into the

darknesses of evolution. I ducked my head, bobbing Alexander against my shoulder, and entered a long cave beneath the
earth where, once, about four hundred years ago, a glowing
river of lava three times as deep as *Homo erectus* is tall ran under
the friable skin of new land from Kīlauea down through a
chain of tributaries to the sea. Cynthia and I held hands as we
walked through the little segment of it improved for tourists,
and, after a few dozen yards, emerged out of a dank world into
a sun-shower of light dousing mossy blocks of basalt on the
other side. Voices echoed in from the cave, children skipped
and skittered by, couples with babies in strollers trundled, and
klatches of Japanese tourists dressed in black shorts and white
polo shirts snapped color pictures of each other, setting off a
chain of camera flashes. I was bored. We left quickly, hurrying
back to the cabin.

What bored me was the superficiality of it. That there
wasn't more to know besides what the Park Service or guide-
books told you. That there wasn't any more to *feel*. I wanted
an encounter, an embrace or a showdown with the past. I
wanted to stand in the presence of whatever ghost of my father's
past might be there for me, take up whatever representative of
my grandfather I could conjure, and grab him up by the col-
larbones until his face was warmed by my own and he would
acknowledge me, grinning like a gambler who owed me money.

I said "Fuckit" a lot, grumpy whenever I became aware
of any triviality. I treasured washing dishes with a rag full of
detergent because I could look through the kitchen window at
the blue water tank beside the house slowly filling with runoff
coursing through the gutters as an afternoon's drizzle drained
from around the roof of the cottage. It mattered to me that smells
from a wet earth alongside Volcano Highway triggered no vi-

sual echoes except images of a tiered forest of barkless, silver-limbed trees, tree ferns, and the green froth of staghorns. The rain fell and clouds raced up-mountain toward the summit. I flung civilized scorn on the wet grasses outside the cottage and began to sing in my own flesh, reeds in my bones, passion like an owl whooing from the dank hollow of a tree.

Devastation Trail

One day, after lunch, I went off alone with Alexander while Cynthia did some chores. I drove us through the National Park again, went left at the Chain of Craters Road cutoff to the parking lot near the lookout where I'd seen the schoolchildren trooping across the black caldera under a light drizzle. I planned a short amble across Devastation Trail, the planked walkway across the 1959 cinderfall from Kīlauea Iki that burned down the portion of the *'ōhi'a* forest closest to the little cindercone between the calderas named Pu'u Pua'i.

In November of 1959, Kīlauea erupted with a keenly dramatic episode of lava-fountaining. The cliff walls of Kīlauea Iki burst open with *pāhoehoe,* pouring over the old caldera floor, then began blasting vertically in a fire-fountain nearly two thousand feet high. My relatives, who drove up from Hilo to see it, told me that the cinders had drifted away from the fountaining and fell down on them and their parked cars. They held up newspapers to cover their heads while they watched, and the hot cinders would start the papers smoldering. They told me that the ground sang like old plumbing and the sound seemed to shake them from the insides, from their *organs* rather than their bones. The spout and plume of lava looked to my family like a whale's breeching the sea and steaming up a red cloud rather than a white one. The little hill that the ashfall made even began to look like a whale—a buff-and-brown one, unmottled and virginal, a fine new calf sporting under the sky.

I saw this in photographs and postcards of the eruption— the plume of lava opening from a fine corolla into an expansive blossoming of cinders as the lava chilled and darkened from red to gray and brown. It made a "hard rain" that tended to fall southwesterly with the prevailing trade winds, settling among the fern and 'ōhi'a forest that had sprung up since the last major ashfall of 1790. That year, an ashfall and outburst of gas had surprised and killed an army of Hawaiians crossing Ka'ū to Puna to oppose Kamehameha, the warrior king who became the first to unify all of the islands. The forest burned again as it did in 1790, down to its roots, and the 'ōhi'a, hāpu'u, 'ama'u, and *uluhe* had to start again under the bleached, spindly ghosts of the old forest trees. Devastation Trail was the path the National Park had made so tourists could pass through the regrowth area and see the forest coming back with new, pioneering plants.

The cinderfall came halfway up the trunks of many of the old trees. I saw an old highway speed-limit sign that had been nearly swallowed up by the new soil level. It was buried past its wooden throat all the way to the metal sign. The old road around the crater rim had been partially lost too. The '59 cinder-fall took away the section of it alongside Kīlauea Iki, and the road we went on now passed farther on away from the old ledges of the craters. Later, I'd become familiar with road closures and losses. Kīlauea regularly buried the land, burning forests, covering roads, even taking away an entire village. An earthquake dropped a section of land along the East Rift Zone several feet in 1971, cracking and collapsing the portion of Crater Rim Road beside the ledges between Iki and Kīlauea, alongside Waldron Ledge near the bluff by the large tourist hotel overlooking the main caldera. When the volcano was about its business, it did what it wanted. Trees and traffic were no consideration.

When we got out of the car, we surprised a pair of *nēnē*, brown and nearly the same color as the cinder itself, foraging for berries amidst an old stand of *'ōhi'a*, now understoried with *'ōhelo*, the plentiful heath shrubs full of a tangy red fruit. It seemed to me amazing that food could spring so directly out of rock, so easily and plentifully. I found a little bough with a few berries still nestled in among its tight and tiny camellia-like leaves, and plucked a few, offering one to Alexander peeking out of the Gerry pack over my shoulder. He gummed and sucked on them, smacking his lips. I felt the warm skin of his cheek against my neck, and jounced along, setting out for the little trail.

Since '59, dozens of plants had come back in, many of them exotics. The *'ōhi'a* was growing, and the ferns and sedges and the *'ōhelo* too, but blackberry bushes crowded in, and a green shrub from China called "anemone" with huge, ball-shaped, handkerchief-white flowers that looked to me like cow's-eyes. We escaped the little grove of newsprung plants and out onto an expanse of buff-colored cinder unblemished by growth of any kind. A buffeting wind flung a cold but kindly force into our faces. It felt to me that the soft, cool lips of the universe were blowing upon us. I felt a faint burst of

faith, and walked a little more quickly, wind in my ears, little
flaps of assurance and susurration whipping me along to finish the day.

'Ō h i ' a

Of all the plants I was trying to get familiar with, it was the
'ōhi'a, a species of myrtle with the scientific name *Metrosideros
polymorpha* ("heart of iron with many forms"), that was the
most important tree in Volcano's rain forest. '*Ōhi'a* grows
throughout Polynesia and probably came to Hawai'i in sea drift
thousands of years ago on a packet of rafting plants or in wind
drift borne on the gales of a hurricane. It can be a shrub or a
tree, depending, with smooth bark and hairy or smooth leaves
that radiate out from its branches like soft green spoons on short
stems.

Sherwin Carlquist, a biologist I met in California who
has written several books on Hawaiian plant life, says that '*ōhi'a*
might have made multiple migrations to the islands, coming
first as a bush or shrub with shiny, glabrous leaves, then next
as seeds of a tree with hairy leaves, or vice versa. Not unlike the
California woodland oak tree, the Hawaiian '*ōhi'a* exists in a
kind of hybrid swarm of closely related and genetically com-
patible subspecies, capable of radiating into many adaptive
forms, occupying multiple botanical niches in the forest at altitudes from seacoast to subalpine.

In Volcano, in the rain forest at three thousand to four
thousand feet, '*ōhi'a* was everywhere around me—out in the

front and back yards in little stands of saplings, as mature trees sixteen to more than eighty feet tall in the deep forests forming their upper canopies, as seedlings in little perched botanical colonies in a patch of butchy green hair among mosses and worts colonizing on the wet stump of a fallen tree or growing epiphytically at the top of the trunk of a host *hāpuʻu* or even from rain gutters and the tops of telephone poles in Volcano Village, as stained and crafted salad bowls and varnished cribbage boards, as a curio jewel box whittled into the shape of a short but thickly fluted brown penis erect in a display case at the Volcano Art Center.

As wood, there are a lot of other uses for *ʻōhiʻa*. I read in Hawaiian-language dictionaries and regional field guides that the Hawaiians used *ʻōhiʻa* for the gunwales of their canoes—it withstood wear better—and a musical history of Hawaiʻi said that, because they lasted longer and stayed put once tuned, entertainers preferred the keys on their ukuleles to be made from *ʻōhiʻa*. When weather was cold, I called a number posted on the bulletin board outside of the Hongo Store, and a *haole* guy came over with his battered Ford pickup piled high with a half-cord of cut *ʻōhiʻa* he got from a stand behind his lot on old ʻIʻiwi Road. The wood was wet and mossy and suspiciously clumped with bog mud, but I took it and tried to get it to dry in my garage, under the floors of the house, themselves made of *ʻōhiʻa* cut in long strips, stained a deep brown and polished to a subtle, dark tannish shine by years of wear from the tread of bare human feet.

ʻŌhiʻa leaves and blossoms showed up in the Christmas wreaths our neighbors made. *Lehua*—the puffy pom-poms of red filaments like the erect crests of mating cranes—were prized and woven into *lei*. I'd see raiding parties of local women gathering *lehua* blossoms in the vacant lots around our house, pruning the little *'ōhi'a* trees of their scarlet beloveds, the crimson warriors that were the flowers of the tree. *Lehua* could mean "sweetheart," the lover's familiar in a figurative Hawaiian. The gatherers would have been from a *hula hālau*—a dance school—converging on Volcano to find what they needed for head garlands and wristbands, for *lei* used in performances. They would have met near the summit or along Mauna Loa Road on the dry side, where they would have first gathered *palapalai* ferns. It was a belief that no one respectful of the old ways should pick *lehua* on the way *up* to Kīlauea or while coming *in* to the rain forest. Its violation would anger Pele, the strong goddess of the volcano. You were only to pick *'ōhi'a lehua* on the way *out* of the rain forest. Otherwise, a covering mist might overtake you, and you'd live in bewilderment, too enchanted to leave the place.

Dieter Mueller-Dombois, a biologist retired from the University of Hawaii who now makes his home uphill from an old strawberry patch near the Japanese Schoolhouse in Volcano, tells me that *'ōhi'a* can die off all at once in one huge generational stand that can cover gigantic swaths of square miles along an entire slope of Mauna Loa. This is because mature *'ōhi'a* takes over the biological zone and completely fills it up all by itself, creating, for all intents and purposes, a botanical monoculture, choking off light to other plants and even new seedlings of *'ōhi'a* so that, for scores of years, nothing but the mature *'ōhi'a* can grow there. Until, that is, some kind of environmental disturbance or catastrophe occurs—not just a burn or a superheated flow of fresh lava, which is an obvious cataclysm, but a subtle shift in soil chemistry or an alteration of groundwater availability—to the point where the entire stand of trees, essentially a cohort generation at exactly the same age and relative stage of health, might suddenly die off simultaneously, creating strands of dieback, whole sectors of the forest in senescence in a mosaic pattern of decline, yet making way for new seedlings to seek the light. What might at first look like a disaster would thus enable renewal. Together with *hāpu'u* and *'ama'u* ferns, young *'ōhi'a* inspire a botanical symphony of succession, making way for the club moss and *'ōhelo* berry, the raspberry and black coffeeberry *pilo*—botanical diversity. Young *'ōhi'a* flower at the height of only a meter or two, and, in concert with neighboring adult trees, they spurt forth a vast and covering seed-rain showering down invisibly and, says Mueller-Dombois, nearly all the time, alighting on lavas and burns, on matted ferns and the neck fur of your neighbor's cat, rooting in catchment crevices and fallen, water-soaked stumps.

I loved the way *'ōhi'a* looked, whether carved or corded, living or in senescence and dieback, in silvery branches stretching up to a blue cerulean canopy of sky by Volcano's dump and transfer station, remnants of a five-acre burn in '87. *'Ōhi'a* like the long digits of powder-white finger coral fronding up from a black reef. I liked the wind-shimmered leaves of *'ōhi'a* in the sunny three o'clock afternoons, green coins mullioned in the slanting light of a mustard-yellow sun, and I liked the gray Rip Van Winkle beard of aboveground roots balling and shrouding down from an old sentinel trunk alongside Crater Rim Drive near Kīlauea Iki.

Though the effects of pollution and global warming I'm sure don't help much, and though land developers and private owners have slowly cut into forested areas for homes and garages and flower farms, *'ōhi'a* still persists in patches of growth and decline around Volcano. In a checkerboard of clear-cuts and teeming life in the village, out in the National Park in rich floristic provinces side by side with new lava flows and fresh burns, thickened canopies of old stands run alongside upstart adolescents letting in the light to the forest floor, their differing ages synchronous with the chronology of multiple lava flows that slipped by and over each other, that braided and buckled, that burned and beatified equally well.

Wāwae-'iole

Other plants I was able to recognize and identify those early days in Volcano were as conspicuous as *hāpu'u* and *'ōhi'a* but less plentiful, parts of the forest's lowest level and not a dominant band of the ecosystem. These were things like the *'ama'u* fern (a native), the bamboo orchid (an invasive exotic), and club moss—the three-foot-high native plant called *wāwae-'iole* in Hawaiian, translated as "rat's-foot" in my illustrated trailside guide, the pendant spikes of strobili curved and clawlike. Its shade was that light emerald-green of cedars in the Pacific Northwest, and the texture of its branches seemed a bit cedar-like if I didn't look too closely.

For a while, *wāwae-'iole* seemed to me just another yellow-green plant that grew in the thin soil of Volcano, distinguished partly by its diminutive size and smallish numbers, but memorable most for its wonderful formation—a low, green fan of the forest; a coral-like, fronded moss of long scales; its overall shape like that of a petite Christmas tree trimmed with the little forked scissorhands commemorated by its Hawaiian name. *Wāwae-'iole,* like each element of the environment here, was a distinctly benign and clear message from creation to anyone who might care to bear witness to it. A resilient but quivering plant only lightly rooted in the black grit of soil leached out of lava and the nitrous mulch of 'ōhi'a and ferns, the club moss signified to me all of charm and de-light as well as fragility.

I'd spot them along the roadsides throughout Mauna Loa Estates, springing up beside telephone and electric poles, pok-ing through the leaf litter and mulch of decomposing sedges. The Latin name is *Lycopodium cernuum,* and the common Eng-lish name is nodding club moss, acknowledging the way its branches are fixed in a perpetual droop. They reminded me of little green fingers rather than feet, poised over a keyboard. Ru-binstein and Horowitz and Ashkenazy fingers hammering out delicate arpeggios, played *pianissimo,* for a Hawaiian rhapsody, droplets of gray rain like dotted eighth notes clinging to the slen-der, scaly tips.

Later, I read in O. Degener's affectionate and generous field guide, *Plants of Hawaii National Park,* that the plant I was seeing was, in fact, an asexual adult. It reproduced strangely and miraculously, in secret, out of sight and beyond the awareness of most animals. It was neither male nor female, neither father nor mother, but a grandparent in a way. In the tips of its scaled fin-gers, it bore tiny sporangia that, when mature, exploded into nearly invisible clouds of spores that, if successful, then them-selves grew into miniature sexual plants called gametophytes, the male and female, swain and maiden, of the species.

The gametophytes ferret themselves into minute cracks in the lava, hidden away in the microgaps of basaltic rock where moisture collects from rainfall and where it condenses from the sulphurous vents of steam billowing from the cliffsides and cracked earth near Kīlauea. Swain and maiden find both their underground nursery and their darkened bower within the scores of gaping fumaroles and sulphur banks along the rim of the summit caldera. They swarm into life inside of volcanic vents, sustained by heat from the volcano and hidden by its crevices, a Paolo and Francesca of biology, thrilled in inno/ cence, embryos of sexual experience perpetually sequestered in the dark infernos of earth. It is their very immaturity, their prim/ itive but abundant adolescence (the gametophytes grow in un/ countable swarms), that produces offspring, those "adult" plants that are the sexless green *professori* greeting me, nodding under cool, gray robes of afternoon rain, sleeves full of a hid/ den energy. For the club moss, it is its embryos that are the par/ ents, giving birth to adults and not to children, its existence an evidence of life sent into a strange reversal of the conventional, anthropomorphic narratives of maturity.

On a hike in the National Park, taking the trail from the old *hula* platform by Volcano House along the sink of land thick with dying *uluhe* and newsprung colonies of *wāwae-'iole*, I can no longer tread in any damned innocence of my own. The steaming maws of Kīlauea's fumaroles gape like sexual lips along the ground, yellowing labias of volcanic rock opening to the eternal wind of Paolo and Francesca, who sing to us to read no more.

IN MY NOTEBOOK, I wrote down a short list of other plants I'd spotted and wished to learn more about:

kāhili ginger—escaped from cultivation, an exotic with fragrant yellow flowers in foot/long inflorescences at stem tips; resembles a Hawaiian *kāhili,* or "feather standard," hence the name *'ākala*—Hawaiian raspberry and rose-leaved thimbleberry; in abundance (*Rubus*)

māmaki—nettle plant along Volcano and Chain of Craters Road

'ie'ie—climbing screw pine (related to coast *hala* tree?); short plant with long, swordlike leaves; evening primrose and fuch-sia; introduced by voyaging

This kind of book-work emptied me of the feeling I wanted to get at by living here. It was "busywork," a substitute for what I really wanted, that which was more primary and original. It was a simple matter to teach myself the names of everything en-demic and exotic, to match herbaceous features of the forest to photographs and botanical descriptions in a book. Yet, after only a short while, I realized what I wanted was a thing much harder to know. I wanted to feel deep in my bones exactly what I was learning, to know why I was bothering to learn. But knowing the little I did about the plants of the Hawaiian rain forest couldn't equal feeling kith and kin to a place on the earth. At least not yet. And I even wondered if knowing a lot would make any difference either. Even if I had years to spend here, I wor-ried that knowledge would be a poor substitute for initiation.

Lasiandra: A Tale

Besides the *hāpu'u* and *'ōhi'a* and *uluhe,* the one rain-forest plant I studied was an "exotic," an introduced species despised by the park botanists I'd met and local naturalists I knew. The plant was the one that grew in a bushy hedge next to the Hongo

Store, the one my aunt Charlotte had called *mi-no-sabi,* or "I-don't-know." I'd renamed it "the beauty of sadness," but a botanical handbook I had called it "lasiandra," Latin name *Tibouchina semidecandra.* A cogniaux, it was in the Melastoma family of plants.

I found this out from an old text full of Chinese-style, hand-painted illustrations reprinted by Charles Tuttle in Rut-land, Vermont. The book said the plant came from Brazil and described it in this way: "Flowers of royal purple velvet make this plant conspicuous when in bloom. Prefers cooler tempera-tures—mountain roads. Five velvety petals and lighter pinkish stamens in the center, peculiarly angled. Buds are bright pink-ish red, due to velvety color of calyx. Leaves attractive, thickly piled with green hairs which create a silver sheen—marked lat-erally by several conspicuous veins. Old leaves scattered over the plant turn bright scarlet and are as noticeable as the flowers."

What it meant to me was an end to a small mystery I'd wondered about since that afternoon my aunt and uncle had first taken me back to the old store. Knowing the local joke wasn't enough, knowing what it looked like and where it grew wasn't enough either. I wanted to know something more sub-stantial about it. I wanted to know not only the little lore that science had compiled about it but something of its mythology as well, its *metamorphosis* from a misty, astral light into plant and flower.

I gave a spray of it to my wife. She placed it in a gallon jar she left on our unused woodstove. I began to look for it in the bridal nosegays of old photographs of family gatherings, in the floral arrangements my aunt and her club made. I asked cousins about it. Acquaintances. I wanted a collection of stories, an episode of scandal or the bough laid on the crest of a coffin.

What I got was this: There was a marine back during the war, World War II, who lusted after one of my grandfather's store clerks, a teenager from a neighbor's family in Volcano who had just blossomed into puberty herself, and who, along with her older sister, had been impressed since childhood to help out with the work of the store. One of the jobs was keeping the place well swept, inside and out. The inside job was easy—broom and dustpan work. The outside job could be tricky and tough and frustrating. There was asphalt around the store, black and uneven, and the gas and delivery trucks that came by hummocked the paving so badly that cracks began to appear and pools of rain would collect in the depressions. My grand⁄father, Japanese⁄born and a stickler for appearances, insisted that no water be allowed to pool around the lot of the store and make puddles the village children might splash in, displeasing customers. He made the girl take care of this, handing her a push broom. She was to use it to spread the water evenly around the lot, eliminating the puddles.

She was fifteen or sixteen that summer when a troop of marines from the Mainland began driving by in their jeep. She wore a thin cotton *mu'umu'u* which was a flower⁄print, country girl's shift. It was translucent against the low sunlight of dusk or dawn, and the men would stop at the store for gas, get the young woman to pump it, and point out the puddles in the lot, asking her to sweep up again, as they'd noticed she did each morning. She would, and they would lean forward in the jeep, staring at the outline of the soft curve of her hips inside of the dress, the slender inverted vee of light running up between her legs. They were not loud, but stared in silence, then drove on.

One Friday, one of the marines returned. He came to the store and asked for liquor, which my grandfather kept on the shelves behind the register. He kept *sake* and plum wine from Japan and whiskey from Kentucky and Tennessee. The marine wanted whiskey. He paid for it and took it outside and began to drink. He drank it, a full pint, then threw the bottle across the road in the brush behind the stand of cedar trees. He wiped his mouth with his sleeve. He asked for gas. It was sundown. The girl stepped out from behind the counter to pump it. He watched as she primed the pump, working the crank, seeing the roll of the new flesh on her breast heave as she shoved her arms, making the pump work. She stuck the nozzle in the jeep's rear tank, began filling it, and said nothing as the machine's bell made its soft, periodic ding. When she was done, he asked if she'd like a ride up to the military camp at the summit. She said no. How about a ride just around the parking lot? She said maybe. "Well," he said, "you come up here and sit by me and we'll see how you like it."

They drove off, the jeep lurching, and didn't come back for an hour or more. When they did, my grandfather was waiting for them, a pistol in his hand. He waved it and made his neighbor's daughter get out of the jeep and stand beside him. He told the marine to drive the jeep to the edge of the lot, beside the flowering hedge, and to park it. The marine laughed. My grandfather fired a shot in the air. The marine did as he was told, letting out the clutch a little, coasting to the spot. He giggled as he did it, crouching over the wheel and looking back over his shoulder. Just as he was about to sneer, expecting nothing but talk and a waving of hands, my grandfather walked up and hit him across the face with the barrel of the gun. The marine went down slowly, sliding sideways across the passenger side of the jeep. He put an arm over his face. My grandfather hit at him again, the blow falling against a sleeve. He put the gun barrel up against the marine's temple. He cocked it. He shoved a quart-bottle of whiskey under the marine's nose. He told him to drink it. When the marine looked perplexed, my grandfather hit him across the cheek with his fist. The marine drank. First one gulp, then more until the bottle was nearly empty. Then my grandfather hit him again. Under the chin, picking him up off the seat of the jeep. He told him to drive away. "You go now," he said in broken English. "Nevah come back." And he hit him again.

The marine drove off, the jeep lurching through its lower gears, swerving slowly out of the lot and down the Volcano Highway toward Hilo. He planned to come back with his buddies as soon as he could find them, so he drove more quickly with each mile he made downhill. At Glenwood, halfway down the mountain, near a grove of bamboos and an embankment made out of black lava rocks, he hit a shallow bump and bounced, just a little, up off the seat, and, as he came down, cranked the wheel sharply toward his knee. The jeep veered off the road into the wall of lava rocks, and the marine was thrown thirty feet or so, his head and shoulders bouncing against the black face of the road. He died instantly, drunken, his heart full of revenge, his loins satisfied. A purple oil dripped and pooled under the wrecked jeep from the broken pan. Petals from a violet flower fluttered away from a roadside hedge and mired themselves in the rivulet of oil below the jeep. The woody stem of the same flower had been stuck through one of the buttonholes of his green jersey. Under the white tag of his name— who knows what it was? The flower's name is lasiandra. Petals of a velvet indigo, yellow anthers full of pollen, and stamens the color of pink coral—filaments encircled by a sexual girdle of oceanic flesh. *Mi-no-sabi.* The beauty of sadness encountered and then forgotten, shaded in rage, in disgrace, for me only a whisper from the trees, the gesture-free bounce of a fragrant, conscience-troubled wind against the withering cups of passion's flower.

Chill

Things always seemed to be cold and damp for us—after all, we lived in a rain forest, we said to ourselves, and at a level of nearly four thousand feet—consequently, we spent a lot of time figuring out what kind of clothes to wear and arranging our bedding. Temperatures ranged from sunny mid-eighties to chilly bouts of fifty-degree weather during fogs and rainstorms, dropping off even to the low forties near dawn. Daytime, when skies were clear and the summer sun ruled and dried things out for us, wasn't too much of a problem—we just wore shorts or jeans and T-shirts with cheap rubber beach sandals or running shoes. Then, when things chilled down in midafternoon, we'd snuggle into a sweat-shirt or I'd put on the golf jacket I'd inherited from my father. Nights were the problem, as well as the early mornings, when all the ten thousand things of the forest universe had that most intense and damp chill of dew and darkness upon them.

As the place was without heat or a fireplace, we had to bundle up once the sun set. Our host had left us with a mountain of quilts and blankets—brown Tibetan cotton-covered quilts, an assortment of thin, Hawaiian-patterned ones, and the familiar fleecy woolen blankets everyone has. We used all of them on our bed, plus an electric mattress pad Cynthia had

shipped over from Missouri. We'd turn on the electric pad before getting in bed, ostensibly to warm things up, but more and
more, we realized, we needed to dry out the dampness that had
accumulated in the cotton batting of the quilts during the day.
Then, we'd switch the current off sometime during the night,
relying on the mound of covers and the warmth of our bodies.
For Alexander, we used a Japanese *futon* coverlet over the little
drawerlike bed under the shelves of the cabin's library. It was
a complicated arrangement we kept adjusting and readjusting
all the time, never finding the perfect solution, but waking often
during the night, groping for the mattress switch, fumbling out
from under the mound of quilts and picking our steps through
the cabin to the deck and outhouse, and finding darkness and
thick fogs or else the startling bright haze of the galaxy shining
timelessly down on us as we shivered.

Eruption

One night, around the third week we'd spent in the cabin, I
was annoyed awake by a rumbling I sensed underneath the
futon. I heard a whining moan like water rushing through a big
pipe, a groaning like a big bus cranking through a gearshift or
going uphill. It made the floorboards of the cabin shake a
little. It made the windows rattle. It was sometime past twelve
o'clock and it should have been nearly completely dark, but as
I popped up, hugging the bedcovers against the chill of night,
I saw the sky behind the back windows of the cabin illuminated with an infernal, fiery red light that cast the stand of for-

est trees nearby into silhouette, black and skeletal against its glowing. The sky had gone entirely red outside except for the stark fringing of ʻōhiʻa trees. Kīlauea was erupting full force from a vent about nine miles away from us.

In the sleepy fog of my mind, I thought, *Oh, an eruption,* and I laid myself back down, trying to fall back asleep. I guessed the vibrating to be lava moving through the rift zone, its huge earthen conduit miles below us. I was happy in a dumb sort of way. I thought, *Oh, an eruption, and I'm here for it.*

Geologists had been expecting a new outbreak. I'd been reading the papers and hearing news bulletins and volcano up-dates on the car radio. There had been reports of seismic activ-ity coming from Puʻu ʻŌʻō, a new vent site about nine miles from the summit of Kīlauea and about a quarter mile from the site of the last outbreak at Kamoamoa. Lavas from a flow em-anating from Puʻu ʻŌʻō had oozed along the line of cliffs that had once made up the coast of this island some thousands of years ago, and ran down to burn a few homes near the ocean-side village of Kalapana. Pele, the Hawaiian goddess of vol-canic creation, had decreased her activity somewhat after that, restricting herself to fuming, steaming, and a little shaking at a spot along the East Rift Zone on old Campbell Estate land just outside the boundary to the National Park.

The East Rift was a vague line of recent activity running in a northeasterly direction from the summit of Kīlauea near Volcano Village down to the sea near the village of Kapoho. It was as if a huge underground conduit had been laid from Kī-lauea Summit (where most of the nineteenth-century activity had been centered in the lava lake of Halemaʻumaʻu) easterly down to the sea. It was believed that magma came up below Kīlauea and filled a gigantic storage chamber under it about a mile deep, then, once filled, it ran out along this East Rift Zone until it simply overstrained the leaky plumbing and burst out in red blossoms of molten rock. The Kapoho eruption in 1960 had happened this way—a fountain of fluid *pāhoehoe* first break-ing out in a papaya patch, rupturing the earth and sending up small, attractive fountains; then it erupted in a huge and terri-fying curtain of fire a hundred feet high and forty yards long be-hind the village stores; finally, it evolved into a huge cinder and spatter cone that sent flows of *ʻaʻā,* that clinkery rubbled lava, enough to bury the entire village and surrounding farms. Kapoho—a cluster of houses, agricultural buildings, and a string of shops along the highway—was entirely lost.

One of my uncles had land out there then, planted in vanda and dendrobium orchids—the fleshy purple-and-yellow ones—and my eldest cousin remembers running through the or-chid fields, grabbing flowers, shoving them into buckets in the back of a running jeep, and smelling the sulphur fumes of the flow heading his way. All the recent activity had been along this line, from Kīlauea Iki in 1959 and Kapoho in 1960 to Mauna Ulu (the Darth Vader of all spatter cones) from 1929 to 1974. Since January of 1983, the eruption had been at Puʻu ʻŌʻō, another site along the East Rift Zone, and episodes of fountaining had been occurring there about once a month. I knew this from having read up a little, from having had con-versations with relatives, from remembering stories from my own childhood. I'd never witnessed an eruption, but I vaguely knew how it would go, or so I thought. In my drowsiness, I wanted to sleep a little more.

My wife, sitting up and gazing at the red glow in the win-dows, was aghast. She saw my sleepy nonchalance as pure fool-ishness. She thought I was irresponsible.

"I'm calling the neighbors," Cynthia said, prodding me with her knee.

My wife, from Oregon, and I, from Hawai'i, had very different responses to volcanoes. Her knowledge came from the eruption of Mount St. Helens near Portland in 1980, an explosive and deadly, bomblike blast caused by the buildup of energy released in the collision between two massive geologic formations—the Pacific and the North American plates. Mount St. Helens blew the top off itself, knocked down forests, vaporized lakes and leveled towns. It killed. But, from the reading that I'd done, my idea of a volcano was Kīlauea—a beautiful, almost continuous flowering of volcanic energy that, over eons, had slowly built this chain of islands. I'd read that eruptions here were fountains, lava displays, rivers of heaven. They were spectacles and illustrations of the world's splendor. And, given a good night's sleep, I felt completely ready to cherish them.

"Look," I said, calling after her, "if you have to call someone, why don't you call the Volcano Observatory? They'll have the news and you can ask them any questions."

The Hawaiian Volcano Observatory was a field station of the United States Geological Survey built during the early part of this century to monitor and study the activity of Kīlauea. We'd been to a viewpoint adjacent to the observatory once. It was on a high bluff with a spectacular view of Halema'uma'u, the remnant of the lava lake, and the old, gigantic caldera of Kīlauea. I noticed then that there were geologists inside one of the buildings who seemed to be on observational duty around the clock.

She phoned through, getting a technician on the line right away. "What's going on?" she asked.

The technician, a local, explained that this was the nine-teenth episode of the current eruptive phase of Kīlauea that began in 1983, that this was an episode of "high fountaining—to one t'ousan' feet at leas'," and that lava was geysering out of Pu'u 'Ō'ō, the main vent site just upslope from the prehistoric cone of Kamoamoa. His explanation, Cynthia told me later, was fairly technical, his delivery almost deadpan, except that he seemed to be suppressing excitement, as if he were speaking to her while staring through binoculars at the eruption. I imag-ined him to be a local guy dressed in rubber beach sandals, jeans, and a T-shirt while manning the hot line, stirring a cup of coffee with a wooden stirstick, checking seismographs and jotting measurements, spotting the eruption through binoculars fixed on a metal stand, holding conversations with Civil De-fense and USGS headquarters, and talking to my wife all at the same time.

"Where should we go?" Cynthia asked finally, getting to her point.

"Where are you?" the technician asked.

"In Mauna Loa Estates, twelve streets in from the twenty-sixty-mile marker," she said, citing our coordinates.

"Oh," he said. "You're only a few miles from the vent. All you have to do is get in your car, drive out to Volcano Highway, go down *makai* [seaward] about five miles to Glen-wood. There's a turnout there across the highway from Hirano Store. Drive up to the horsegate and park. Guarantee you can see it real good from there."

"See it? I don't want to *see* it," she exclaimed, "I can *already* see it. From my window. The sky's all red. All the windows are red. The forest is *glowing*. What about the danger? Where should I take my family? I want to get them *away* from it!"

The technician laughed. He asked her where she was from. She told him. He laughed again. "There's no *danger*," he said. "I thought you were calling to find out the best place to *see* it!"

"Oh," Cynthia said, and she hung up, a little mad and a lot relieved. "I guess it's no big deal," she said, turning to me. We hugged each other.

"Let's go look at it," she said.

I drove us according to the technician's directions, then downslope along the highway to the turnout in Glenwood, pulling up alongside the horsegate he spoke of. We looked out from the car and saw only a veil of overcast tinged red from the erupting volcano. It was vapor from the eruption that made the clouds that hid its light.

I drove us still farther downhill, hoping for another, clearer vantage point, a little turnout along the highway where a crowd of locals might be gathering to witness the emergence of Pele. At Kea'au, a crossroads town only a thousand feet from sea level, we spotted a car pulled over near a power-switching station, and a local-looking man, heavyset, bearded, dressed in shorts and a flannel shirt, leaning over a guardrailing, was gazing fixedly over fields of sugarcane at a point nearly on the horizon. I parked the car, we got Alexander out of his baby seat, and we walked over to where the man leaned against the metal railing.

Nearly back to sea level, the air there was much warmer than in Volcano, the obscuring fog high above us. We were on a slight overlook above a field of lands cultivated in orchids, black plastic and white cotton sheets of curved awning and canopy in neat rows below us. Beyond this was old caneland, abandoned to flowering, and stretching out for acres and acres

in the distance on the long lava plain of Kīlauea. The man gestured with a lift of his chin, we turned to look, and we saw a
thin wire of red fire lifting itself from under white and graying
clouds out almost on the edge of all that we could see. Far away,
from where we could make out the bare outline of a small cone,
there was the rose-colored stem of light that illuminated a plume
of white vapor billowing out into a sea of cloud cover spreading
over the land. This was the eruption, the fire-fountain of lava, a
tiny jewel of a glimpse into dread and delight.

The man was friendly. He explained he'd been watching
the eruption from there for nearly an hour, how the fountain
had been higher earlier on, how there had been less cloudiness,
wider spreading of the lava as it spumed out from the vent. We
stayed there only a short while, though, since there wasn't that
much to see, and it seemed to me as if we were breaking in on
the man's peace, his meditation. We drove back home, no
longer excited, but feeling something else, all of our foolishness
gone.

VOLCANOLOGY

Pāhoehoe

THE FIRST RAW LAVA I saw close at hand was down alongside Highway 130 at the seacoast south of Kalapana in 1987. In April, I'd heard news reports that the flow had over-run the highway and that lava had burned down a few homes and was pouring into the sea. Curious to see it, I drove down from Volcano.

I went through the villages of Kea'au and Kapoho, by-passing Kaimū Black Sand Beach near Kalapana, stopping at the road barriers on the low hillocks of old lava flows. I was near an area along the seacoast called Kapa'ahu. The air was warm and humid, full of an ocean wind, but I could feel a singe and an acid in it, a weight in its vapor.

I stripped off my jacket and sweatshirt—the added layers of clothing I wore up in Volcano all the time—and parked the car along a line of other tourist rental cars pulled off by the shoulder of the road. They were parked beside the cutaway of a lava hill. I could see the layers and layers that had built up over time—a period which could have been centuries or merely a few years for all I knew then. I got out of my car and strolled down the center of the highway, still almost new, its asphalt the matte black of being freshly laid. I could see a spot of palm trees off in the distance, some smoke clouds below them, and a large white ribbon of steam trailing from a point that must have been the coast about two miles away. There was no glow of red, but I guessed the steam plume marked the point where lava was entering the sea.

I had to walk about a quarter mile downhill, cutting through the black expanse of a flow that was almost entirely new lavas, a wide sheeting over a swath in the land like a roof freshly drizzled with tar. It eddied in little fans and swirling shapes, mounding in doughy black hills beside the road. Close up, its sheen was silver and metallic, shining like the lead on a sharpened pencil, flaking like packed shards of ice, giving off a low heat and some sulphuric-smelling kind of gas. The highway surface was hot from the tropical sun, and there was something extra in the air—a sizzle of molecules stirring and restirring the atmosphere, heightening the senses, giving off a fume like ozone channeled down from the upper air.

Hummocks of new black rock rose up alongside the road, and I could see how it eddied in the flats, pouring like mud through gaps and shallows on the plain around me, fanning out and crusting, rippling into a hardened skin. This was called *pāhoehoe,* lava of the relatively fluid kind that congeals with a smooth and billowy surface. It cooled from its outside inward, at first forming a thin, sheetlike layer of crust on the large, flat flows. If it ran into an obstacle, the forward part of it blocked by a feature on the earth, or if it was slowed by a momentary slackening in the flow's volume or momentum, the crust might start to twist and curdle like a bedsheet lifted by one of its corners. *Pāhoehoe* would twist in ripples, gyring around a center of resistance, sending purling rays out from where it was being pulled and tugged, bending over itself, forming a littoral radiance that would be preserved. When it mounded, it made a wonderland of silvers and blacks, a topiary of fantasy shapes covering the land and everything on it. I saw *pāhoehoe* that looked like the thick, fattened bodies of walruses and sea lions. In other spots, the moving lava had buckled and rolled and solidified like the weave of a basket made from silvered fronds of palm. When it sluiced through a channel, it made frozen spillways and little pans that seemed like a deck of black cards fanned out and placed on a black slate table. Little toes of rock, shining like quicksilver and swelling from the inside out, dropped into the ditches alongside the road, cooling and hardening into strings of silver sausages that singed the asphalt boiling under them. A smell like a sauce of faint smog—I thought of the air around the L.A. airport at dawn—pervaded the atmosphere, and I rubbed at my eyes.

I'd been reading a textbook called *Geology of the State of Hawaii,* written by Harold T. Stearns. He wrote that its eruptive temperature—in a fire-fountain or fissure eruption sending red gouts of it in a long curtain-of-fire sheeting upward—is over 2000 degrees Fahrenheit. The flow temperature, when it slides like a fluid red cream over the land, is no less hot. *Pāhoehoe* is emitted containing a lot of volcanic gases, which dissipate as the lava cools. If the lava cools and loses enough gas so that crystallization starts, *pāhoehoe* changes into *ʻaʻā*, the lava that is rough and clinkery. I had yet to encounter a live *ʻaʻā* flow.

Pāhoehoe presents itself in a myriad of shapes and spreads from an eruptive vent through a system of conduits that can range in size from a few inches to more than twenty-five feet in diameter. Nahuku, the Thurston Lava Tube, is that huge. There were layers of flowing *pāhoehoe* upslope of me then, made up of several smallish flow units spreading and forming glass skins a fraction of an inch thick, hardening over, then swelling open in squeeze ups (fractures in the hardened skin oozing fresh lava), or cooling down in blocks and slabs of tumuli and pres- sure domes where the land was flat and the lava had spread it- self out in widening and thickening sheets. Up close, its surface could look like asphalt in one spot, then a shining elephant hide or sharkskin in another, crusting into shapes like entrails or a swirl of ropes and cords, tessellating in blistered and filamented surfaces, pumiceous, festooned, puffed up in small, intricate, and shelly chambers. When *pāhoehoe* pours over a cliff, it forms a lava cascade, a Niagara of molten red rock—a lava-fall. When it flows into the sea, it makes a lava delta that can be as big as a football field, a new piece of land that might suddenly crack away from its brittle tie and slide itself into the sea like a sounding whale. Or, if it maintains flowing in the shape of a tube all the way from vent to ocean waves, it can spew forth as a glowing fire hose of lava, *pāhoehoe* streaming in a sluice of lantern-orange sperm churning into rock and black sand in the liquid staggers of froth and spume from the sea.

After walking down the road awhile, I came upon a place where a house had been. It looked like a junkyard or lot for auto wreckers, shells of scorched cars here and there in the black puddles of the flow, the blackened frame of a bench seat off by itself, round and rusted wheels half submerged in hardened lava. The flow had swung around a little hill and come down a gully—maybe there was a creek or small gulch here—and sliced through someone's property—someone who liked cars and trucks, someone who had to leave about half a dozen of them behind. There was the husk of a flatbed pickup immersed up to its wheel wells in lava. The steel on it looked like it had sat in rain for twenty years—all paint, upholstery, rubber belts and hoses and tires incinerated away. The hood was caved in and buckled. Its bed was buried under solidified lava. I thought of Ice Age mammoths mired in pools of tar. Ripped sheets of corrugated steel were strewn around too, sticking up out of the black puddings that held them at funny angles like stiffened sailboards, like metal sculpture left unbronzed. All was black and rust-colored. Pieces of flat metal like posters or signs lay about, burned of their messages, black and rusting, pocked and curled from the heat. There was nothing like a house any-more—just a few steel pilings sticking up here and there, like the ribs of an old pier exposed at low tide. Indeed, the remnant world around the burning seemed like an eddied land of tidal flats after the ocean had pulled away, draining, full of things half-alive, exposed and shriven of their flesh.

I came to a black hump, like the carcass of a gigantic slug, lying across the road. This was where the flow finally cut off the rebuilt part of the highway. I'd heard that it had been rerouted each time that lava cut it off, keeping the way open for residents to come in and out. I'd heard there were people still living on the hillsides. They watched television while lava chan-neled through the slopes around them. Along the flatland that had been overrun with lava, other families who had evacuated were still coming back to pick up what was left of their things. I met a Hawaiian man who trekked miles across the flowfront just so he could get to what was left of his property—a crop of ripening mangoes hanging from trees still standing in a small pocket of green cut off from the road but left unscathed, an emerald island among the stark blacks and grays of the flow.

I stopped at a point where the flow had mounded up higher than the roof of a semi. It seemed the lava had crested here, burying the highway, inflating from inside until it grew higher than a man standing on another man's shoulders. I hopped up onto the edge of the flow, stepping on lava for the first time, worrying, gauging angles and footholds, measuring myself against its folds, crevices, and gaps.

It was still hot, giving off shimmers of heat, and I could feel the skin on my face prickle, the heels of my feet getting warm. I wasn't wearing shoes, just a thick pair of beach sandals. I wanted to *feel* that lava, would've gone barefoot over it if I could've. It held me up, bearing my weight like a mound of green Japanese floats held together with a seining net, crackling under the spongy rubber of the sandals. It flaked and made a grinding sound as I walked over it, building its heat up under my soft arches, keeping me on the move, taking me farther and farther away from the road. I was spellbound out there, suddenly in a world strangified by this rare phenomenon—a kind of silvery ocean on whose waters I could walk. I felt wrapped inside of a brittle shroud of birthing. The heat did not matter, nor did the faint charge of acidic air annoying my breathing. The sting in my eyes seemed part of the awareness, the joy of feeling something was new. I stalked from mound to mound, making little leaps across gaps and gullies in the flow, playing like a child among fresh dunes of sand when the tide was far, far out.

I came to a place where the skin of the flow was ripped. A red, dermal gumminess glowed from within it. When I got close, I felt a radiant heat as from an opened kiln. Lava was alive under the surface of the flow. There was a thick red taffy of it still churned up inside the steel-colored skin. What made things so hot out there, rock to rock, gray pillow to lead-colored mound, was the inner paste still red and movable underneath like a lagoon engorged with a tide of luminous plankton briefly masked and then revealed by the sheet of hard-ened kelp that floated on its surface. I'd walked on the living rock. I was separated from its temperatures only by the thickness of what had cooled—perhaps inches, perhaps feet—a mere skim of time for the cooling to take place, a dimension's distance be-tween the states of solid and of liquid. The radiance swam past my face and arms, curling as the wind curled around me. I saw more streaks and scarrings of red where the lava was inflating from underneath the hardened paddies of rock, cracking open a piece of its surface, stretching from the inside out, pouring through and dripping down, glowing from within.

There were soft sizzles of rose in the rock surrounding me. I'd walked past the cooler point of the flow and stood along-side an expanding pond of its red dough pushing upward through the gray coating of its surface. Heat salved up the skin on my ankles and gripped my calves. My breath shortened. A shimmer of sweat came to my brow, a cold spray of panic broke through the skin on the back of my neck. I turned and moved back the way I'd come, taking shorter steps, making fewer leaps, watching carefully the color under the surface of the sil-ver rock I walked upon.

In minutes, I got back to the roadside. I'd only gone a few hundred yards, but, within myself, I felt an upwelling like an orange glimmer of pride. A globulous, cooling mass loomed beside me. I went and put my hands on the lava again. It flaked and came off in my palms in gross scabs the color of silver and black. Small fires touched off in the dry brush alongside the road. Around its bend, swizzles of burning grass sent up tiny flames and swirls of slate-gray smoke. The white plume of steam I'd seen ribboning out from the coastline was still a mile away across the shining gray sea of *pāhoehoe*.

Channels and Lava Tubes

I started going out for hikes over the old flows—out down the Chain of Craters Road that led away from Crater Rim Drive around Kīlauea and down to the ocean and the east coast of the island to where Kalapana was with its beach of black, volcanic sands. I'd drive out from the crossroads near Iki under the canopy of the three-tiered forest, and head out past the chain of pit craters, moguling in my little car through *'a'ā* flows, scrubby *'ōhi'a* stands, and volcanic tumuli sprout-ing with little tussocks of grass. The land, which had been full-blown rain forest near Kīlauea Iki, gave way quickly to a kind of dry scrubland of *'ōhi'a* and ferns pioneering fairly new lavas. From the sparseness, it seemed that the rains, com-ing in from the sea and up Kīlauea, had bypassed falling on these lower slopes of the mountain. What was dramatic was that all of this was within a mile or three of the summit, less than a mile from the thick fern forest that swaddled the land around Iki.

I found a place I liked. It was an automobile turnout just before the road sank and started switchbacking down the face of the Hōlei Pali, a gigantic fault scarp formed when massive shelves of earth slumped away and left majestic cliffs hundreds of feet high and miles long. There was a large lava plain that had built up around Mauna Ulu, a fairly new dome of black lavas that had come up during the 1970s, and it was all acces-sible from the highway. At one end of it was a huge channel built by 'a'ā, the rubbly stuff that cut you if you fell against it.

I knew from my reading that an 'a'ā flow can be massive, building up walls of clinker that act like levees holding in a lava river that can be five to thirty feet wide. This one was one of the bigger ones for Kīlauea. I'd walked over and by the chan-nel a few times where it crossed Chain of Craters Road, and imagined it full of lava, flowing slowly, glimmers of red like the living tissue under its rough black skin. The channel had ten-foot levees which its own flow had built up along both its sides, and its bed was wider than my car was long, big as the California aqueduct, but with banks of roughened black rock. There was a crested ripple on one side of it where it took a turn and bent toward the sea, spuming up like the huge face of a black wave, smooth and frothing rims of rotted action, fallen at its lower lip, full of agglutinated splash and veneers of glassy vesicular rock.

When I walked down inside it, stumbling over the bro-ken bits of 'a'ā, I imagined a current of lava like a gigantic, molten eel thrashing over my body. Its face was red and pussy, and its body surged with sublime strength and incan-descence. My body smoked and became vapor, ghost and flesh both incinerated in an instant. There would be no afterlife, I thought, no heaven but this rock and its absence of spirits.

The wind would whip up a little, tussling my hair or flap‑
ping up my jacket collar, and then I could feel a primitive
nothingness slashing its way past me without dimension or
conscience.

I began to take longer hikes, away from the turnouts,
cutting past an old crater, circling a cindercone, crunching my
way over iridescent fields of *pāhoehoe,* emptying myself of ex‑
pectation. I liked going over the flows radiating away from
Mauna Ulu, still a smoking dome near the road. Mauna Ulu
had erupted for several years during the seventies, growing up
as a spatter cone on the East Rift of Kīlauea in 1969. It had
phases of fissure eruptions, high fountainings, and lava‑lake
formation during the time it began shaping itself into the
"Growing Mountain," which was what its name meant in
Hawaiian. After a while, another lake began forming itself
within the summit, and then a spatter cone built itself over
that too.

The succession reminded me of a pagoda, a kind of Ori‑
ental pavilion of lava, and I thought of the miter of wisdom
that Odysseus captures near the end of the modern *Odyssey*
written by Nikos Kazantzakis. It was a totem made up of the
heads and faces of a succession of religious and philosophic
thinkers. There were beasts at its base, an eagle or whale rep‑
resenting religious animism, but above it was an image of
Adam or Christ, then an image of Muhammad or the Bud‑
dha over them. Mauna Ulu, in its quickly changing phases
of growth, seemed to stack itself in this same way, a volcanic
scepter on the earth built from lakes and shields and spatter
cones each succeeding the other.

'Alae Tube

Hiking away from Mauna Ulu down the rift zone toward the sea, I crossed and recrossed a long *pāhoehoe* channel of brown lavas. It broke off huge shards of itself along its sides, sharp-edged tablets blank of inscription except for scores of minute bubble holes left over from boiling gases. I had to leap over these, stepping on them too, making slow progress on a barely discernible trail back from an old crater to the still steaming dome of Mauna Ulu beside the highway. They made a clink and a crunch under my bootheels, glassy rocks I worried might be sharp enough to slash my legs if I fell. I did fall too, scour-ing the skin under my Levi's, but kept going.

Once, I jumped into the channel and walked on the hard-ened lava bed. The trail had gotten so rugged, so intricate with broken blocks of lava, that the smooth bottom of the old chan-nel looked the easiest way to get along. I dropped down from its curling lip, thinking of the slathering momentum of liquid rock. I hit the floor, stumbling, and it caved in under my feet, and I crunched through about a two-inch chamber of rock, like a little cell of lava formation, a layer that gave way to another layer that finally held me up. The entire floor was like this, and, walking on it, I kept busting through, as if walking on con-centric glass eggshells. When I dropped down once to a layer that swallowed up my ankles to a point just over the stretched Achilles tendon, I realized I could be in for a much deeper fall, rocks cutting through my calves and thighs as I crunched through its chambered layers. I scrambled up a curve of the lava bank shaped like the concave inner waist of a skateboarder's pit. I cut my hands, but I made my way out.

The channel I scrambled out of might have eventually clogged up or skinned itself over, forming at first a veil of thin, shelly *pāhoehoe* over its flow. Gradually, the shell would thicken, the flow starting to freeze inward from its edges, adding bit by bit to a kind of roof forming itself over the still fluid center. The movement would become cylindrical, a pipelike zone forming at its center as the flow became more restricted. Initially, there is no air space between the roof and the flowing stream, but a space gradually develops because the moving lava erodes the hardened lava at the base of the pipe and cuts down to deeper and deeper levels. As the tube forms, a layer of magmatic gases fills the space between the moving rock and the hardened canopy built over it. From overflow and spillage, the roof could grow from mere centimeters to inches or even feet in thickness, adding to it-self, hiding the moving incandescence and tremendous heat under layers of insulation. There would be a blazing red eel, in diameter large as a New York subway, sloughing itself in secret under the surface of the earth. I walked over tubes like this.

Near 'Alae Shield, a former crater on the trail from Nāpau to Mauna Ulu, lavas had filled in and swollen the surface of the earth. The *pāhoehoe* could be green and translucent as an old Coke bottle, then darken into the color of seaweed, rocky, rope-like kelp slithering under my boots. I would come upon a miss-ing piece, a plate of lava bigger than a manhole cover, broken away from the surface, a section of the tube's roofing fallen away. I'd creep up to it, crack away carefully with my bootheel, kneel down, and look inside, probing with a flashlight or sim-ply letting my eyes adjust. Under the column of light, in the bounce of luminous rays making visible its insides, there would be a tunnel of rock that had the appearance, momentarily to me, of the fatty tissue inside of blood vessels, an opened vein on the inner arm and princely wrists of the earth. Outside, all along the flow's surface exposed to light and air, its color was that continuous and regularized metallic gray of model airplanes before they're painted. But inside, I'd see its innards were clay-colored, shaded like the flesh of the thoracic cavity, lined with a smooth stain of iron red oxides and pancreatic yellow sulphurs, a body tuned to music in a brightened glance.

Skylight

Once, out with scientists from the Hawaiian Volcano Observatory, I stood on the roof of a tube while lava still flowed through it. I was beguiled by skylights, holes where the roof had luffed off, fragments that had torn themselves away from the surface so there were viewports into the tube. We'd found two—one on a clinkery surface and the other on smooth, ropy *pāhoehoe*. I studied one, drawing myself closer, feeling the heat wafting up past my face, my arms, toasting the cotton fibers of my Levi's. I stood too close, enraptured, and one of the scientists pulled me back. I was trying to gaze in, looking down on the little red river I could see sliding by through the portal of the skylight.

"Don't stand over it," he cautioned.

I moved back, seeing from his immobile face that he wasn't kidding.

"It's about two thousand degrees Fahrenheit," he said. "It would sear your eyeballs." He nodded and I gulped.

I saw a little band of orange run quickly—the way sea‑ water surges through a narrow, pipelike channel cut through tidal rocks. The skylight could have been a tiny blowhole spouting fiery spume, but the viscid matter instead ran steadily in its channel, sending heat shimmers up from the gray folds of hardened rock. It was an endless sauna out there—but its cur‑ rents encircled me, putting me into a little cell of convection. So long as I stood near the beautiful thing, I'd have to steel myself against a mild agony.

A few feet away was another skylight, larger and more like a hatch had been cut through the roof of the living tube. A thick orange light radiated from it, making visible the out‑ lines of stalactites that hung down into the moving liquid. I watched for a while, trying hard to see the visible pulse of the land. A column of light spewed from the hole. Downslope from where I stood, ropes of bluish gray lava piled up like short, pliant chains of pearls hiding the sags of flesh on an aging neck.

The scientists shooed me along, and I turned away, an up‑ raised hand shielding my eyes against the heat. I realized then I was standing on the roof of a tube, earth shoving its way be‑ neath me like a baby sliding along its mortal red canal.

Kapu *Tube*

From neighbors and friends around the village, I kept hearing about a gigantic tube that ran from one of the old Kīlauea flows, down under the land behind Hongo Store, and onward through Mauna Loa Estates on the other side of the highway. Geologist friends said it was thought to be a continuation of Nahuku, the Thurston Lava Tube, which ran downslope from Kīlauea Iki. You were supposed to be able to walk it, to fit a moving van inside of it, and you were supposed to find another world down in there. I'd heard of cave petroglyphs and burial bones, about huge ʻōhiʻa root systems that hung down from the surface like bristly Spanish moss, teeming with hissing bee- tles—an underworld Shangri-la, alive with shadows made into flesh, fed by what drained from this one.

I told myself I'd find that tube, and asked around about it. Someone in the village would say, "You could drop down into it and walk all the way to a papaya patch back of Moun- tain View." That was over ten miles downslope from Volcano.

Geologists would say, "Oh, yeah, this tube is probably some major conduit off of Kīlauea—but I never heard anything about walking to Keaʻau or Mountain View—where'd you hear that one?"

Finally, a neighbor admitted he knew where an entrance was.

"Get one *beeg* skylight in dah lot next to mine," he said one day. We were hanging out at Hongo Store, drinking bad coffee from plastic, cone-shaped cups. "Get dog skeleton in dere. I t'ink one family of pigs use to live inside too."

He described a hole in the earth behind a stand of fire trees and brush, rimmed with sword ferns and a few bamboo or- chids—the kind of collapsed tube you were supposed to stay away from if you were buying property to build a house on. But a scientist had bought this lot—a Stanford biologist living in the village—and was using it for a special study on evolution inside lava tubes.

My neighbor had trespassed. He told me he'd gone exploring there one Halloween with his wife and child, taking a picnic dinner and flashlights.

"Evening time, aftah dah sun go down, we juss drop insighe, eh? Dat was dah easy part. We went scramble ch'rough sword fern patch down to where not so deep, grab and hol' on to one treelimb, den juhlike *skeed* down to dah tube floor, yeah? Juss a few fee' chyeah? We juss poot on slippah, hop dah realtor streeng on dah property line, and slighe down onna long grass until we wass insighe dah tube. No problem. Wass easy."

Villagers liked to make events for themselves this way. A family might take in a night out on the lava flow to be under the stars, camping on the beach from where lava emptied into the sea, taking box lunches and beach chairs and ice coolers filled with beer down to the spot where the road was covered by the latest flow, laughing it up listening to the radio and the pidgin patter of a "local boy" deejay. The dread skylight became, in this same way, an occasion for a family outing, transforming a small piece of science and regional lore into part of a Halloween memory.

I got him to take me there one afternoon. It was a formation about twenty feet across and from six to fifteen feet deep under the opening. Part of the old skylight was like a little hummocked lip or awning over the old bed, which had a multilayered surface that was cut and channeled and terraced up its sides partway. It was old. The rock had turned soft gray and lost all trace of the metallic sheen of freshly hardened lavas. Its deepest blacks seemed the product of mosses and the accumulated dankness of time. Epiphytes hung down over the rim and water dripped over them, plashing in a coppery pool on the bottom of the hole. The tube undulated where it opened to the light of day, then plunged away like a tree root down into depths and darkness beyond my seeing.

My neighbor had been quiet as we walked over, and there was a zombie's look in his green eyes as we stood over the opening to the tube. He was part Hawaiian—the term for someone with a little Hawaiian blood. But he was part *haole* (Caucasian) and part Filipino too—a mix of races, like so many of my neighbors. He had tanned skin and a large frame, his brown hair was wavy, and his eyes seemed to have sunk back into their deep sockets.

"Hear dat?" he said.

"Hear what?" I answered.

"Dat *howling.*"

I shook my head, my mind changing cast with his remark.

"Ju' lissen more careful," he said, "like you went cross bot' ears or somet'ing. Try listen in *3-D.*"

I paid attention to him for things like that, for teaching me these little local tricks, taking the techniques of one of our senses and applying them in another. He was *evolved,* as good dreamers used to say back in the sixties. I listened in 3-D and heard my heart first, then I heard the wind through the tops of the 'ōhi'a trees around us, and then a lot of miscellaneous white noise of the forest. And then nothing for a while.

I looked at him out of the corner of my eye.

"No move," he said, placing his palm on my belly, steadying my pose.

I noticed the rhythm of my own breathing then. A bird twittered. It was an *'amakihi,* a little green piper of the lower forest giving off a chirruping whistle somewhere close by. I heard the heavy heads of the broom grass brushing against themselves, and I heard, or thought I heard, drops of water falling into the pool at the bottom of the tube.

"No breathe *hard*," he said, touching my chest lightly with his index finger.

I sighed, mind racing to thoughts, when I picked some-thing up. It was a low moan. It was a sob and a light chuff-ing. It was like the low note of an end-blown flute, a faint, harmonic warble on the edge of human hearing. I picked it up through the skin around my testicles first, and then my anus clenched. I felt something on my breastbone where a ghost might have stood cold against it.

It was the wind, of course, atmosphere moving across the opening of a cave, vibrating, sending out a note like a shaman singing into the mouth of a body recently dead, summoning its wisdom from the other world. It was the afterlife speaking, and we felt it.

"See?" my neighbor said, not looking at me, but gazing at his feet. He was watching a beetle track its way over the brown grasses by the sloping earth we stood upon. Its black antennae worked like digital filaments, trying to pick up signals, listen-ing in 3-D. I cleared my throat.

"Hey, man," I said. "Maybe this is *kapu*. We don't have to go down."

He nodded. We stood there silently for a while, waiting for the moment to trail out. Then we walked away. Traipsing through the forest, I bowed my head, and neither of us spoke until we got to the road. My neighbor had brought me to the brink again, to a feeling I recognized, a sense of belonging to the land known to me at five but not twenty. I'd fallen back to a spot of consciousness, a belief in the power of the land.

Kapu was a gambit I had used as a child sometimes when I was afraid and needed to save pride among playmates. If I feared crossing a private beach, if I didn't want to swim in the cold springs at night in the dark end of a particular lagoon, if I balked at the notion that a bunch of us neighborhood kids had to pass through the trestle ribs of a WPA bridge and over a shallow, mossy-rocked creek on a night of the Turkish moon, I said it was *kapu*—forbidden by sacred law. It was a reference to the old Hawaiian system of prohibitions, creating differences between rulers, the *ali'i*, and commoners, the *maka'āinana*. When you said something was *kapu,* it meant a line was drawn that couldn't be crossed. It meant a border between one world and another. *Kapu.* It meant a body that could not be held.

GHOST

Ghost Showers and Impatiens

THERE WAS an outdoor shower Cynthia and I loved to use.
It was part of the detached bathhouse—an outbuilding adjacent to the main cabin, joined by a wooden deck, containing
the privy and a sauna. You got to the shower by walking along
a planked runway, smooth and almost constantly damp with
the rain or mistiness from the forest. Like any bathroom floor,
it could be dangerous, and, after a fall or two, we took care to
keep our steps short, to heel and toe carefully, digging in with
the balls of our feet, almost grasping with our toes.

The medieval Japanese method of walking, perfected at
imperial court and in the *shōgun*'s castle, made a lot of sense to
me suddenly—the deliberate slide of the foot *before* the lifting of

the toes. Kind of a reverse of normal human ambulation. I tried it, gliding a bare foot on the runway in front of me, lifting it toes first at the end of the step, then dragging the other foot along beside it, skating along. The motion is what children use to polish wooden floors, feet skidding and wrapped in rags or pillows brown with wax. In medieval Japan, the style was considered decorous, respectful, part of etiquette and good breeding. Its origin, though, might have been in practicality— stockinged feet on slick pine and cedar floors, cloud trousers emblazoned with silvered cranes trailing. Who would want to take a tumble, toe over teakettle, in front of an emperor or a *samurai*? You might lose not only composure and status but your guts and head as well. You took care to walk, sir, and skated if you had to, but you did not fall.

I fell like a bear on ice skates. No harm, though, and my bones did not rattle. I got up and walked the "regular" way, and foundered again, feeling my heels skidding a little on a patch of surface scum on the wood. I stopped in my tracks, meditated, and tried another approach. I tried *wading* my way along, as if fly fishing the Henry's Fork of the Snake River in Idaho. That seemed to work much better. I went slowly, imagining eddies of mist and the forest's milky blackness swirling around my knees and thighs and ankles, and I was fine from there on out. In Hawai'i, in the rain forest of 'ōhi'a trees, under the sign of Kīlauea's steaming vents and sulphurous bluffs, I imagined moose and trout in the waters of the night, reeds and the rushes of the Nez Perce, sandhill cranes bedded off beyond the cindercones and *pu'u* hills of Volcano.

During daylight, the shower was a station in the garden surrounding us. The view seemed planned. There was the brown paneled outbuilding set against the lavish earth tones and

greens of the rain forest—an understory of emerald mosses and
sea-green *'ama'u* ferns, the tans and browns in the stalks of the
hāpu'u tree ferns standing over them, and the foliant shimmer of
'ōhi'a leaves, soft and glabrous medallions scattering an aquatic
green light throughout the canopy overhead. But, in the understory just beside the building, someone had planted impatiens,
little popcorn and starbursts of white, pink, and red surrounding the shower's little corner like the decorated panels of a folding screen. You washed up as if wearing a loose-fitting gown
of forest-colors and a spangle of decadent jewelry. Your own
nudity was glorified and made the central detail of a painting
that had charm and even some elements of romance. When the
water came, it was a hose of fertile gray light.

Though nights were misty and chilly, it wasn't a problem
to shower under the stars either. Our bodies steamed, pale suns
with white prominences furling off our skin and into the black
milk dark of the forest. One of us would be showering, and the
other would walk out of the house and then down along the
planked walkway around the sauna. We used flashlights, orbs
of yellow light probing the way. When it threw the bather into
the relief of the other's sight, it was a marvel that made us laugh
and could reconcile any difference of the day.

Cheerios, Raisins, and Papayas

We had changed what we ate, going back to what I knew as a
child in Hawai'i. For dinners, I bought simple things—fish
when it was cheap (it wasn't always), local-grown chicken and

pork, some fresh vegetables, a jar of yellow Japanese pickles made from fermented *daikon,* and brown rice. For lunches, we got by with a variety of Oriental noodles. With most meals, I made *miso* soup from powdered fish stock or dried bonito flakes and dabs of brown peanut-butter-looking soybean paste. The broth steamed on the little propane stove and fogged the window by the sink and the sky-panel over the back door. As the frothy ocean-smell filled the little cottage, the task of meal-making became a wayside of culture and memory. I tried to remember tunes my grandfather hummed while chopping scallions with a big Chinese knife, Japanese *ondo* from a diner's jukebox on Kamehameha Highway circa 1956, a Portuguese *chang-a-lang* melody made over into a *paniolo hula* and spinning on the 49th State record label on the family hi-fi. The smells were there, the staccato chopping sound of the knife on the cutting board, the hands wet from preparing food, my wife setting the little table, and my own son the baby in the kitchen now. Try as I might, though, what came to me were blues and jazz tunes, Gershwin and Erroll Garner. "Look at me," I'd croon, sweeping the little green flags of cut scallions into a *bizen-yaki* teabowl, "I'm as helpless as a chicken-of-the-sea,/Not knowing my *shoyū* from my *poi,*/My hat from my glove,/ I get misty and too much in *lava.*" Alex would bang a wooden spoon and grunt, or throw his pacifier onto the dirt floor, disapproving, making me stop the silliness. I'd pull out a box of breakfast cereal from under the counter, sprinkle a handful of Cheerios on the table, add a few raisins to it, and go to the fridge for an apple or a pear, or to the windowsill over the kitchen sink for a ripe papaya or a mango to slice and place in a plastic bowl for him. He'd gum them all, chewing and sucking almost at the same time, point and mew, helpless as a kitten, to the bottle of apple juice I'd left on the counter.

Cynthia liked to dress for supper. I'd wear any old pair of shorts and some local-style T-shirt (a humble, powder-blue LOCAL MOTION, an ornate and purple TO BE OR MUSUBI with designs of rice cakes wrapped in seaweed printed on the back, the rattan MAUI THE DEMI-GOD, etc.). When it was cold, on a rainy or a misty day, I'd throw on a navy kung-fu jacket and black rayon Chinese vest too. That would be it for me. But Cynthia found rayon skirts in tropical pastel colors, silk blouses dyed aquamarine and gold, and Chinese slippers made of black cotton. The colors fit in with the rain forest, blazes of Shantung bronze, Italian turquoise, and viridian from Indonesia against the brown-and-green backdrop of ferns, the slender, aspenlike trunks of 'ōhi'a. I took a photograph of her in her silks and rayons, holding Alexander, himself dressed in an "aloha suit" (trunks and shirt) of orange-and-purple birds-of-paradise blossoms against a dark blue field. They stood framed in the back doorway of the cottage, emerging out of the rectangular shadow into the brilliant daylight of a mistless day in Volcano. Next to them, suspended from a nail on the side of the cottage, was the round zinc disk of an old-fashioned washtub beaming with the same silver-gray light that shone off the trunks of 'ōhi'a trees rising over the roof of the cottage. Bow ties of impatiens blossomed around us.

The Blue Hand

I went into a specialty store called The Blue Hand in the little neighborhood of shops along Kamehameha Avenue on the old

bayfront in downtown Hilo. The *tsunami* of '60 had taken out
Torakiyo Hongo's two homes and tiny insurance building, but
most of the rest of the old, prewar structures still stood, and I
liked going in there and getting a little of the feeling of an older
Hawai'i that it gave me, strolling in shorts, aloha shirt, and
beach sandals along the clutch of storefronts and walk-up
hutches. I used a copy place, the bank, a hair salon inside of
the old Lyman Building, a *sushi* takeout stand, a Ben Franklin
for toys, and a travel agency.

I was looking for a present to give my wife. I'd heard about
an antique store and curio shop next to the old Hilo Theater in
the building that had once been the Hilo Hotel. On one of the
side streets. There was a big placard sign above the storefront—
a slender, mudra-posed hand painted in slate-colored blue over
a white field. The blue was the color of demons in the Buddhist
paintings I knew from Japan. There was a large, epicanthic eye
nestled in the center of its palm just above the mound of Venus.

The Blue Hand was a shop that took up two floors and
two storefronts. It could have been located in the fashionable
district of any town with a sizable upper middle class. On the
first floor, there were dolls and masks from Mexico, jewelry
from Tibet and Thailand, blouses and shirts from Ecuador and
China, *happi* coats and silk *kimono* from Japan. On the staircase were locally produced ceramics and rattan furniture from
China and the Philippines. In the three second-floor rooms
were African masks and icons, Polynesian tikis, and wooden
toys from Russia and Scandinavia. I marveled at the splendor
and its careful arrangement—Mayan rugs draped across the
walls on the lower floors, *kimono* hanging from an antique
wardrobe, Thai metal necklaces spread across black velvet in a
glass case.

I found a rack of Chinese silk blouses and washed silk Japanese *happi* coats. I chose a shining black thing, a little frilly at the bodice, long in its line for something made in Asia. I took it up to the clerk and struck up a conversation with her, a middle-aged woman with dark hair and a fair complexion. I asked her to try on some of the jewelry—her coloring was like my wife's—and she obliged. She tried on necklace after necklace and we talked. I went about choosing one of them and maybe some earrings too. I asked to see the Mexican carnival masks of a green donkey and a yellow jaguar I saw hanging from a pillar in the corner. She asked me what I did and I told her. She said she read everything—novels, magazines, *The New Yorker*. I told her I was having trouble, that I couldn't bring myself to write yet. She just nodded. She seemed to know quite a bit about the jewelry I was looking at, about the history of Southeast Asia and the Buddhist religion too. She'd spent the sixties and early seventies in Berkeley and San Francisco listening to Alan Watts's radio show on Zen.

"It was on the Pacifica station, you know," she said, looking into my eyes for some sort of recognition. Perhaps she thought we were of the same generation. Knowing the reference would reveal my age. I knew nothing.

I spotted a Tibetan meditation bell on a satin pillow in a glass case behind the counter and said something about it. She asked if I knew how to ring it. I said I thought I did. I remembered how acolytes had rung bells during the chanting sessions when I lived in a monastery in Japan. They struck the bells sharply and let them vibrate over the chanting. The clerk turned and pulled out a thick wooden stick and handed it to me across the top of the glass case.

"Here," she said, "go ahead," and turned away.

I wet my lips and struck at the bowl-like bell, trying to make it ring, but it only clanked for me. It was like the one in the loft in our cabin, the bell I'd tried to ring on one of my first nights back in Volcano. I hit it softly and it clanked again. I tapped it and it clanked, frustrating me. I kept this up for a few minutes until the salesclerk stepped back to me.

"Oh," she said politely. "Sometimes it doesn't work for me either. Let me try and see if I can get it going."

She reached for the bell and cupped it in her left hand, evenly supporting it at its base the way I'd seen Fish and Wildlife biologists handle 'apapane, 'amakihi, and 'elepaio—those little baitfish-sized birds of the forest they'd trapped in soft nylon netting up on Mauna Kea. With her other hand, she picked up the lacquered stick and held it in a strange, double-jointed grip I can't explain. She closed her eyes, audibly let out her breath, breathed in again quietly, and then twirled the stick above the metal bell.

She brought the stick, still twirling, down around the outer circumference of the bell, making a circle around it, beginning to stroke it just slightly, trailing the stick along its metallic skin as if giving it a light, whirling massage. As the stick twirled, the bell began emitting a soft hum and a fine-pitched, central note that oscillated higher and higher until the clerk broke the smoothness of her motion and clanked the stick hard against the metal of the bowl, stopping the radiant humming altogether. She started up again, twirling the stick, and the Tibetan bell hummed and rang like a shimmering gong. When she stopped, the bell clanked and its ringing ceased. When she kept the stick going without flaw or pause in her motion, the little bell whined to life and sent out its purest, longest notes—like Te Kanawa singing Villa-Lobos.

I thought back to the anthropological film I'd seen once on Tibetan lamas and their meditation. The film was in black and white and full of glitches that made the people in it jump forward like comedians in old twenties silent movies. But the soundtrack had chanting and temple bells in it, the Heart Sutra in its Tibetan version, an emptiness translated into words—the rhythmic and doleful chanting of the lamas—and then their motions—a lurching circumambulation of the Tantra housed within their central altar, what would be the Vehicle of the Law—their faith—kept alive within the temple. Besides the deep, groaning chant, like the murmurings of a herd of devout cattle, the sound I remember was that of the bells—deep, percussive gongs and then high, radiating tolls over them, a concert of resonating brass. The sound I heard in The Blue Hand was like the higher-pitched ones from the film—an aural radiance more than a ring. I was moved. And I was shamed.

"You're afraid of your own vision still," she said calmly, her eyes looking down into a ledger lying open on the counter. "That's why you haven't written anything yet."

She was jotting out my receipt for the Thai necklace of silver leaves and birds, the black silk Chinese shirt, and the Mexican carnival masks of papier-mâché. She looked up at me, briefly, maybe to see if her words had registered. I don't know what showed, whether spark or dimness, but I sensed she was right.

"The land here," she said, starting her sentence a little backward. "You don't feel you can speak from it yet." Her head dipped and nodded as she spoke. Her chin moved with her talking and her voice was low. "You don't have the feeling for it right now. But when you do—and you will—you'll write."

She looked up from her book and smiled at me in a wifely way. I took her words to be a little prophecy, the writer's version of Macbeth's vision of the soothsaying witches in the forest. I wanted to be part of the earth I walked upon, body of a woman. Beginnings might be easier after that.

I took up the gifts I'd bought, wrapped in a thin, translucent yellow plastic bag, quite oversized, and made for the door—a cute, heavy glass thing that belled as I opened it, making me look, a little nervously and out of rhythm, back into the shop. Beside the register, the clerk was giving me a circular wave of her hand the way a sitting cat paws the blank air alongside its whiskered face. When I raised my own hand to respond, I felt the eye in it folding open like a lacquered blue fan. The traffic noise blared in from the street and, through my loosened clothes, I could feel a lash of warm island wind stroke my skin.

Ghost

I was frustrated. I'd been looking for my grandfather's ghost in everything, and that gave everything an undercurrent of dissatisfaction. I came up with almost no poetry daily, while the rain dazzled down through the sun-showers and the fluffs of forest light outside. Birds called *ee-EE-vee!* and *pip-pip-a-WHEEYOU!* and I made no move to the picture windows to spot them bouncing through the upper limbs of the 'ōhi'a. I stayed indoors and read blank verse, free verse, *vers libre,* variable feet, compositions by field, long lines and short lines,

end-stopped and heavily enjambed lines, and made myself
an expert on their nothingness. I yearned for another music.

I spent a morning reading Witter Bynner's translation of
the T'ang Dynasty anthology. It was called *Three Hundred
Poems of the T'ang Dynasty* in my version. I'd gotten it in a Los
Angeles Chinatown bookstore one December a few years before. It was a charming thing with a red-and-orange cover and
black lettering across a little burst of color that looked like a sun
or an unfolded Oriental fan. There was Chinese on the left-
hand page and English on the right. There were notes at the
back, and the individual poet's name appeared at the foot of the
page. When I read the works, I felt good. I'd read a poem,
think on it, then read another, sort of like practicing a song. I'd
let the thought and sentiment of it penetrate me like good
weather, like a draft of liquor, even an "ichor" of spirit, as John
Keats thought of them, the little romantic Buddha of the odes.

I got up the next morning and took a long sauna, stoking
the little fire inside of its iron stove, wadding and rolling up the
sheets of newspaper from the kindling box, breaking the kin-
dling, shoving in a few sticks of dry *ōhi'a* and scrap two-by-
fours. I was usually bad at fires, but this lit up and got hot
quickly, drying out the cedar planking of the little sealed room.
I took in with me a candle, a flashlight, a bucket of water, and
an empty coffee can for a dipper. I also took the *Poems of the
T'ang.* I fell into its world, reading about melancholy, grief, and
loneliness twelve centuries ago. I read about border guards
and courtesans and civil servants sent far from the capital and
into the provinces. I read poems of wine-drinking and moon-
viewing, of hard traveling through high mountains. I read the
pledge of the river merchant's wife to come halfway down the
road from her home village to meet her husband, returning from

a long journey. Monkeys cried mournfully from the trees, wine
rose to a scholar's lips with the silver shimmer of moonlight
dancing on its surface like the trail of a courtesan's gown as she
crossed a footbridge to meet her lover. The bells of the temple
sounded a festival, and the mountains folded into the distance
like pitching winter seas. I saw the world again, inwardly,
reimagined as pure beauty, as *feeling*. Every image had its sentiment, every hint of emotion was figured forth in catalogues of
phenomena. The autumn light of dusk fell, slanting on the
mounds of temple moss, and Wang Wei felt in it the end of
days, the cosmos come round to another age. The world turned
like a verse, one wheel of karmic time. I felt in me the echo of
my own birth, and I stepped out of the sauna, shining with
sweat in the damp, foggy Volcano air. I'd given myself a little
ceremony, and I wanted to write something.

I'd heard from him. I imagined the man, my grandfather,
and I felt a catch in my throat that could have been his own
voice. I felt a focus of emotion, a way of seeing, of addressing
myself to the world as if through the mask of my grandfather's
face, flat like mine but dark and with the high forehead we both
shared with my father. I'd seen a photograph of him only a couple of times, and no spirit had come from them, no personality. He was a blankness to me, though stories of him came from
nearly everyone.

Kazu·the postmaster told me that Torau Hongo had once
opened an *onsen* in Volcano too. It was a reprise of his salad
days in Nu'uanu. During the war, with a gambler from Honolulu named Johnny Au, Torau converted a small warehouse
into a Japanese teahouse. They brought liquor and girls in from
town, from Kaua'i, from Honolulu. The Greek, Lycurgis,
came over a lot, the man who'd built Volcano House, the big

hotel overlooking the crater in the National Park. "Your gran'-faddah was dah only Japanese he talk to. None of us could in-terest him, beeg shot. But your gran'faddah was dah only wann could spark him. I don't know what was said. . . ."

My mother told me Torau would just stand around, smoking his custom cigarettes, twisting the butts into his little bone holder (he imitated FDR), letting everyone else do the work at the store. He was retired and he pointed. "*A-reh, a-reh,*" he said. Do this, do that. Keeping his back straight, his cigarette in his mouth, his lips frowning. He was handsome and surly. His hair was white, white. He was six feet. He spoke only Japanese.

When he was dying of cancer—throat cancer—he coughed a lot in the morning, my mother said, but he could talk fine. No one could stop him going over to the post office side to talk story with the customers. I'd heard he'd died on a day when the mountain frosts came early, killing off the lettuce field in back of Hongo Store. While waiting for the funeral, my mother, three months pregnant, obsessed on the smell of the rot-ting plants, and was vomiting every day, vomiting whenever the sun shone on the lettuce field, whenever the wind shifted from over the saddle of Mauna Loa and blew toward her window and the village.

He kept a gun—a shotgun—loaded but uncocked, be-hind the counter of the store during the Depression. He sold liquor, you see. '*Okolehau* from potatoes distilled in Kea'au or Hāwī. He got *sake* from the Japanese sailors who came up from town for his *onsen*. He ran a whorehouse in the big, warehouse-like building with the galvanized roof a hundred yards up Vol-cano Highway, the one called The Big Store now, the *Onouye* Store, the Upper Store. That was the *onsen,* that was the teahouse, that was the brothel. Fern Grotto, it was called, and the soldiers and Lycurgis and the fancy pants from all over came by, dropping their trousers and their money in Volcano. Old Hongo was a businessman.

That was Grandpa, my oldest cousin said, six years old and incredulous at the mundane evidence of death, pointing to an urn of ashes on the kitchen windowsill. That cup of trouble was the old man! He ran outside, skipping past the gas pumps under the eaves and awning Hongo had built out over the service station to shelter customers from the constant rains. He picked up a pebble and heaved it across the highway at the stand of Japanese cedars Hongo planted there before the war. *That* was Grandpa? He thought of the black porcelain jar, he thought of the man who smoked cigarettes in a bone holder, he thought of the smell of incense and no tobacco burning in the house. *That?*

A chant came to me. A kind of warble that rose like the ghost of a huge jellyfish from the green sea I imagined in the grove of *'ōhi'a* behind Hongo Store. It hovered over what had become of the lettuce patch. It rose like a fogline and held itself midway up the tallest trees, just at the tops of the tallest *hāpu'u,* the lantern ferns with their heavy boughs like the wings of huge green eagles. It wavered over the land, a bank of gossamer spreading itself until it enveloped all of the land the old store was on—the field of calla lilies, the pond of carp, the decrepit garage, the white house in back where I'd been born, the kitchen of the store behind the counter, the rusting water tank and its screen of old bamboos planted to shield discriminating eyes from the displeasure of practicality. It rushed across the highway, vapor and silk, and took up residence in the voice that I held in my throat as I bent over the writing table and took up a pen.

I'd heard that Torau had written a death poem, a seven-teen-syllable *haiku* or even a *tanka,* that longer poem of thirty-one syllables and higher training. He was supposed to have written it in the weeks before his death—an act that would have been as much like the legend as the man. Japanese of the upper crust, the *samurai* class or the merchants who'd become Japan's bour-geoisie, had it as a custom to write a piece of stern profundity and insight just before the moment of death. The tradition dic-tated that it be framed in somewhat classical terms—allusions to the tradition, perhaps a famous opening line from the fourteenth-century poem of Tsurayuki or the twelfth-century poem of Shunzei. A favorite approach would be to quote a Buddhist proverb—in essence, a passage of scripture. Jakuren's "the foam on the water of the lake" would do. Or Issa's "They say it is a world of dew,/And yet . . . /And yet . . ." My grandfather was supposed to have written something, but no one had it, no one knew where it could be, no one had it memorized.

"The poem was read at his funeral," my aunt said. "I re-member I came across it once written down somewhere, but I haven't thought of it in years. Only the old folks seemed to care about it, and we knew it was appropriate, that's all. The priest read it aloud before he chanted. The *minister* read it at his memorial service in Hilo. Someone paid for an artist, a callig-rapher, to write it down nice in Japanese lettering on rice paper and we hung it from his crypt and put flowers in front of it and his picture above it and we went there all the time, espe-cially on Fridays and Sundays after church. I remember it hanging from the glass in front of his urn. I remember it curl-ing and getting old. No one thought to replace it, have it writ-ten out again. I guess it just disappeared one day. No one thought about it. I wish I had it for you, so you would know more about your grandfather. He was a special, talented man, you know. He didn't only cause people trouble. He had *ideas* about things. He was going to open a department store, but then he got sick, did you know that? He was trying to round up investors in Hilo when he got the news he had cancer. It wouldn't have stopped him either, except he got serious about that too, preparing himself, reading books, talking to the priests, buying *Okyō,* and learning to chant. He wrote his death poem and he was so proud. He showed it to the postmaster when he had it finished. He showed it to the old-timers, his old regular customers, and they looked awkward, not understanding all the complicated words of it. I think it had Buddhist words. But boy, it made a sound! Like nothing heard in Volcano before! I wish I had it for you so you could see it. Maybe you could understand the words."

I imagined my grandfather, walking his grounds, strolling through the field of calla lilies behind Hongo Store, coughing, counting his blessings, reflecting on his life. I imagined him talking to me from the fogs of thirty-five years, refusing to explain himself, confessing no crimes or shortcomings, giving me nothing except his pride and resolve. Maybe he called me *kimi,* "little one" or "thou" in Japanese, but I kept it outside of what I wrote. I gave my words over to him. His ghost rose within me, from out of the cold, from the fens of the rain forest, from the glimmer of gray light in the hazes over the crater. He spoke to me. For a moment, death flickered away. A ghost came to drink. And I gave him his poem, a draft of ichor.

THE UNREAL DWELLING

The Unreal Dwelling:
My Years in Volcano

What I did, I won't excuse, except
to say it was a way to change,
the way new flows add to the land,
making things new, clearing the garden.
I left two sons, a wife behind—
and does it matter? The sons grew,
became their own kinds of men,
lost in the swirl of robes, cries
behind a screen of mist and fire
I drew between us, gambles I lost
and walked away from like any bad job.

I drove a cab and didn't care,
let the wife run off too, her combs
loose in some shopkeeper's bed.
When hope blazed up in my heart for the fresh start,
I took my daughters with me to keep house,
order my living as I was taught and came to expect.
They swept up, cooked, arranged flowers,
practiced tea and buyō, the classical dance.
I knew how because I could read and ordered books,
let all movements be disciplined and objects arranged
by an idea of order, the precise sequence of images
which conjure up the abstract I might call
yūgen, or Mystery, chikara . . . Power.
The principles were in the swordsmanship
I practiced, in the package of loans
and small thefts I'd managed since coming here.
I could count, keep books, speak English
as well as any white, and I had false papers
recommending me, celebrating the fiction
of my long tenure with Hata Shōten of Honolulu.
And my luck was they bothered to check
only those I'd bribed or made love to.
Charm was my collateral, a willingness to move
and live on the frontier my strongest selling point.
So they staked me, a small-time hustler
good with cars, odds, and women,
and I tossed some boards together,
dug ponds and a cesspool,
figured water needed tanks, pipes,
and guttering on the eaves
to catch the light-falling rain,

and I had it—a store and house out back
carved out of rain forests and lava land
beside this mountain road seven leagues from Hilo.
I never worried they'd come this far—
the banks, courts, and police—
mists and sulphur clouds from the crater
drenching the land, washing clean my tracks,
bleaching my spotted skin the pallor of longtime residents.
I regularized my life and raised my girls,
put in gas pumps out front, stocked varieties of goods
and took in local fruit, flowers on consignment.
And I had liquor—plum wine and sake
from Japan, whiskey from Tennessee—
which meant I kept a pistol as well.
My girls learned to shoot, and would have
only no one bothered to test us.
It was known I'd shot cats and wild pigs
from across the road rummaging through garbage.
I never thought of my boys,
or of women too much until my oldest bloomed,
suddenly, vanda-like, from spike
to scented flower almost overnight.
Young men in model A's came up from town.
One even bused, and a marine from Georgia
stole a jeep to try taking her
to the coast, or, more simply,
down a mountain road for the night.
The Shore Patrol found him.
And I got married again, to a country girl
from Kona who answered my ad.
I approved of her because,

though she was rough-spoken and squat-legged,
and, I discovered, her hair
slightly red in the groin,
she could carry 50-lb. sacks of California Rose
without strain or grunting.
As postmaster and Territorial official,
I married us myself, sent announcements
and champagne in medicine vials
to the villagers and my "guarantors" in town.
The toasts tasted of vitamin B and cough syrup.
My oldest moved away, herself married
to a dapper Okinawan who sold Oldsmobiles
and had the leisure to play golf on weekends.
I heard from my boy then, my oldest son,
back from the war and writing to us,
curious, formal, and not a little proud
he'd done his part. What impressed me
was his script—florid but under control,
penmanship like pipers at the tideline
lifting and settling on the sand-colored paper.
He wrote first from Europe, then New York,
finally from Honolulu. He'd fought,
mustered out near the Madison Square Garden
in time to see La Motta smash the pretty one,
and then came home to a girl he'd met in night school.
He said he won out over a cop because he danced better,
knew from the service how to show up in a tie,
bring flowers and silk in nice wrappings.
I flew the Island Clipper to the wedding,
the first time I'd seen the boy in twenty years,
gave him a hundred cash and a wink

since the girl was pretty,
told him to buy, not rent his suits,
and came home the next day, hung over,
a raw ache in my throat.
I sobered up, but the ache
stayed and doctors tell me
it's this sickness they can't get rid of,
pain all through my blood and nerve cells.
I cough too much, can't smoke or drink
or tend to things. Mornings, I roll
myself off the damp bed, wrap
a blanket on, slip into the wooden clogs,
and take a walk around my pond and gardens.
On this half-acre, calla lilies in bloom,
cream-white cups swollen with milk,
heavy on their stems and rocking in the slight wind,
cranes coming to rest on the wet, coppery soil.
The lotuses ride, tiny flamingoes, sapphired
pavilions buoyed on their green keels on the pond.
My fish follow me, snorting to be fed,
gold flashes and streaks of color
like blood satin and brocade in the algaed waters.
And when the sky empties of its many lights,
I see the quarter moon, horned junk,
sailing over Ka'ū and the crater rim.
This is the River of Heaven. . . .
Before I cross, I know I must bow down,
call to my oldest son, say what I must
to bring him, and all the past, back to me.

VOLCANOLOGY:
TRAILS, PONDS,
AND TREES

Nāpau Trail

I WENT ON HIKES from Mauna Ulu to Nāpau Crater
where the lava fields went on mile after mile. Scraps of rock
and iridescence shattered under my feet, tiring my eyes with the
range of gradations in its blacks and grays. And then I would
come to a meadow of bamboo orchids and scrub *'ōhi'a* dotted
with a few soapberry bushes dandling their little bracelets of red
jewels in zircon chains of rain. The plants sprang waist- and
shoulder-high, out of lavas only decades old, and I would see
across a meadow vista back over the bleak patches of dark lava.
After a walk of only a few more yards, I'd come upon a fern
forest, dense, wet as a lagoon, and the trail full of a light brown
mud that itself seemed like part of the land's growth too, a soft,

carpeting plant flowing over hard, black ground. *Hāpu'u* ferns ten feet high mixed in with taller *'ōhi'a* and Portuguese fire trees.

The fire tree was a species that damaged the Hawaiian earth, changing the chemicals in the new ground, altering the system. It was a transplant, an invasive exotic that made things over so that none of the native things could grow around where it had sprung, fouling the land a little, depriving it of its more fragile, endemic beauties. I was told by local naturalists and park botanists to uproot these whenever I came upon them, turning them over so their roots would dry and rain would cleanse them of the earth. In a fern forest, I'd come to a patchy place under a sparse canopy of *hāpu'u* where the fire trees had sprung up and started to colonize. Often, if it was a juvenile grove, dozens of them—small shrubs tall as floor lamps—would be completely upended, drying like tobacco plants in a shady barn—the work of some scientist or park ranger on a periodic traverse. The way might be flagged with blue strips of ripstop nylon here and there—the sure mark of a predecessor—and I'd feel less alone, less isolated from what I'd started to feel was the beginning of all things. There *were* companions.

I'd cross another flow, a long field of oxidized lavas, buff-colored in stark light, and then another little meadowland of things wet and green and teeming with the sweet sizzle of bird-calls. The land would drop away before me hundreds of feet then, opening like a great rift in the earth large enough for entire cloudlands to fill, and I'd be at the cliff rim of a caldera stretching out before my vision like some huge bowl of a knowable sea evacuated of its waters. This was Nāpau Crater, a gigantic pit formed by the subsidence of volcanic matter from underneath the earth's surface. The ground suddenly sinks, the volcanic material which had once held it up now withdrawn from underneath, and the ground collapses, forming a rim of growing circumference as its sides collapse too. What's left is an ovoid pit like a giant pockmark—a scar on the face of the earth. At Nāpau Crater, a stubble of trees froths across the flat brown plain of its floor like the burble of green tea in a *bizen-yaki* bowl. I'd think of canyons carved out of the soft sediments in Arizona, of the gorge of the Columbia in the Northwest. I'd think of the work of the earth, steaming to be born in the distance, the slate-gray cone of Pu'u 'Ō 'ō a spume of land on the crater's far rim, smoking with a long ribbon of white gases falling away toward the sea. I could feel the earth's turning under me, the escape of the planet from under its own aging skin, spouting itself away in gouts of rock and flattering incandescence. I thought of weather like a sailor's words carried on the wind, to the memory of a lover trailing the wake of the moving ship like a flock of white birds dipping and wheeling and dancing alongside a green shadow furling over mutable water.

Perched Lava Pond

On return trips, curling around the back of Mauna Ulu, things might be clear or rain might have condensed into little waves of mist and fog ribboned around its base, rainsheets moving low and laterally. I would worry about an instant eruption sometimes, irrationally, seeing lavas filling the tube I was crossing, spurts forming at the summit of the mountain, fountainings, then a red cascade moving toward me down its slope. Imagination would bring what observation had not, and I felt briefly an excitement brought by fear. Broken fingers of *pāhoehoe* tamed me, and I crossed old tubes without interest, getting lost sometimes, slowly finding my way back to the trail, a narrow scratch across spatter and broken tumuli. On a mound behind the smoking cone, or walking the pinched rim of a collapsed tube like it was a girder on an unfinished highrise, my nerves would start to scramble again, living in the height for an instant, feeling the strange, abyssal dread of pinnacles and surroundings all of colorlessness. Stepping over broken chips and crumbled ropes of lavas always helped this, and jumping down to lower depths, even flying ten and sixteen feet down to the bottom of a tube, was good. I'd only fall and roll a few feet. It was material presence touching me again, giving a good jolt to my bones, and whatever dire thoughts I'd been having would quickly end.

Sometime or other, during one of these hikes, crossing a plain that might have seemed endless except for the companionship of a pressure ridge cracking a line of lava blocks along the earth for a hundred yards or so where I walked, my mind began to accept these as perfected images of solitude and isolation. I trekked over the filled pit of 'Alae Shield one day, rain spattering against my glasses. It made for easier going if I took them off, though my feet stumbled under me. The world was all drizzle and basalt and shades of gray.

Before I walked too long, the monotony that became like rapture was relieved by the great sight of the perched lava pond on the side of the lava shield of Mauna Ulu. Its ramparts and outer walls, formed by the slow buildup and spillage from a tiny lake of lava that sprang from the side of the cone, seemed like the protective sides to an old castello of black adobes. From up close, it felt much more remarkable than it did when seen

from a helicopter. Even the view from the top of nearby Pu'u
Huluhulu (a seventeenth-century cindercone about five hundred
feet high) seemed to diminish the perfection of the lava pond's
symmetry, the evenness of its wall engineered by the simple
accidents of gravity and the gentle pressures of the volcano.
Close at hand, I could see the round forms of its sides and the
top of its banks. The walls looked extremely thick—huge toes
and tree-trunk formations became apparent as I made my in-
spections. Its surfaces were full of deep wrinkles that made it
look like the hide of an elephant. On a much larger scale, the
lava pond in Halema'uma'u must have formed in this same
way, and I liked extrapolating, coloring things in, imagining
what it must have been like for Mark Twain or Charles
Wilkes, more than a hundred years before me, to come upon
and stand nearly beside such a thing, a great bubbling pie of
liquid fire, a shallow tureen of glittering reds and blacks swirled
in convective movements first this way and then that. My mind
eddied in realities, in the richnesses of captured details.

Lava Trees at Huluhulu

I found lava trees. Out on the black plain of new lavas between Chain of Craters Road and Pu'u Huluhulu, I found
a black swarm of pillars that were shaped by the stately movement of *pāhoehoe* making its way across a spot of low incline.
New lavas from Mauna Ulu had moved in a funereal march,
eddying out in fans and radiant toes stretching themselves
along like elephantine amoebas, gluing their way along in a

slow slaloming time. As it fell away from its highest levels, the receding lava had swirled around the trunks of tree ferns and *'ōhi'a* standing in its path, incinerating them. The flow chilled and hardened into rock where it came into contact with the cool bodies of these plants, while the interior of the flow continued being molten and fluid. When the viscous curls of molten rock subsided away from the trunks of these trees, they left behind the black lava casts of an entire forest. After cooling, what remained looked like thick and broken hangmen's trees stippling the flat plain of 1977 when the lavas last flowed here.

There was a smooth trail from the turnout to the old cin-dercone, and I'd park and get out for the short hike out there in rainy weather or sunshine, alone or with friends out from Honolulu or the Mainland for a visit. It was a congenial grove, more part of heaven than of hell, though I did think, from time to time, of the bleeding suicides in Dante's wood as I walked it. Like Dante's, these trees seemed to talk too, but often in a mood more of beneficence than anger. They did not pummel one another, and if you brushed by them, if you snapped at their bodies with a hand or bootheel, they did not weep or bleed or rail against you. More a grove of sponsors than of suicides, they seemed free and authorizing, like standing stones on a heath on a Scottish isle, sentinels to a time eons past; in terms of the acquired innocence of knowledge, in terms of the pure seeing I craved, they were only a heartbeat, a breath away.

Once, I strolled up a little rise in the asphalt-colored trail, thrown up by a hummock of lava that was inflated from below, pushing up in a slow adagio under its older surface, fracturing only a little, making pressure cracks and a gradually sloping tu-mulus that lifted me up the few feet I needed to see a little black

vale between myself and the cindercone. It was seeded with ju-
veniles, I thought, black adolescent trees without crowns
arranged in the pattern of replanting as in a clear-cut in Oregon.
But I could also see a flock of hundreds of long-legged flamingoes napping on a black sand beach, their black bodies tucked
up and silhouettes obscured into the wide absence of light.

It was nearly sunset, and the regular rains of the afternoon
had let up, though there were still a low-lying fog and patches
of cloud cover that the sun did not quite manage to break
through. A slanting light came straight at me from behind the
vast field of lava trees. They looked then like black mesas
densely packed and backlit by the setting sun. Their profiles
made me think of Monument Valley and the Painted Desert,
except that the scale was much smaller, the space more intimate.
It was such a congenial panorama—a stark profile repeated
again and again all across the lava field still glistening from the
last shower of rain in the late sunlight. When I walked a little
farther ahead, the angle of light changed, or the intensity of light
itself shifted. I was looking at a few trees standing over swirled
mounds of lava made hazy in the misty light. I strolled and
strolled, empty of breath, gaping as I passed under the torn arms
of the first tree I could touch.

I stepped up to it, finding definition in what appeared
from far away as an almost smooth, featureless surface. The
formation was a small tower, a kind of chimney built up
around what had once been an *'ōhi'a* tree maybe fifty years old.
Lava had clothed the living tree in a winding sheet that
burned it until it smoked at one end and spat a sizzle of juices
out of each of its limbs and branches. The whole tree might
have erupted in flame at one point, incinerated almost completely in the grip of the hardening stone. What was left, I

could see, was a hollow where the trunk had been, a column partially filled with a cutaway of what had once been its cross section, a radiance of blackened phloem like a charcoal anemone inside the small cave of the absent trunk. I stepped back to measure it, sizing it against my own body, finding it half again as much as I was, a monster except for its gentle-ness as infant rock.

It was a dark, black thing, a torso lifting itself out of mire. There were niches in it, burbles in the rock, fungal growths pocked up its trunk. It looked at me and winked from under its charcoal skin, and the mineral world seemed made into flesh that day, rock into a softer presence alive with comedic insinu-ation, like the gigantic caterpillar in Wonderland. And yet it was the shadow of all matter—lavas wound in a coil that pre-served a distorted semblance of a tree's shape, like the dark cast a high sun makes of the body when one stands between it and the surface of the earth.

A white limb hung from out of the tree's hollowed cen-ter. It was blobbed with lava at one end, burned like used kin-dling at the other, a bone that had snapped off and then exploded into burning when the mold was being formed. I picked it up and swung with it in one hand, turning my wrist like it was a miter, feeling its weight, a heavy counterbalance at the end of the light stick. There was a fine ash from the old burning, a silver slip of color shining within my palm.

A chorus of voices came from down in the vale of shad-ows, then a jet plane's echo sounded from where the black flamingoes had been at rest. I tested the snapped limb against owl-shaped hornitos, swung it against rounded driblet spires rising like black mushrooms at my feet and around the dark lava tree.

What was memory and what sense furled together in spi-
rals. Before me was a plain stripped of its comfort of forest.
Kīlauea, an innocent shadowland, tilted itself gently skyward
into fists of wind, crimson dreadlocks of nimbus clouds gan-
jaed over the sponsoring grove of relict trees.

LEAVE-TAKING

Rodrigues's House

NEARLY A YEAR had passed, and now, we were leaving
Volcano in less than a week. Cynthia and I both knew we
wanted to come back. But we needed to find another place to
live. It wouldn't be easy renting from long distance, and we
couldn't have the same cottage again. Our host would be living in it with her son as soon as the year was over. If we wanted
to come back to Volcano for any like length of time, we'd have
to locate a decent place to rent. We'd have to line it up.

Idly, over the last weeks we were there, Cynthia had been
scanning the classifieds in the local paper. I was supposed to be
asking around too—asking my cousins, perhaps posting a note
on the bulletin board at the Hongo Store. But I was completely

embarrassed. I didn't want to advertise my wanting. I felt
abashed to be exposing my wish for a place, my need for help
finding it, my lack of resources, friends, and finances. There was
the fact of my shame involved, my fear of being exposed and
found out, a feeling that if people knew how strangely passionate I was about wanting to return, they would find little sympa-
thy and, instead, feel scorn and pity for me for my silliness and
self-indulgence. *What?* I imagined them saying, silently. *The little Hongo boy needs charity? Needs a house so that he can live in his
Hawaiian dreams?* I sequestered myself in imagined derision,
avoided dealing with finding the house, procrastinated until we
had only a few days left before we had to leave.

Cynthia found an ad. "Custom 3-br," it said, "2 bath,
carport, 1500-gal. tank in Mauna Loa Est." We called the
phone number, and a man with a soft local accent invited us
over right away.

"I think you'll like it if you come see for yourselves," he
said, pronouncing the plural, the complex conjunction of
vowels and consonants *l-v-e-s* exceedingly carefully, grammati-
cally, modestly. The sound was a little difficult for the local accent. Yet, there was a slow, confident note in the way he spoke.
There was power.

The house was easy to find—just about six streets closer
to the highway than our cottage and a block up-mountain. It
was on a corner lot just past where the asphalted streets gave
way to unpaved lanes dozed right over the lava. There were
hydrangeas lining the driveway, *hāpu'u* ferns shading it, and
clusters of *'ōhi'a* left still standing throughout the grassy yard.
Two bare-chested men, one older, both looking as strong-
shouldered and purposeful as marines, were hard at work,
bundling up a pile of slash or tree trimmings, lashing and tug-

ging and industriously knotting neat little bales together. I figured the house would be cherry. As we drove up, the older man
came down the driveway to greet us. He was Tony Rodrigues,
a Hilo plumbing contractor who had built the place as a weekend cottage for his family. And it was built immaculately, a
cedar A-frame. Rodrigues had done all the work himself, digging the cesspool, clearing the lot, replanting the *hāpu'u* into
rows, landscaping, pouring the foundation, framing it out,
plumbing it, wiring it, customizing the interior and roofing it,
seeing to every nail and joist, each pipe and piece of shingling.
Things looked and felt *tight* and I knew the place was a steal.

"Allah kids grown now and we don't have dat much use
for it," he explained. "Plus, I got one oddah, bigger place I'm
building way out on Wright Road. Frankly, we could use the
cash a rental would bring in to finish it."

I liked this Hawaiian way of explaining yourself, of revealing what was behind what you did. I gave him a little of
my story—the Mainland college professor coming home. Cynthia walked up from the car carrying infant Alexander asleep
in her arms and finished out the picture of my sincerity. I felt
we were reaching an accord with Rodrigues already.

He pointed to the house next door, a blue one looking
vaguely similar in overall design to the cedar A-frame. He said
he'd built that too, only gave it a bigger water tank—three thousand gallons—twice as big. It was painted blue, like the house.
He said he learned from building the first one. He abandoned
the fancy crank windows for regular, vertically sliding ones on
the second house, went for cheaper siding and plastic interior
paneling (no cedar), and added the bigger tank. "For dah laundry, eh?" he explained, slipping into pidgin. "For wash clothes,
no worry about use 'em up, drought, anyt'ing like dat." So he

pointed out what he felt to be the cedar house's only flaw. It made me like him.

I said that we'd call him from Missouri, from the Main-land, once we decided to come back. He seemed only a little perplexed we were looking so much in advance. We needed a place, maybe for a year, I said, for the *next* time we'd be through Volcano, but for sure we would be.

He nodded and gave me a card, wrote another phone number on the back of it, and told me he couldn't guarantee it would be available, but that he'd welcome my call if I was in-terested—"when-evah," he said, casually, musically. He gave me an idea of what the rent would be, and I was pleased it was so low. Even an assistant professor on leave could afford it if he fed his family dry tuna fish and peanut butter sandwiches for a while.

We drove away, feeling strong about making these plans. The skies were that silver-gray of haze and volcanic fog. Alexander, awake now, was banging a toy against the window of the car, spuming and razzing and sputtering, making a spit-song to accompany the hope Cynthia and I felt swimming through Volcano and each of us.

Eveline

We'd be flying off to O'ahu in a day or two, to spend a month in a beach shack on Kawela Bay on the North Shore near where my Kubota grandfather had *his* store. We had only a cou-ple more days left in Volcano.

I decided to drive to the house behind the Hongo Store one evening. Soon, there would be no time left to meet Eve line, the woman from Hāwī who had married my grandfather a few years before his death, the woman who had inherited what was left of all his gambles. I put on the off white golf jacket, undersized for me, that my father used to wear, and an nounced I was going to the store for milk or bread or the evening paper.

It was misty, drizzling softly, and the roads were wet, the trees around the village and the highway dripping. I used the wipers on the windshield of the little rental car. I disconnected the car battery from the cable to the cottage's water pump, nosed the car out of the narrow driveway, and drove across the checkerboard of roads of Mauna Loa Estates, crossed the high way, and drove the short way up mountain along the bypassed strip of old Volcano Road to the Hongo Store.

I drove down the graveled lane *beside* the store, down the little track that led to the house Torau Hongo had built for my father and mother the year before I was born, the house where Eveline Hongo now lived. Surely, she would have heard by now the story that I was back, living in the village, that "a Hongo" had returned to Volcano. I wondered if she had ever thought to prepare for a meeting with me, how her own relatives, themselves now installed in the grocery business in the village, might have given her the word and speculated what I might have been up to in coming back. Once, I'd heard her name called out at the post office, and it sent a shiver through me, but, up until this moment, I'd sought no meet ing with her myself.

I had glimpsed my grandfather's old house before, dur ing my first trip to Volcano, when I was taken there by my aunt and uncle. I remembered its oxidized, white-painted sides, the flumes from its roof gutters that led to multiple water tanks. I remembered the gigantic field of calla lilies that made up most of the grounds surrounding it. I pulled up behind a carport with a new, silver-gray Japanese compact car parked under it. I got out of my car and walked up to the door at the side of the house. There was a front door as well, under an awning that seemed to run from the back of the Hongo Store to the rear house, but I doubted it was much used. The side porch had a collection of shoes, rubber beach sandals, folded umbrellas, and an alcove for *bonsai* that told me folks came in through there. I trotted up the stairs, ducked my head inside the entranceway, opened a screen door, and walked into an anteroom cluttered with stacks of old newspapers and maga-zines, tubs of bagged trash, and a few buckets filled halfway with water and cut lilies in several grades. I could hear the crackling speaker of an old television tuned to the evening news inside, and a gaggle of conversation in Japanese. The voices were women's. I banged on the frame of another screen door inside the little porch. It was dark inside there, damp, and the smell of cooking wafted out to me through the flabby wiring of the door's old metal screen.

"*Gomen kudasai!*" I shouted, speaking in Japanese, loudly but politely announcing my presence. My back stiffened and straightened itself out, and I could have almost bowed.

The voices stopped, interrupted by my firm outcry, then picked up again with a mild flurry of excitement and sorted themselves out.

"*Ehh, eh!*" an older woman's voice said, musically, from deep inside of the house. "*Dareh deshyo wah neh?*" It asked, po-litely, decorously, who I could be. The flurry of voices guessed a salesman, the paper boy, a neighbor named Yamamoto, then they died away. Who could it be?

"*Hongo de gozaru yo!*" I said, my voice booming a little, "*Namae wa Hongo dah.*" I sounded absurdly mature and manly—like the actors in *samurai* movies. "It is *Hongo,*" I said, "The name is *Hongo.*"

"Who is Hongo?" a higher, bewildered voice asked in Japanese. "Mrs. Hongo is in here with us."

"*I* am Hongo," I answered in Japanese. "The grandson of Torau."

The women's voices came in a burst of exclamations then. *Hurry up*, they said, *get to the door, don't make him wait, who can he be? Where did he come from? Go to the door! No, you go to the door!*

There was a flurry of negotiation that fell quickly into whispering, then silence. I heard soft footsteps pad out to me, and a short, slim woman in blue polyester came out of the dark house to the doorway. Her face was dark, pleasantly wrinkled and angular like a Spaniard's—I recalled Edward Weston's portrait of José Limón—but she was clearly Japanese. And she had poise.

"Yes, Mr. Hongo," she said calmly, opening the door, "but you *must* come in." She held the door open wide, sweep-ing it outward over the porch and the clutter of footwear arranged like little coffins between us.

"Are *you* Mrs. Hongo?" I asked her, knowing instantly that she wasn't. There was no spark in her eye, no fear of me, no anger, no hint of suppressed emotion. She held the door open against its spring, gestured for me to remove my own shoes, and waited while I did so.

"No," she said. "I am Nakamura, Mrs. Hongo's younger sister-in-law. We are here, all of her sisters-in-law, visiting her in Volcano. I myself come from Maui."

Shoes off, I crossed the threshold, ducking my head under a short curtain of Japanese-patterned kitchen cloth, sucking in a short breath—the Japanese male gesture for asking pardon. Stepping into shadows, I noticed a flicker of light in the room beyond.

Nakamura from Maui led me through a cluttered, ramshackle kitchen with a greasy pan still on the stove and dishes piled in the single sink. There was an oil-spattered calendar of a Japanese temple garden on the wall, pink hydrangeas or purple azaleas under spreading spots of brown grease. There was a canister of thin-pressed dried seaweed and lobelias of dried Chinese plums wrapped in colorful papers and strung into wacky *lei* that hung from a nail driven into the wall. We crossed quickly through another little room—the breakfast nook, crammed with newspapers and cardboard boxes full of magazines and old clothing, stacks of varicolored canned goods like blue Spam and green tuna and red corned beef.

In the large room we entered last, several women were seated around a square table. Another woman was seated on a love seat, and another in a club chair. A basket of knitting spilled out onto the rattan rug on the dark, brown floor. This was the living room, and it too was crammed full of things. A large, round table took up one entire corner of the room. Its top was rife with clutter. There was room on the sofa, a love seat, and there were empty places at the square table, which was set for dinner, chopsticks and teabowls and small *chazuke* plates arranged around its sides. An automatic rice pot, a flask of soy sauce, and a bottle of Tabasco took up the center. The women around me were all old, modest, and countryish in dress. Their hair was white or silver-and-black, done up in buns and full of hairpins. They wore sack dresses or polyester pantsuits with Orlon sweaters added against the Volcano chill. They sat or stood stiffly, and my entrance, I knew, had transformed the room and their quiet, family-style dinner. These were widows, and my youth and maleness had completely changed the equi-librium of their evening. They flapped their cardigans, adjust-ing the fit of a sleeve or a shoulder, cleared phlegm from their throats, and quieted themselves, waiting for what I'd say, what I'd do, whom I would address.

"This is my sister-in-law," the Maui woman said. "This is Mrs. Hongo, your grandmother."

She gestured toward an extremely short, flat-faced woman with gnarled, leathery skin gathered over her skull like a sock doll's cinched at the throat and eyes. The woman's lips parted and smacked, but before she could speak, another's voice spoke up sharply.

"*She* is not his grandmother!" said a porcine woman, dressed in a checkered dress. "He is the grandson of her *hus-band*! They are *not* related. Their names are Hongo, but they are not related!"

The gaggle of voices murmured and assented. *Oh yes, oh yes,* they said, *don't we know the story?*

"Please, take a seat, we're having dinner," the voices said. "Please join us, it's no trouble, we'd be honored." And heads nodded, hands gestured toward an empty metal chair uphol-stered in a light-colored, Formica-looking Naugahyde. There were spots and flecks of rust on the tubing of the frame. An-other tiny woman who hadn't yet spoken grabbed a small, flat pillow, upholstered in a purple velour, and placed it on the chair's seat. There was a silence, a held moment. I glanced at Eveline Hongo, who stood stiffly, making no invitation, no protest, but holding herself fully frozen in indecision. I sat down, thanking everyone, nodding at Eveline, agreeing.

"Tea only," I said, holding my hand up and dipping my head for an instant, Japanese style, though I knew I'd commit/ ted everyone to serving me.

Eveline stood and served up steaming white rice in every/ one's bowl. She ladled it out with a bamboo paddle, hefting and flicking little dollops of rice sideways into the bowls. She kept her eyes on what she was doing and did not glance at me.

I saw that the whole room was doused in an extremely pale, greenish enamel paint that reminded me of every old, plantation/style shotgun house I'd ever been in since child/ hood. There were two square pillars spaced across the middle of the room, bracing up the center pole of the roof, and the floor was a dark, unvarnished wood I guessed to be 'ōhi'a, plentiful and perhaps plantation plain at one time, but now a luxurious affectation in the Honolulu homes of the bour/ geoisie. There were cans full of pencils and pens all around the room, little fuzzy and woolen things, silk pillows and balls of yarn, stacks of cheap yardage, a clock, a new Sony portable radio, and a Sears sewing machine out of its box and lying on a cluttered end table in a corner. There was one large overhead lamp that lit everything, but there were also two oth/ ers, their shades woolly with dust, at the corners of the room. In the air was suspended a mixed fragrance of liniment, fried foods, and mildew.

I got a dollop of pale, red spaghetti on my plate, then a patch of boiled and chopped spinach, deeply green. A plate of soft white *tōfu* was being passed around too, sprinkled with amber flakes of bonito and seeds of blackened sesame. I plucked off two dainty squares with my tapered red chopsticks. A couple of cans of tuna made the rounds too, bathed in soy oil; a plate of flavored and toasted seaweed; some yellow morsels of pickled Japanese radish. A sweet thing—perhaps a cake of sugared bean paste—came by as well. And brown rice tea. All the smells and tastes of a country meal. I ate like a crow pecking out the eyes of a corpse.

The porcine woman in the checkered dress sat across from me and explained she was the oldest of four sisters and that she had recently been widowed, like two of the other sisters. She gestured toward Eveline, who had suffered widowhood the longest, and another woman who never spoke the whole time I was there. She said that her sister from Maui, the thin one in the blue polyester suit, the one who had come to the door, had *never* been married, but was here to help Eveline with the store, help all of them grieve. They were gathering to rally themselves, to get reacquainted with each other, and since Eveline had the biggest house, they had chosen to come to Volcano for a reunion.

She introduced a tiny woman at the end of the table, who nodded politely at me while shutting her eyes. She was the one who had gotten up from knitting. She was not related to the rest, but was a neighbor here, Mrs. Yamamoto. She told me she lived in a house across the road from Hongo Store, the one with the little glass greenhouse in front next to the driveway. Her son grew orchids there. She said she thought that he knew my father, that another son, a retired policeman, knew my father too. Someone grumbled, switched the subject, and the group began discussing a bingo game in Ka'ū for a moment.

Mrs. Nakamura asked about me, my family, my father. I told them a little of the story. My father was dead, I told them, first thing. My brother and I buried him on a knoll in Los Angeles overlooking the harbor, a piece of the Pacific that he never recrossed to Hawai'i once he left. They expressed sorrow, condolences. I said that I had grown up in Los Angeles, hankering a little for Hawai'i all my childhood, had returned periodically, to O'ahu and my Kubota grandfather's home there, in order to keep it part of my life. But, I said, this was only my second trip back to Hawai'i, the Big Island where I was born, and only the first time I'd come for any length of time. Had I been staying here long? someone asked. Would I be making plans to settle permanently in the village?

I answered I was already about to leave for O'ahu, and Eveline nodded, speaking finally, acknowledging me, affirming to herself I wasn't a ghost, bobbing her head, punctuating my little narrative with a little accompaniment of musical verbal assent. When I said that I was a university professor, that I'd gone through college and graduate school in literature, she broke in and spoke a full sentence.

"Your father bought you a good education, did he?" she said. "Oh, that's *good,* that's *very* good! He used his money *wisely!*"

I remember thinking then that she meant to imply that what had come of things here in Volcano had resulted in my being educated, that my father had *bought* a life for me out of whatever he took from the store. Her eyes flickered alive at that moment, and they looked into mine. *Leave me be,* she seemed to be saying. *You have what you have, honored by the world. Now leave me be.*

I held her gaze and felt the spark there, firing through the empty space between us, and I let it go, answering her with silence. I dropped my eyes to the dinner plate, congealing with grease and swirls of black soy sauce, and then looked up again. Eveline had already glanced away. But the character of the expression on her face had changed. It had been frozen before, pained and vulnerable, exposed and without any electric impulse of thought or emotion, but something calm had descended upon it now, and she seemed to me like a girl awaiting a blessing from the priest at church. She seemed bathed in the brief aura of some innocence, shriven of guilt or defensiveness.

She must have known I would exact no material revenge. Retribution, if it was just, would have to come about through another route. She must have sensed it before I did. Her property would remain hers, and my presence meant no challenge to possession of it, either legal or moral. I felt her eyes shift under a half-lidded, obscure smile, then look away again, sliding across the morsels on her plate.

I clattered my chopsticks together across the rim of the dinner plate in front of me, shoved myself away from the table, announcing I had to return to my family waiting for me across the highway, and I got up, refusing the little gift of fruit or a can of soup someone offered me. Two of the old women got up with me, and they all bowed, saying goodbye, how good it was to meet me, how illustrious I seemed, how wonderfully I spoke Japanese, how surprising I could, how wonderful that Mr. Hongo's grandson had returned home. Eveline rose too, but someone else walked me to the door. In the departing, someone must've asked if there was anything I wanted that they could offer.

I asked to photograph the grounds, the house, the carport under the drizzle of rain. All the women came out with me then, putting on their rubber sandals and *geta,* the Japanese

clogs. We tramped over the driveway to the field of calla lilies
and the old fishponds my grandfather had dug for *koi,* the ornamental carp he tried to raise once, before I was born. The
fish were long gone and lilies had overgrown their ponds. I
took a picture of the end of the house where I fancied my parents might have had their bedroom. I took a picture of the
shingled and hatted water tanks. I took a picture of the oiled-
dirt and graveled lane from the loop of driveway as it curved
through the field of white lilies buoyed upward in the drizzle
on their green stems. I thought of birth, of nursing, of the calla
lilies as the breasts of my beginnings. I walked out along the
lane, the porous crunch of lava rock under my feet, a past of
veils and feints and spatterings of humanity vanishing in the
track behind me. I got into the rental car and drove away, un-
illumined ghosts bristling with envy in the dark that was
descending.

Chickens and China Nights

In the end, all I wanted to do was walk around outside the little cottage, mostly with Alexander drowsy and gurgling in my
arms. The ground below and forest surrounding us seemed to
gurgle too, spitting up and swallowing itself all the time. Water
was everywhere, as dampness in our clothes and throughout the
house, in drip and dew on the broad leaves of ginger plants and
staghorn ferns shooting from the forest floor, in muddy and
crumbling ground, in the spongy trunks of *hāpuʻu,* in rivulets of
rain rushing under the crawl space of the house, in the sump

and gurgle of catchment gutters and flumes filling up, in a gauzy curtain of fog and mist drawn across the silver face of a stand of *'ōhi'a* trees.

I liked to hear the ground suck and crunch under me as I walked over it, padding along the tiny pathways worn over the patches of planted grass. Bare lava mounds sometimes stuck up in the walkways, a crazy quilt of trails around the cottage that led to two things: our neighbor's house about an acre lot away and an abandoned system of pig-hunter and pig trails wandering through the forest's understory. Sometimes I'd slip a little on my cheap rubber beach sandals, my wet soles skid-ding on the slick face of a worn piece of rock, and I'd wish for the tough clunk and digging grip of nineteenth-century Japa-nese *geta*—rectangular clogs raised up on two ridges of thick wood running perpendicular to your foot.

I wore *geta* as a child walking muddy plantation roads, and wore them again as an acolyte in a monastery in Japan. Once, I tromped up a favored moss garden of the master, not thinking to remove the clogs and go barefoot on the soft natural carpeting. My *geta* left trails of treadlike depressions all over the delicate green, a planting centuries old and nearly perpetual. The head monk tapped my shoulder briskly and gestured for me to look behind to what I'd done. He laughed and said that in three hundred years, no one had ever accomplished that. I never forgot the lesson—tread lightly on beauty. And so I did in Volcano, heel and toe, cat and foglike through the ferns.

For company I had not only my child, lolling himself to sleep on my shoulder, but a bunch of my neighbors' chickens running loose through the forest and foraging on whatever worms and kitchen scraps they could scrounge. The cottage was without a disposal, so I'd been taking out our kitchen scraps every afternoon and scattering them on a barren part of the pathway between the houses so the chickens could get to them easily. I threw papaya seeds and rinds, eggshells, coffee grounds, crusts of bread, leftover pasta and noodles of varied sorts (Chinese *mein*, fat Japanese *udon*, slender Japanese *soba*, and generic Oriental *saimin* and instant *rāmen*)—all of which the hens pecked and gobbled with gusto. They screeched and bug-gawed lovingly, came running whenever I'd emerge on their turf, pecked away, then hopped and bobbed along, disappear-ing and reappearing around the bronze stumps and trunks of the tree ferns as they dispersed.

There were two roosters—a large white Japanese cock with an intense red crest and gnarled claws, and a small, russet-colored one who seemed more in authority, smarter and spryer. The Japanese cock was silent, stolid, and earthbound, heavy and ducklike, waddling over the pathways and foraging through the lower ferns of the forest. But the russet would hop up in the abandoned chicken coop on the property line, take up a perch on a piece of doweling, and crow until you wanted to hit him with a lava rock. He'd be the one to wake us morn-ings, cockadoodling at daybreak, spurring us on to make hay and *pulu* while the sun shone.

The hens were black bantams, reds, and Japanese whites. Their feathers sometimes shone iridescent in the Volcano driz-zles, their beaks yellow as light breaking through a fault line in the clouds. I thought of chickens running loose in my childhood village of Kahuku on Oʻahu, the plantation camp on another island where my parents moved after they'd given up on Vol-cano. I thought of the people who kept those chickens—thin, bandy-legged Filipinos and Japanese in khakis and flour-sack *muʻumuʻu*, rolling Bull Durham cigarettes on their unpainted clapboard wood porches, nodding and talking story and calling to me "*Boy-san! Boy-san!*" and cupping and uncupping their hands in the repeated soft, mouthlike clap that meant *Come hither.* I gave myself to memory again, to a legacy of images lost in my growth and travels and scattered upbringing. I returned to a natal world of lavish colors, rich in sounds and abject in its poverty.

I sang songs, lullabies to my baby, slumped on my shoul-der like a twenty-five-pound sack of cane sugar. I sang "Des-perado" mostly, a croonish cowboy tune written by a Laurel Canyon band. But I also sang Roy Orbison's "Blue Bayou," practicing the virtuosic end-yodel on my slumbering son. I sang Hawaiian-language songs I liked and tried to learn—"Ipo Lei Manu" and "Tuba Roses"—sweet, melodic, and mournful. And I sang one Japanese ballad, "Shina no Yoru"—in Eng-lish, China Nights—a tune my father and grandfather both liked, spinning it on the restaurant jukebox while they sat cross-legged on *zabuton* floor cushions and played hand after hand of *hanafuda,* a Japanese rummy game.

"Shina no Yoru" was a 1939 hit in Japan, brought over to Hawai'i through the old Japanese community, and its nar-rative is about a poor, forlorn Japanese foot soldier sent abroad to fight the Chinese in Manchuria. Its verses are sung by his hometown sweetheart, a tenderhearted and loyal maid who re-minds him never to forget where he comes from, what his roots are, what the color of light is like in his village. Its Japanese is beautiful, reminiscent of classical *samurai* court po-etry, elegant in syntax and powerful in its paradoxes and *peripeteia*ic narrative twist. The maid sings, *Minato no akari, murasaki no yo ni/Noboru junku no yume no fune. . . . /Ah-ahh, ah-ahh . . . /Wasurarenu/Kokyu no ne/Shina no Yoru.* It means something like "As you board the junk,/that boat of dreams,/forget not the shining lights of the capital/nor your own village roots, alas,/during these distant China nights." Like Petrarchan sonnets, the images are part of an old allegorical machinery as well, full of sexual puns and allusions (violet lights like a *geisha*'s hair) and warnings and bearing a strong reminder regarding origins and one's loyalty to them. On one level, its message reminded me of the Antaeus myth, the story of the Moroccan giant Hercules had to fight whose strength came from his contact with his mother, the earth. Once Greek Hercules realized this, the embattled hero picked African Antaeus up by the waist, lifting him from the ground, and, the previously invincible giant thus weakened, Hercules was able to crush him to death. On another level, the song's message was one about birth and sex, a feminine loyalty to origins. "Forget not the womb or your loins, dear warrior, for you are of the earth—a woman—and not apart from her." It is a commandment calling for gentleness. It was likewise for Petrarch and the Earl of Surrey, his English Renaissance translator— allegiance, for them, had a lot to do with a fleshly love and a loyalty to place. But later interpreters and sonnet-practitioners had abstracted these principles much further to mean allegiance to the state and to Christian religion itself—and thus, the sonnet tradition became a poetry that had inscribed within its blunt sexuality and spiritual traditions a competitive martial tradition as well. "Shina no Yoru" had a soldier in it, but there the resemblance ends. For this 1930s Japanese pop tune, loyalty was fairly basic—given primarily to homeland and to the sweets of a village sweetheart. I took it as my own reminder about Volcano, the place that was my center, and about the roots my soul should remain loyal to. Its most moving line, for me, had to do with having been sundered from village roots and then being reminded to return. It was a poet's reminder to stay aware of origins in a confused time, and of identity with one's people and a specific place.

In those last afternoons, I rocked my infant son, crooning as romantically as I could a *sake*-drinking song, a "chune" on the Japanese hit parade of 1939, scattering a flock of perplexed chickens through the foot trails of the rain forest, feeling myself lucky and alive in the place where I was born, where the earth steamed and vented, giving birth to still newer lands. On a horned junk, a boat of dreams and meditation, I returned. I let loyalty inspirit my breast and inflame the chambers of my heart. Dripping boughs of the fern forest, gnarled limbs of Hawaiian myrtle, a shower of sunlight from a break in the clouds dazzling down the path I walked.

Snails and Star Trails

Early on the morning we were to leave, I woke long before dawn, wriggling out from under our heavy bed quilts, and opened the back door so I could walk outside to the toilet. A small swarm of jungle slugs was making its way across the little deck in the back. I'd noticed their slime trails from the start, lacy dribbles appearing overnight across the smooth wood of the deck. Showing themselves now, these were large, hummocked things about the size of wrens without their wings. Without feathers. Without skins. Raw flesh on the move, pasty gray and mottled red and orange. Their fresh slime trails shone like stardust. I took a breath and picked my way past them to the john, then turned away and stood at the edge of the deck-ing instead. Already naked, I hissed at the dark. I wanted to feel the night.

Stars were out, necklaces and bracelets glittering across the maroon velvet of sky, the smooth neck of Pegasus and pelted shoulders of the Bear. Fragments of their stories flickered dimly alive in my thoughts. I felt bathed in the chill, drenched and stained by the night's dark zenith, mottled in starlight. I could hear my own breathing and the plash of runoff dripping from the trees onto the fern-thick understory around me. I turned back.

The slugs had moved. There was a hole in the deck where the house opened itself up to the bottom of the earth. They came from that. It was a kind of open well of junk our host used to store plastic milk cartons, soda pop cans, and other scraps and leftovers. There were empty boxes and crates down there, carefully folded pieces of cardboard alongside the torn and dissolving. I saw a few child's toys, a rake and a hoe and the aluminum tubing from either a television antenna or a Sears clothes palm for hanging wet laundry. Either one was useless in wet and remote Volcano. *Dampness is all,* I joked to myself, twenty-nine miles from Hilo and cable tele-vision, toes soaking up the dew. I had yet to confront one more ghost.

Inattention had put me at risk. The slugs had moved past the refrigerator and the woodpile to the decking around me. I was cut off from my path back to the house, and the shining skin on the backs of my bare heels raised up invisi-ble hairs. The slugs trooped along to the forest swelling in from the dark.

K i r i u

A few days later, we were in Honolulu, having lunch at the
Pagoda, an old-style Japanese restaurant near the public golf
course. It was in a neighborhood halfway between downtown
and the university district. The Pagoda also had rooms to let
and, before the huge seventies and eighties boom in Japanese
tourism at the luxury market level, had once been the most popular hotel among the trickle of visitors coming to see their country cousins in the islands. There was an old-fashioned grace to
its rooms and grounds, and its restaurant was still well known
and written up in the chichi tour guides. There was a multi-
level carp pond and waterfall, filling the dining area with the
regularized sound of a gentle plashing that did help incline the
soul toward a bit more graciousness than the rattle and clink
and short-order chatter of a Denny's. The sound system piped
in the sedate music of *sankyoku*—a classical Japanese trio of
shamisen (a three-stringed, plucked banjo-like instrument), *koto*
(a fifteen-stringed lute), and *shakuhachi* (the eight-holed, end-
blown flute of Zen meditation). I noticed black enamel chairs,
slate tile floors in the main dining room, and *tatami*-mat rooms
with sliding doors on the floors above the main level. The atmosphere was a mixture of corniness and Tokyo metropoli-
tanism to me. I could smell the spicy sweetness of a gentle
teriyaki in the air, and guessed that the food would be good—
delicate, presented well, sliced and sized with complete precision,
with sharply defined flavors and balanced colors in every meal
selection. Efficiency and accuracy. I also guessed I wouldn't be

paying. Katayama—the man who'd married my grandmother, the dancer, all those years ago—*he* would be paying. Cynthia, Alexander, and I were his guests and he would insist.

We'd flown over from the Big Island to Oʻahu the day before, gotten a funkier, Honolulu version of the same red rental car we had in Hilo, and driven out to the little beach shack in Kawela I'd rented over the telephone. We'd settled in, taken in one magnificent sunset firing out over the lagoon, and then gotten up early to make the luncheon date with the Katayamas. I'd called and asked my Aunt Charlotte to call them first, preparing them for the contact. Katayama, the old plantation boss, called me in Volcano then, introducing him-self, inviting Cynthia and me to lunch or dinner with them once we got to Honolulu. I remember he'd given me direc-tions, in English, and started them from Wahiawā in the pineapple fields near Schofield Barracks, where the freeway into town began. They brought us in past Pearl Harbor and the cutoff to the Arizona Memorial, by the airport and past the lit-tle financial district to the old Japanese neighborhoods that dot-ted the upper end of the little river valleys along the Koʻolau Mountains, the green cliffs that are a constant backdrop to the city. "Take the turnoff to Makiki Heights," he'd said, and I'd followed the directions, winding us past stacks of cheap apart-ments and old, temple-roofed Japanese houses up the little pal-isade into a little area of condominiums and bourgeois swankiness. I pulled into a wide driveway area that served a triplex, a complex of town houses, and a single home, all cramped into a tight lot against the hillside. Katayama opened the door. He was dressed in gray polyester slacks and a silver-gray patterned aloha shirt. He bowed to me, taking up my hand and saying "Gran'ma" would soon be down, that she'd

left something upstairs and had gone back for it, that we'd car
avan over to the restaurant.

They had the upstairs of the triplex, and when she de
scended its stairs an instant after we'd arrived, she seemed to de
scend sideways, the line of her hip emphasized by a stylish and
shibui (elegant but understated) gray silk clutch she held against
it. She was done up, eyes thick with mascara, brows plucked,
her face powdered pale and cheeks lightly rouged. Her hair was
mixed white and black, done up high in a Nefertiti-like do, and
she wore heavy, square-heeled shoes that clunked as she de
scended the wooden planking of the stairs. A black silk scarf
waffled out in the wind, and she brought it over her hair like
a little parachute dropping down on the bole of a cultivated,
arboretum-bred tree. She seemed to me not the god or demon I
half expected, but merely an old woman of some means, dressed
in good, Japanese department-store clothes. I'd seen many
dressed just like her—elegant and tasteful in a style recom
mended by the consensus of cultural mavens haunting upscale
Shirokiya, a kind of Japanese Neiman Marcus chain store in
Ala Moana Center, the huge shopping mall near Waikīkī that
claimed to be the biggest in the world. The way she carefully
picked her way down the staircase made me think of Gloria
Swanson in *Sunset Boulevard,* the film paean of the fifties to the
glory days of a silent-screen beauty. And my grandmother was
larger than most Japanese women of her generation, full-figured
and busty, and her voice, when she spoke, had a rough, low
register timbre and sounded like the blast of a plantation-mill
whistle.

In Japanese, she told her husband to apologize to me for
not being outside to greet us, for her having to go back upstairs
to retrieve the handbag she'd forgotten. He began to translate,

and then they fell into a jabbering exchange about which one
of them was to bring the cash. Then smiles and greetings and
a huge amount of admiration expressed for Alexander and his
cuteness. Here was the ritualized greeting-style of Japanese
social custom being enacted among a family which had been
dissolved and had no history or affection. I must have performed my stylized role as well, bowing and snapping my head
forward, as I'd learned to do during my year in Japan.
Katayama would translate, and I didn't let him know I already
understood. My grandmother spoke little English, and she let
her husband relay whatever she had to say, looked to him for a
translation of our English. I was a little rude. I kept my Japanese to myself, sensing it might be easier, better for me not to
let them know. It was a betrayal, of course, but I gave myself
justification many times over, thinking of runaway wives and
mothers, orphaned children, and the goodwill my father wasted
imagining a parent he never got to know.

   At the restaurant, about a half hour after we'd arrived, I
used my Japanese. The conversation had been drifting, and
Katayama was attempting to restart it, asking about my job,
my schooling, Cynthia's "home country"—anything innocu-
ous and bland enough to sustain our mild boredom. I broke
in and asked the old woman why she had left her children,
why had she left my father? The meal had come—Japanese
teishoku—*teriyaki* beef cut in decorous strips, some barbecue
chicken, raw tuna slices garnished with shredded *daikon*
radishes, pieces of deep-fried shrimp rolled in a light batter—
and we'd been eating awhile, slipping the food into our
mouths with the black chopsticks, slurping up the clear broth
in the black, lacquered bowls, masticating, gulping, holding
it all down.

Why did you leave? I said again in Japanese. It seemed she hadn't heard me. She mugged at my child, gurneying her face around a quartet of absurd expressions, holding one for an in‑ stant—it was a look of mock astonishment that entailed that the breath be held as well—then she was all plain cheerfulness and laughter. She concentrated on Alexander, trying to make him giggle or buzz his lips. She ignored me.

I put my chopsticks aside and said again, louder, in the most ornate and polite Japanese I could muster, *It is said that you were not treated as well as a mother should have been, that there was cruelty in the family, that you were delicate and unable to endure it. Is this so?*

There was an instant of silence. I had fixed everyone's at‑ tention. Her body, long trained in dance, held a pose, but her face would not turn my way. She held Alexander still. She fixed a stare onto his face, and it was without mark or under‑ standing, a pure innocence with no expectations of her other than amusement.

Katayama spoke. He said, *Gran'ma is hard of hearing.* He said, *Gran'ma has forgotten many things. She cannot recall. What can be said of the past?* Then, of himself, for me, to my father's mem‑ ory, he offered me only one thing. *It is indeed unimaginably sad for one to outlive one's own child. Be pleased, out of kindness, that life is with you and your wife in this child of happiness. It is a fortunate thing. We are pleased for you, though sadness has made a visit. Why not let it go now and reside with the past? We here have life and joy is over so quickly.*

He picked up the teapot that was squatting between us on the dining table. He poured a dram of its coppery liquid into my porcelain cup. *Here,* he said, *I have let your cup become empty. I am so sorry.* And I let the moment pass. The desire for my questions to be answered, for my yearning to be put to rest, left me even before Katayama had begun his little speech. I'd seen the fear and frailty on my grandmother's face, seen that there was more confusion there than anything like guilt or culpability. She was a stranger and would remain so. She was like an old neighbor woman who outlives all the children on the street, with no children of her own.

We finished the rest of lunch uneventfully. Cynthia took Alexander back from Yukiko, and we strolled outside among the pathways and ornamental shrubs of the restaurant gardens. We let Alexander, a toddler now, romp among the trimmed and sculpted pines. Katayama produced a camera and took snapshots, and I did too, hefting the heavy Nikkormat I'd brought along out of the diaper bag.

We posed for shots on a path of rock tiles, beside a stone lantern and the spreading horizontal bough of one of the pines braced with an ornate crutch of bamboo and twine. Yukiko posed with Alexander in her arms again, Cynthia standing beside them, and I snapped group and head shots while they posed, turning sideways and holding smiles, passing Alexander between them. I may have posed with her too, but I hardly remember it. Whatever feelings I had, they were buoyed above my heart by a meaninglessness that seemed to give to everything material and conscious nothing other than a pure airiness that inspired forgetting. It was like a dream, pure effacement.

A week later, when I got the pictures back from a little photo kiosk in the supermarket parking lot, they were all hazy and overexposed. In every print, my grandmother's face was burned away by the amount of light my lens had let in over the film. In one picture—a head shot I'd taken of her and Alexander against the Honolulu sky—a pale chin and rouged mouth poked through pure cloudiness and an almost complete absence of color that descended over the upper half of the frame. There was no face there. And so it was in the others, in frame after frame. She was ghostly, a puff of gas in every picture. My hands shook as I shuffled the prints and let them fall on the pavement as I walked. I picked them up, and a little rain from my eyes spattered down on one of them.

SELF-PORTRAIT

BMW

I WAS SEVENTEEN, driving in my father's car, a four-door BMW 1800, white, with a flip-up brodie on the wheel that my father had attached there to make cool left turns. I took it driving around South Bay, to Palos Verdes, up through the Santa Monica Mountains. I drove it back and forth to night classes at UCLA Extension, where I was taking college-level literature, though I still hadn't been admitted. My father sat in the passenger seat beside me, and I was driving southbound in the fast lane of the San Diego Freeway, Interstate 5. We were south of West Covina, coming back from a coin collectors' show in Santa Monica, crossing underpasses named Sepulveda and Pico and approaching Century—the International Airport

District. I was yelling, complaining loudly, whining about a fight with my mother about college.

She wanted me to go to UCLA, essentially a *free* school supported with state taxes, to study engineering or prelaw or premedicine or *anything* that would guarantee me a comfortable living. She wanted me to take chemistry, biology, math, economics, and business English—whatever it would take to secure me a place in America's professional class, America's *middle* class. We were poor, simple workers, she said, and money didn't grow on trees. I'd have to plan, I'd have to sacrifice, I'd have to *gaman*—give up personal preference and desire and tough things out.

I wanted to go *away* to school, to one of the small, private liberal arts schools I'd heard about from my high school English teachers. I'd get admitted, they'd award me a scholarship, and I'd study literature and philosophy. I was thinking maybe I'd try my hand at short stories and photography. I'd meet bright professors and pretty girls. I'd be introduced to things artistic, and I'd *grow*. It was the late sixties.

We'd had a blowup. My mother had yelled at me. She'd put her hands on her hips, indignant at my dreaminess, at my defiance, at my obliviousness to sacrifices, and she'd lit into me with a punishing, vengeful stream of belittlement. She wouldn't pay a *cent* for my education, she'd said. If I thought things were so easy, then I could pay for my own education myself. But if I wanted support, if I wanted to continue living in her house, I would have to do as she said. I'd have to go to UCLA, register for engineering and sciences, do mathematics and economics, and prepare myself for earning a living in this world.

I was pissed. I'd thrown things and said a few choice words of my own. I'd grabbed car keys and run out of the house, burning rubber in the short suburban drive, and roared off cursing at the top of my lungs. My mother chased after me, waving and gesticulating as she raced alongside the drive and then the sidewalk by the street I drove away on. I put music on full blast. I pounded the dashboard and steering wheel. The rage I felt was pure. I was as helpless and angry as I'd ever been.

Weeks had gone by. I'd gotten responses from the colleges and universities I'd applied to. I'd gotten into the University of California system—they'd offered me one of the satellite campuses. And I'd gotten into two of the liberal arts colleges. Neither offered me aid. One of them was out of state, but one was in California and eligible for sponsoring the tuition scholarship I'd earned as a good high school student. I could go there on state aid, but there was room and board to pay for as well as tuition.

"I geeve you diss kaah," my father said flatly.

"What?" I shouted. It seemed he'd spoken a non sequitur to me. He'd said something about cars, and I was whining about *college*. What could he have been thinking? He often couldn't follow what I was saying when I was excited—his hearing loss was particularly a problem talking on the phone or riding in a car. The hearing aid distorted things badly. "What?" I yelled again.

"Diss kaah," he said again, "I *geeve* 'em to you, you know." He gestured by jutting his chin forward in that Hawaiian, localboy manner meaning to reassure, to approve, to sponsor.

I scowled, not understanding anything. I thought he was speaking in a conversation he'd imagined, that he'd missed all that I was saying. He'd goofed it all up and was answering some question I hadn't asked. I was annoyed.

He leaned forward then and popped the glove compart-
ment. He rifled around in there until he found what he was
looking for. He got the broken plastic shield visor-pouch that
had the car registration in it—the "pink slip"—slid it out,
turned it over, pulled a ballpoint pen from his pocket, then
signed it. He slipped the paper back into the plastic shield and
tossed the whole thing onto my lap.

"Here," he said. "Dah kaah yours now. You do what you
want."

We continued southbound, and I slowed the BMW and
drifted to the right a little. We dove under an underpass,
through banks covered in green ice plant, flowering with yellow and white cactus-like blossoms. A Union 76 sign loomed
like an orange moon over the embankment when we emerged.
I could sell the car. It was worth *thousands*.

Cello

In school at Pomona College in Southern California I took on
extra courses my sophomore year to fulfill some requirements. I
wanted the luxury the following term to study with Bert Meyers, a poet I'd heard about who taught at Pitzer College, an af-
filiated school in the same town. You could cross-register, and
the course would count for my graduation. Other students I'd
admired had studied with him, and they'd written poems that
impressed me. I had to find out about this poet. I wanted to
study with Bert Meyers.

I'd seen him around the combined campuses. He was a Jew. The story was, Meyers himself had never gone to college but had been admitted to a graduate school in literature on the strength of his poetry. He'd been hired, then, without completing the Ph.D. He was a *poet*. His face was sharp like an axblade's, his hair silvery and wiry and full of curls, ruffled like the surface of a lagoon just before a big rain. It rode up against one side of his head and seemed to crest there and hold itself like the high face of a large wave, poised just before crashing. He had eyes like a dromedary and smoked long brown unfiltered cigarettes that came in a red cardboard box. But it was his voice, a deep and resonant baritone rising to tenor, that summoned everyone when he spoke. It seemed to me that he did not actually speak, but was softly bowing, with the velvet cords in his throat, the strings of a tiny Cremona cello that was embedded there. His sentences came slowly, lavishly, with music and deliberation as if they were scored. At a public lecture, I heard him talk about "Baud'laire," and it seemed as if he were speaking of a beautiful, sickened forest, restored to life by energetic rains. He talked about Aimé Césaire of Martinique, about the Caribbean and the poetry of "Négritude," and his words sparked fresh thoughts through my mind concerning my own native land. A visiting poet from the Midwest, decked out in a varicolored Mexican poncho, once teased him about the largeness of his eyes, and Meyers said "Fuck you" out loud and flipped the arrogant visitor the bird. I decided this Meyers guy was for me. I took his class the next term.

It met in the evening, and I arrived a little late for the first session. The poet nodded to me to take the only seat available, which was next to him in the small seminar room. There were less than a dozen others in the class, all scruffy and long-haired, pseudo-hippie types of the middle to upper class.

I noticed Meyers had brought his own thermos of coffee to class, a big blue-and-silver stainless-steel thing like the one my father carried to work on the night shift. The poet sipped while the little workshop of student poets talked.

A man with long blond hair and a puckered face that gathered down to a ginger beard introduced the topic of Walt Whitman and his homosexuality. A woman with long, braided brown hair, smelling of patchouli oil, cited some crit- ics and a discussion she'd been involved in at a writers' con- ference in Vermont that past summer. I felt awe at how complicated their acquaintanceship with the subject was, how *socialized*. I'd barely begun to *read* poetry, let alone discuss it with adults in a public place.

The poet said "That's bullshit," then proceeded to pro- vide us with an extended critique of this particular *journalistic* and decidedly unliterary approach to the discussion of Whit- man. He said that Whitman was a *poet* who may have been gay, who may not have been gay, who might have been multi- sexual or bisexual or nonsexual, but what was important about him was that he had this *feeling* for humankind, for the wounded dying in the Union hospitals, for the *workers* and *builders* and *teamsters* and for *women* that compelled him to write a strange, prosaic, but chantlike nonmetric verse, slightly imita- tive of what he thought *Indian* vedic scripture was like, slightly imitative of what he thought Native American *storytelling* and ceremonial *chant* were like, and taking off on what he'd vaguely heard about as *vers libre* from the French; borrowing certain common American *religious* ideas; joining all of them to what he felt was the elite fashion of literary Transcendentalism; and from *that*, he, Walt Whitman, a newspaperman and profound sentimentalist, had accomplished the building, along with Emily Dickinson, a spinster, of what had come to us as our *American* poetry. Homosexuality was *not* the issue, nor was *heterosexuality*. It was *poetry* that was the issue and he, Meyers, would not allow our discussions to be turned over to whatever fashionable or scholarly controversies had arisen to divert attention away from what was important. *Poetry was poetry,* he said, and although gay rights and women's rights and minority rights were important, it was *poetic content* and *poetic style* and *poetic tradition* which we would emphasize, and not the social controversies, not the debunking and not the dismissing. Unlike my usual literature professors who cultivated a studied mildness, Bert Meyers had passion, he had opinions, and he was not afraid to state them. He had an *attitude,* and he felt confident in exposing us to it. And that attitude had the music of eloquence.

There were some student poems handed out and read. Meyers said critiques would begin the following week. He ended the class session by reading aloud some translations from postwar Polish poetry—poems commemorating the work of rebuilding the country and its culture in the aftermath of World War II. He read from a pamphlet—an issue of a literary magazine. No books were yet available, he said. When he was finished, he tucked the pamphlet into his outer coat pocket, reassembled his coffee thermos, and started for the door. He asked if I'd walk with him, as I'd said nothing during class and it puzzled him.

We left the building through a glass door. His wife and teenage son and daughter were there to meet him. They were walking the family dog, a black Labrador, and invited me to trail along. We trudged back through a foggy night, across asphalt tennis courts, azalea-lined walks, and under olive trees through one college's campus and then another. I found myself walking beside the poet, who'd produced a pipe and was having trouble keeping it lit. He'd stop from time to time, relighting the tobacco, and I'd stop with him to keep him company.

"I know why you're so pissed off," Meyers said, sucking on the stem of his pipe. Sprinklers hissed on a lawn somewhere nearby. His wife and children and dog were up ahead of us. I was stunned, fixed to the sidewalk in my sturdy tennis shoes. He stared at me.

"Your parents were in those Camps," he said, and a puff of smoke swirled around the dark blade of his face.

He said he'd been a kid in high school in Los Angeles. It was World War II, a few months after Pearl Harbor. He was a gymnast at Marshall High. There were lots of Japanese American kids in his school. He'd grown up with them. He'd gone to the picnics in MacArthur Park, where the Nisei would bring their kids every weekend and share food—rice balls and fish cakes and sweet pieces of marinated meat—he'd run around, he was a kid and could ask anyone, a Jewish kid with his Jewish parents, Sephardic Jews from Spain via Brooklyn, and he'd grown up with them, playing baseball, stealing hubcaps, trying to get dates, when, all of a sudden, one morning, *all the Japanese American kids were gone!* Just gone. He couldn't believe it. Our government had taken all of them, rounded them up like cattle and marched them off into trains and shipped them away to God-knows-where, to Kingdom Come, to concentration camps in the desert. His schoolmates were stunned, but everyone seemed to accept it after a while. His father Manuel raged about it at home. It was a crummy deal.

Bert Meyers knew about it. He could tell me. He could look into my eyes and see into the history I was not myself ready to address, to live by. He knew part of my story, the part no one else knew or seemed to want to know, and he said he would help me with it. He was telling me that. I followed him.

O - m e n

It was early summer, a heat wave had come, and I was in Hōfukuji in Okayama Prefecture in Japan. I was twenty-two and a year out of college. All through that previous fall and winter, I had been in Kyoto at another temple, sweeping the grounds, getting thinner, watching the pines of the surrounding gardens spear moon and stars and hunting owls at night. In the mornings, a gray light drained away all darkness. Crusts of frost hardened on the tough mosses throughout the temple lands. Now, the seasons had changed and I'd made a journey across southern Japan to have an audience with my teacher's teacher, an old master who spoke a rough dialect and held a fan, whipping the air, his light brown summer robe decorated with a gold-and-red sash. He had been pouring me tea—a rich, creamy, amber brew full of earth and stone and completely without froth. We had been seated at a low lacquer table, eating sweet rice cakes, letting the conversation wander. He'd gotten up, straightened his robes, and whisked himself off across the large hall into a smaller chamber. He'd said something to Genshō, my teacher, his disciple, who'd been sitting behind us, ready to intervene.

"The master wishes to talk to you more efficiently," Genshō explained. "Please get up and go immediately to that room." And he gestured with a nod of his head and the direc-tion of his eyes toward a pair of sliding doors just across the hall.

In the tiny room I entered, there was no table. I bowed to the master, a deep genuflection, head to the mat, palms upraised but flat on the floor. I lifted my hands slowly, bringing them past my ears in a small ceremony of humility before the incar-nation of the Law who was before me. I rocked back on my heels and haunches, folded my legs under me, and sat with them tucked under my rump, the worn Levi's and T-shirt I wore soft and full of my body's heat. I tried to slow my breathing.

The master asked me about poetry—*what is it?* He asked me something about Bashō, whom I professed to admire—what was the great *haiku* poet doing traveling so much? *Was he wan-dering or staying?*

I felt a buff light like a haze of California dust powder-ing the air between us. I started to say something, using my Japanese, then I stopped, thinking in English about poetry. I halted in mid-sentence, forming a long and studious answer.

"Halt!" the *roshi* shouted. *"Get out!"*

The master ordered me away, flapping his fan and scowl-ing. There was no expression on his face. It betrayed no feel-ing, no disapproval or impatience. But in his voice had been a bark sharp as a curse.

"You must leave now," my teacher said, touching my shoulder. "The master has asked you to and you must go."

Genshō, a high monk who was vice-abbot of the monastery, had come to America to my college to study West-ern religions. There, he had taken on some followers—a few American students of his own, disciples more curious than

committed, more ardent than adventurous. He had seated himself beside me during all of this, my first *dokusan,* my interview
and dharma combat with the master. Only I hadn't quite
known it was this. I'd come prepared only for tea and had spoken as if we were idly chatting—as an *inferior,* as a *student.*

"But why is he so angry?" I whispered in English.

Genshō frowned. He looked deeply into my face and saw
that I simply didn't understand, that I was confused and not
prepared. I simply was not ready. I had wasted my time and
the master's.

The master, sitting behind him, grunted and cleared his
throat, adjusting his robes by shifting his shoulders, rocking
forward on the legs under him, Japanese style, then leaned back,
in perfect position again. Then he barked something—something rhythmic and poetic and repetitive like a rhyme, only not
a rhyme. It was forceful. It was spoken clearly, but in a dialect
I could not divine. He flapped his fan and the tawny light of
the hot season rose like dust in the tiny, four-and-a-half-*tatami*-
mat room.

Genshō turned back to me then. He was smiling like a
cat cleaning its whiskers.

"The master says," Genshō began, "that the poet must
learn to intone the song, which is music. Must learn the dance,
which is the body's movement. Must learn the word, which is
the speech of man in the universe. He must learn to write them
all in his own face."

"Whose own face?" I blurted in English. "Mine?"

Before I could make my question clearer, Genshō's own
face darkened and, for the barest of moments, it took on the
look of Fudō, the demon-warrior of furrowed brows and deep
scowls who is the guardian of heaven.

"*Go-jibun no O-men!*" he said, his voice suddenly deep, impatient, and commanding like the master's. He tilted his shaved head forward, sharpening his eyes against the gaze of mine. "You remember. You bring them all together."

He made a motion with his parted hands then, and I noticed he was holding a fan folded flat between one half-opened palm, poised on the rump of his thumb, and his fingers straightening into the air between us. Then, he brought both hands together and bounced them, gently, in space, on their knuckles, in a little chalice of a motion he made, the fan like hawk wings outriding the body of his fists.

"In your own face," he said, smiling kindly again, tapping my shoulder with the pinion of his fan. "Now go."

I walked into the dusty summer light of the provincial temple, over the swept grounds toward the black bell in its well of wood framing, and toward the heavy temple gates and their discolored bronze fittings. I went through them. Above me, a falcon gyred upward in the azimuth between earth and heaven. I never went back.

Soul

I was twenty-three and had just dropped out of language and literature studies at the University of Michigan, where I'd spent a cold year working on modern Japanese. Only writing poetry had saved me. I was fleeing academe again, wanting to meet writers, seeking to find elders. In an anthology of Asian American writers, I found a Nisei short-story writer's poetic remi-

niscences about Japanese American farm life in Southern California before World War II. The writer's name was Wakako
Yamauchi and she was a Nisei, or second-generation Japanese
American. Yamauchi had been a teenager during the war, the
endnotes said, and began to write while an internee in the Pos-
ton Relocation Center in Arizona. She was a "housewife." The
story I read had the rhythm of song and soliloquy, was pitched
to an emotional note I wanted myself. In Los Angeles, back in
Gardena again and living with my parents, I found Wakako's
name in the phone book one morning and called her up. She
answered, I explained myself, and she invited me over immediately, asking me to breakfast.

Over the years, she fed me dinners, lunches, more break-
fasts, and New Year's feasts too, showing me her scripts-in-
progress, talking to me about my wishes for my own literary
life. She introduced me to the stoic and shamed emotional
world of Mainland Japanese Americans. Through our conversation and her telling stories, I learned that what mainstream society perceived as "shame" and we younger Japanese Americans
called "silence" or "passivity" was actually a great burden of
pain and disappointment for the Nisei and for the Issei first generation. After the dispossession of the war, after the loss of
farms, businesses, and homes and half a lifetime of building a
life, the Issei who'd translated themselves over into becoming
Americans were simply heartbroken and exhausted. Many
could not face starting over again, and they certainly felt little
inclination to *explain* themselves to their grandchildren. Perhaps
detachment, a Buddhist recommendation, was the most they
could muster. The Nisei, on the other hand, were full of pluck
and positive thinking. They wanted to roll up their sleeves.
They wanted their chance. Who had time to reflect on the past?

On the Camps? Who wanted to? It was too *painful*. An embarrassment. An *anomalous* experience that all of them wished to put behind them. Feelings about Camp were things best left forgotten, and, anyway, what could anyone come up with that wouldn't be deliberately shallow or so painful that they would be completely withered by the recollection? The silence my generation had felt around the issue of the Camp experience, the barrier to a link with a prewar history was a necessary thing. It didn't arise to *deny* us, the younger generation, but to protect us and to protect the older generations from succumbing to the dire power of its tragedy. Wakako taught me, with regard to the Nisei and the untold stories of the prewar and relocation periods, about emotional charity, intellectual forgiveness for all the stoicism and denial I'd felt had gone on in our community.

I learned much of feeling from Wakako, much of yearning for the poised mind of artistry. I learned that a gentle stoicism can quell passion in the singer at the same time that it awakens passion in those sung to. I learned that a generation has an emotional note which can be captured in a song, that entire lifetimes of experience, of trudging through lettuce fields with a hoe on your shoulder, of migrating from agricultural camp to coastal village, of a life of loneliness and itinerancy sleeping in bunkhouses and bachelor hotels—essentially the lives of the Issei, the first generation of Japanese Americans—could be figured forth in a story of only a few words so long as those were the *right* words, in the right order.

Wakako would recall a tune one of the old men used to sing, taken from a riverman's song from Nagasaki, its lyrics about poling a junk through the harbor, Western ships full of Portuguese traders in the water. *Santa Maria!* he would sing, and then join the exclamation to new Japanese lyrics he'd made up about bedding and then losing a Mexican lover in the bean- fields where they both worked, the bare ground for their pil- lows, a sluice of irrigation water sliding through their dreams. She told me a story about a beautiful younger man, a farm worker like the older ones, but who carried a violin with him wherever he went, tucking his case under his old coat, opening it up and taking the violin out to play when he came to stay at the hotel her mother ran in Oceanside, along the Pacific High- way the workers all used to travel up and down the California coast during the harvests, moving from beans to corn, then let- tuce to grapes. He played for a while, then asked her, a teenager then, up to his room. Her mother caught them before anything happened, and the man simply left the next day.

"*Otoko,*" Wakako said. "Men who needed."

Once, she sang me a song about the soul's need for beauty, a dance of the heart, a dream in the darkest hour of night. The notes of it chilled my skin, its deliberate and stately intervals jotting out a kind of Dorian scale, the characteristically Oriental minor mode of dirge or lament.

> *Kurai yami no yume,*
> *Setsu nasa yo. . . .*
>
> *Hitori sake nomya,*
> *Kokoro ga odoru.*

> In the dark madness of my dream,
> Things are unbearably sad. . . .
>
> Alone, I drink a blue wine,
> And the soul makes its slow dance.

The tune was a *tai-chi* of melancholia, a stately musical and emotional gymnastic, fluttering from note to note like a res-

olute butterfly captured by her breathing. I found in it an insight into the sadness of a generation, a way through the emotional curtain that was a generation of silence about the war and
relocation and starting over. Whatever I worried about seemed
frivolous by comparison. From Wakako I understood that entire lifetimes of tragedy and passion, of disappointment and de-
sires, could be figured forth in the few lines of a lyric, in an
image collected from the past, in a recollection of the dark mordancy of a Japanese drinking song played by a farm worker on
a battered violin.

Writing Comedy

I was twenty-four, and a play I'd written had gotten some attention. I wrote it for the theater group I'd started in Seattle—
a group made up entirely of Asian Americans and dedicated,
after a fight, to putting on plays about Asian American history.
Some, carryovers from a former group, still wanted to do
"skits" and "revues," showing that Asians could sing and
dance just as well as whites. They wanted to preserve "entertainment values" and worried about offending conservative elders in the community who wouldn't want us "stirring things
up." I wanted to call the group "The Asian Exclusion Act,"
after the Chinese Exclusion Act of the late nineteenth century,
the one that forbade Chinese women from entering the United
States; after the Alien Land Law of the early twentieth, forbidding Japanese to own land; after the Exclusion Order of
1942, sending 120,000 Japanese Americans to concentration

camps. I had a vision of a theater and I wanted to make a point. The entertainers resigned, the conservatives absented themselves from my board, and I had a young, largely student group of players. I wrote a play for them in pidgin English. They took to it with gusto, packing the audiences into a little, two-hundred-seat theater near the University of Washington.

The play was about a small band of Hawaiian bachelors who collected themselves in a bar near Wrigley Field in Chicago, exiles, veterans, men without women, drunks and sentimentalists, all Hawaiian and all talking Hawaiian-style English. It was my young man's tribute to the generation just older than my father's, to those men who could not find women or a place in a new world without plantations, without a war, without families. It was my attempt at dealing with alienation and cultural dislocation.

Only I'd botched the job. I'd made it *funny*. I'd meant to write a kind of tragicomedy, but it was the laughs that made the show, and the young actors—many from Hawai'i—milked every one. The audiences roared at the malapropisms, the charming Hawaiian English, the pratfalls the actors improvised and improved on every night, the broad sexual jokes, and the lovable eccentricity of it all. The actors were indeed lovable—I remember a Chinese American who played a frustrated science-fiction writer. He was hilarious as a gooney dreamer, sketching out his plots and situations out loud to the denizens of the bar, reimagining American history so it was the *Chinese* who were evacuated during World War II—so that *he* could write from resentment, *legitimately,* rather than from the *accomplishment* of having built the railroads. His speech was a satire on minority identity, our wish to translate something subtle, painful, and complex into something as simple and certain and full of pride as fascism—a politics of resentment. The actor was brilliant and got the biggest laughs. The two-week run sold out, and the play and players were written up in a Seattle entertainment paper, in a Los Angeles Japanese American paper, and in my college alumni magazine. People heard about me.

Another playwright I knew, a woman who'd written a play about the Japanese American relocation, had been hired to work on scripts for a Hollywood production company. She'd worked with me. She'd seen my play and she thought I was funny. She was having a hard time, though—her ideas were not working out with the crew of comedy writers and comics down in Los Angeles. The show was in trouble. It wasn't *funny*. She called me up. She talked to them about me. Would I come down? "You're funny," she said, "you'll write good gag lines, authentic Asian American jokes."

Set in Chicago, the show starred a very American comic of Asian descent. Only, because of the sitcom's story line, he was cast as an import-export trader from Japan, one who had a Caucasian American housekeeper, and it was *she* who actually made all the decisions for his business. Sort of the reverse of Robert Guillaume's "Benson," a subsequent network comedy that had a black butler advising the white governor; and the opposite of "Bachelor Father," the fifties series that had a male *Korean* housekeeper and cook making all decisions and devilment for suburban businessman John Forsythe. *This* would be funny. It would be yet another in the hit sequence of spin-off ethnic sitcoms produced by the guy who'd made hits of Puerto Rican yardmen, African American junk dealers, and inner-city Jewish high school teachers. He had a winning touch. About ethnics, this guy was *funny*. I would be too.

So I flew down. I was in Los Angeles again, but at a television studio in Hollywood. I walked through soundstages, air-conditioned offices, and parking stalls marked with stars' names in black lettering on the concrete block at the head of the stall. OLIVIA NEWTON-JOHN said one. GLEN CAMPBELL said another. I was awestruck. Studio representatives gave me a card, charged me a thousand dollars for it, and handed me a cafeteria pass. The expenses would be against my pay, set by the writers' union. I got an office, a chair, and a typewriter. And I was charged for them too. I'd be paid later. I waited for the hoe, coolie hat, and hard boots to be passed along and have them charged against my pay as well. I was an indentured writer on the comedy plantation.

I sat in on a couple of story sessions. I met the cast—an African American guy who played the building's super, the Caucasian housekeeper, an Asian American child star who was the daughter, and the star himself, a tough, quick-witted guy who'd come up through variety shows and Reno dates after doing stand-up in bars and strip joints in San Francisco's North Beach for a dozen years. He wanted me to work on something. He took me aside the first day and proposed that he buy my script, my "Nisei" play. I told him I was still working on it, that I didn't know what I wanted to do with it yet, that I couldn't *sell* it. He looked at me like I was crazy.

He pulled me into the coatroom. He said, "Look, kid, I hear you're funny. Maybe we can work something out. Maybe my character can go out on the town or something. You know, *honky-tonk,* take a night out of the house, get to the bar, *your* bar, do a few gags, have some *real* patter with the regulars, speak *pidgin . . . that* sort of thing. Maybe he's been to Hawai'i before, maybe he's got some relatives there. We can get the producers to *send* him to Hawai'i or something—anything for a good episode, I want things changed—and we'll *all* go. We'll get some laughs. You'll get a story in, and I'll get an episode I can *work* with. Who knows? If it works, maybe it'll change the whole story line? Whaddayasay?"

I told him I'd think about it. And we dropped the subject. I tried working some jokes into the main script, written by one or two of the main writers, balding, cigar-smoking Jewish guys who wore billowy white dress shirts and loose-fitting brown gabardine dress pants. The playwright who sponsored me said that the leaders were old "I Love Lucy" writers and had a certain way of doing things. They dominated, but maybe I could convince them. I was raucous, tough like them, she said. Maybe I'd fit in better than she did, a woman, after all, and a writer of drama. Looking at them, fat, balding middle-aged and older men, it seemed to me that they always had their sleeves and jowls rolled, and I half expected them to pull out green visors and a deck of cards every time we met. They all talked like Jack Klugman to me, ex—pool players with Philadelphia or Brooklyn and the Bronx in every gruff comment or expression. The bitter and sophisticated East, I thought, against the brilliant, tender West. A few others were younger, though not so young as me. We were about a dozen writers all told, including the Asian playwright who'd gotten me in.

I got creamed the first day.

"This ain't *funny,* kid," one of the main writers growled. "You don't know *funny.*"

He puffed on his cigar, then ashed it into an orange tray. I gulped, but said nothing. My lines were cut.

The next day I got creamed again.

"Who says this is *funny*?" the other head said. "Anybody say this is *funny*?"

He looked around the room, waving my little page like toilet paper. No one spoke. Cigars were puffed, sleeves were rolled, and the story conference went on without my lines.

The star pulled me aside after that, again calling me to the sidewalk outside the soundstage. He asked me why I didn't defend myself, why I didn't speak up. He said I should stand up for myself, that I would need to get my lines in, that *he* would support me. The actors sat in on the conferences, he said, and he would be there for me the next time. But I had to chime in. I had to *fight* for my funny, he said. In the old days, some of the guys carried blackjacks, no kidding, he said. *Little saps.*

Fight for my funny—it was a new expression for me. I decided to fight the next time. I thought of a lead-weighted little iron ball wrapped in a teardrop sock of well-oiled leather.

I wrote an entire scene the next day. A *funny* scene, a *humane* scene, and not just jokes or gags or business bits I added to someone else's script. I came up with a few minutes of my own. Ten pages—a minute a page by television's formatting. Audacious. And *funny*. An entire *movement* of funny.

I brought it in at three o'clock—the standard time. I was excited. I was holding my sides, anticipating how everyone would like it, thinking of the laughter. After everyone settled in, lighting their cigarettes and cigars, a secretary passed out my pages.

"What have we here?" the head guy said, leafing through my pages. He was asking everyone else. No one ever looked at me, spoke to me, except the star and the playwright—the other two Asians. People were silent. We worked on another script, on some gags, on some story ideas. My work fell to the bottom of the pile. No one mentioned it for a couple of hours. Then we broke so people could make phone calls, get a cafeteria din-ner, do a little reading. The associate producer waved a clip-board and said we would reassemble in an hour. A script guy waved his clipboard and said the same thing—only *louder*. As-sistants scooted around, picking up the coffee cups, emptying the ashtrays, and scooping up the stray pages of script. The as-sociate producer stood by, waiting for every scrap to be col-lected, accepted them from the head writer, then walked through an inner door that was opened for him by an assistant. I walked out of an outer door.

It was spring in Hollywood, and the days were long enough so there was still real daylight at the end of the work-day. I was disoriented from being under artificial lights for hours, swaddled in scripts and cigar smoke. My skin seemed to be growing a coat of ash and ink. I strolled slowly to the cafeteria, enjoying the hazy brown light of early evening in Los Angeles.

I grabbed a quick bite—by myself, as no one seemed to be around. Between buildings, I could see half of a palm tree around a corner, a clutch of billboards, a public bus-bench with the name of a local mortuary stenciled in green onto it. The Hollywood Hills receded upward across the street, tawny sentinels of earth fading into the gray of constant smog. I strode back to the meeting carrying a cup of black coffee in a white Styrofoam cup. I thought of the monk asked by his master to carry a lit candle from his temple across the city during the busiest part of the day. There were steep steps to descend, a market district to pass through, wagons and bearers and manure-stained streets. He was to ascend to another temple on the opposite mountain. The candle was supposed to stay lit and light incense on an altar—a transmission, an assignment. My coffee stirred, its surface jiggered like the riffle on a mountain stream. A silver light shone on it. A streetlight, like a mechanical palm, winked on above me.

Inside the conference room, I was nodded to, and read my script aloud to the group. I expected laughter, guffaws, cackles, maybe a whistle from the star. I glanced around for him, but he wasn't there. I saw only writers settled around the graphite tables. And from them, there was nothing. Only silence. I finished reading, unstoked, losing steam as I choked a little and muscled myself to the scene's ending.

For a long moment, no one spoke. Then, one of the heads did.

"Look, kid, you're supposed to listen and learn here. This ain't *funny*. How can you know *funny*? How old are you? Whaddayou know from *funny*? So you made some kids laugh up at college. So what? I been through funny with Berle and Jessel and you-name-it from since before you was born! I been through *funny* from the Catskills! From Grossinger's and any-place! I *know* funny. Who *says* you're funny? This ain't funny, kid. You ain't *funny!*"

I choked. I stared at him, feeling humiliated. I'd misunderstood my role. I wasn't supposed to *write*. I wasn't supposed to be *funny*. I was a token, an ethnic name on the crawl.

After a while, when they were done with me and had gone on to other things, I drifted out of the conference room as unobtrusively as possible and wandered along the hardened river of asphalt alongside the building. It was black and seemed pristine to me, about the only clean thing around, though cars and trucks rolled over it. I sat down on the curb next to it, letting my legs spread out over its thin sponge of a surface. It was

cooler, the sun had set, and all was bathed in the grainy twilight of an urban dusk. I saw the star comic across the street,
walking toward me, twirling a beret on his forefinger. He
seemed to me to be whistling, carefree.

He'd been in his dressing room, showering up, changing.
He'd called it quits for the day after the main story conference
and went to wash up, grab a bite, watch the TV news, chitchat
with his buddies in the cast. Why hadn't I come by? There was
food, liquor, he said. Why, we could've talked. Then his mood
changed. He noticed something was amiss. He asked me this:

"Hey, aren't you supposed to be in story conference? What
are you doing out here?"

He was puzzled, concerned for a moment. He looked at
me—*hard*. He must've read then what was the look of complete defeat on my face. I'd said nothing, but he'd guessed my
failure.

He said, "You really hate this, don't you, kid?"

I nodded.

"Well, whaddaya doin' it for then?" he asked, suddenly
abrasive.

I shrugged. Cicadas chirped from the plumes of agapanthus, bathed in mist from sprinklers hissing on.

"Tell me, what do you *like* to do?" He spoke calmly, sin-
cerely, with none of the manic energy he usually had, no swift
mood changes to silliness, to funny poses or the comic's fa-
cial repertoire of mugs and double takes. I thought, *Should I
tell him? Should I let him know?* I'd stood up from the curb to
be next to him, both of us planted in the asphalt, and he
seemed a real guy all of a sudden, an okay guy. So I told him.
Deadpan.

"I like poetry," I said. "I like to write *poetry*."

He blinked for a moment, taken aback. *So now it comes,* I thought. *The ridicule ensues.*

"Then why the hell don't you do that then?" he roared.

I was surprised. I stammered a little, not expecting the advice. I told him that I couldn't make a *living* writing poetry, that I didn't see how I could survive and be a poet.

"Hah," he scoffed, "you think doing *comedy* is a living? You think doing stand-up, *burlesque* in North Beach is survival?"

He was full of energy and certainty then, his body tilted and jittered, though his face was calm. He told me that I shouldn't worry, that I wouldn't be making a living doing *anything* for ten years anyway, that this was the nature of the world, especially in anything artistic—like comedy or poetry—that if I was going to spend ten years busting my ass, then it might as well be doing something that I loved. He said he loved comedy. He loved stand-up. He said *he* was *funny.*

"*You* ain't *funny,* kid," he said. "*You* might as well do poetry."

I resigned the next day, clearing out of the little cubicle I paid for but didn't use (I wrote in the donut and coffee room), cashing in my cafeteria card, toting up my pay versus what I owed the studio. I came out ahead, I thought, taking a few thousand north with me, enough to pay rent for four months or more, buy cheap food, cigarettes, pay the light bill.

I worried over nothing for a few months. I read poetry and I wrote poetry. Or tried to write it. In translation, I studied Greek poetry, I studied Chinese poetry, I studied the South Americans. I read essays about poets and interviews with poets. I found magazines and read what my young American peers were writing. A classmate from college had gone on to Iowa, to the famous Writers' Workshop there, and was already publishing in the best of the quarterlies, appearing with the older generation just then peaking in its fame. I envied her. She wrote about coffee shops and cappuccino steaming in cups, Japanese courtesans in *kimono,* holding embossed golden fans. She'd found an aesthetic and was writing from it. And the lit-mag world we'd worshiped in college acknowledged her. I felt I was falling behind.

All that following year, I worked myself harder, trying to live as much in poetry as I could, carrying paperback books through the rainy streets of Seattle throughout that summer, fall, and winter, denying myself all other life, opening my mouth wide to the dripping cold and holding it that way, calling out the names of the lost, hoping for a dragon to enter my throat, crying for a vision. The books wrinkled with rain. Blossoms in the streetside cherry trees winked on like puffs of light, then gave way to brave ocher-and-scarlet blazes in the boughs of the Japanese maples lining walkways in the public parks. I left Seattle the next fall, surprised to be admitted to a program in creative writing and a little wary too.

Terrible Angel

I was in graduate school at the University of California at Irvine's program in creative writing. I was in the poetry work-shop. I'd flown down to Southern California from Seattle, stayed with Wakako for a couple of weeks, searched out a place to live and found one on the beach. It was an apartment over a garage behind a house that was one block off the strand. Not

cheap, and not clean either. I rented from an old college professor who gave it to me for less than his alimony payments. It
would be okay.

The school was in a large multiversity built during the
sixties boom in higher education. Its physical plant was all
stucco and postmodern, dotted with temporary trailers stuck in
dusty lots under stands of eucalyptus. It had well-irrigated
lawns and walkway planters of agapanthus and cedar. Every
classroom was carpeted and, it seemed to me, had its windows
permanently sealed against the smog, enclosing us in ducted
passageways of air-conditioning. The literature faculty was aloof
and theoretical in bent, all white, highly influenced by Continental poststructuralist philosophy, with offices behind steel
doors along corridors trafficked by sandaled graduate students
in beards or batik dresses.

Our poetry instructor was C. K. Williams, a tall white
guy from the East Coast who was a visitor that term. He was
not yet middle-aged, divorced, hip, aggressive, funny, and de-
manding. He'd gone to Penn, eschewed graduate school himself to "knock around Philadelphia" and write. He'd published
several books already. He'd had a Guggenheim Fellowship. He
was swaddled in prestige. We feared him. He told us to write
a poem a week.

Outside of class, everyone grumbled. How was decent poetry to be written on demand? The students were all about my
age, late twenties, from good schools. They preferred Charles
Wright, the *regular* instructor, a gentle and soft-spoken imagist
who had gone off to teach at Iowa for the term.

Racially, these poets were all white, except one older black
guy who said nothing but brought in his poem every week. It
had a terrific style, but it stumped me with its jumpy, filigreed

rhythms and cryptic, satirical narratives. I wasn't used to it—
it had no overt "message." *What made it black?* I asked myself,
bewildered by this poet's originality and power, free of conventional ideologies. The others wrote even more laconically than
he, imagistically, line by meager line. Caucasian *haiku,* I
thought. Class was a torture. People had a hard time speaking
up. When they did, they praised shit, so far as I could tell.
They *wrote* shit.

    I wrote shit too. I didn't trust anybody. *Poetry?*—I said
to myself. *Not with these people.* Looking across the seminar
room to a scowling man with dark curly hair tight against his
head, I felt afraid and intimidated. Williams looked so fierce
and intelligent, like one of the Caesars in a Roman sculpture.
Critiquing some poor soul's unrhymed sonnet, he'd say, "Let's
come up with a better metaphor!" then leap to the shelf of books
along the wall, tugging one out, reading from it instantly. It was
Baudelaire writing about the streets of Paris, or Prague-born
mystic Rainer Maria Rilke about a panther in a Viennese zoo,
or Tadeusz Różewicz in the midst of life in postwar Poland
incanting on bread and on a knife and on a nation of people
who needed that bread to live. We were being initiated into the
terrible arts of metaphor, cadence, simile, and strophe, in which
endeavors we failed miserably in comparison to the masters.

    Our tall instructor would have at us, bashing, castigating,
lecturing us on our mental laziness, on our lack of ambition. It
was no wonder—Williams himself was engaged in writing
great moral fits against empire, furious and tragic narratives
about Western religious faith gone wrong, acid critiques of col-
lective and individual refusals to exercise consciousness. He
used bleak American cities in his poems, their fragile peoples
masked from each other by denial and bluster and triviality, and

he used his own life, confessing everything—sexual encounters, anger at television news, separation from his children, working factory jobs, scorning his fellow workers, eating slop—likening each of his own acts to passages in the Bible, in Greek tragedy, in the horrific histories of war. We held him in awe. While he charted the possibility for a poetry in the Empyrean, he prose⁄cuted us relentlessly for naïveté, for sloppiness, for insipid im⁄ages unrelated either to the everyday or to the angels.

So I defended. Against him, against the workshop, against *whites,* against my own inspiration. I brought in poem after poem—my poem per week—dramatic monologues im⁄possible to critique. I wrote about Japanese Zero pilots. I wrote long free⁄verse rhapsodies about swimming pools in Southern California (I'd discovered a book on the paintings of David Hockney). I wrote vivid sexual satires delivered in the personae of black soul singers like Marvin Gaye and Wicked Wilson Pickett. I wrote *lousy.* I wrote *to be lousy.* I was afraid to let the workshop and this Turk of a teacher know what it was I cared about, what it was I worried I could not bring myself to be dedicated to.

What I cared about was the inner city, about my teenage life brooding on the social complexities of my integrated high school—unusual in that it was a third white, and a third black, and a third Japanese American. I cared about what it was I *didn't* see a whole lot of where I'd grown up. *Compassion.* I cared about what the family could give that the city did not. I cared that the complete brutality of ghetto life was not compensated for by anything I'd ever witnessed, by anything I could yet imagine.

Once, when I was about thirteen, I'd climbed up on the roof of my parents' house because I'd heard that there was a riot going on in the other side of the city. I was told that you could see fires burning, smoke rising, from the rooftops of our neighborhood. Watts was only a few miles away—across the freeway and down some—and my schoolmates told me to watch the riot from my roof. I climbed up there and saw a red glow, miles off, under a little cover of smoke clouds.

I thought of a classmate—a little guy who'd been caught with a small-caliber pistol on the junior high school bus one day. I'll call him Gerald. The gun wasn't his, but was being passed around from seat to seat, person to person. It was with him when the driver caught up with its illicit migrations. Gerald was busted. He was put out of school on detention, on probation, on expulsion. He went to "joovie," a state-run reform school, where he was raped, repeatedly, by the older, bigger black kids. The Chicanos left him alone. The whites knifed him. He came back, no longer somber and reflective, no longer full of jokes and smiles in gym class. He carried a briefcase now, in which he kept a switchblade, a Filipino dagger, a hunting or a Swedish filleting knife. He was sullen, quiet, and marched quickly between buildings from class to class. If someone laughed too hard or too long close by him now, he'd fix the laughing schoolmate with a stare. If the laughter stopped, nothing would happen. If it did not, we'd soon hear someone was "knifed" in the lavatory, and Gerald would spend the next day full of malicious smiles. It made us cautious about ridicule, real or perceived. I learned about paranoia, about retribution, and little about forgiveness. Watts burned, and all I could see was a red wound across the city and smoke pouring from it. In my dreams that night, I saw my old friend Gerald smiling, a wound opening wider and wider under his own rib cage as he lay on the ground. His eyes did not blink.

Another time, I was riding bikes with my friends from junior high school. But it was summer—hot, smoggy, with no classes and flies in the air around all the Dumpsters in the alleyways we rode through, dodging cars pulling out of their garages in South Los Angeles. We wanted to meet girls, to learn some dances like the bigger guys. We rode around with transistor radios dangling from the handlebars of our Schwinn Sting⁄rays, from the nose⁄sprocket shock absorbers of our clunky Hornets. We listened to the "soul" stations—the black AM channels that played rhythm and blues, the new Motown tunes by the Temptations and the Supremes, the Stax/Volt sides from Memphis by Aretha Franklin and Sam and Dave. We wanted to be "baad" and have soul—like the black kids in our school, the kids who knew all the dances, who did the Slauson and the Twine and the Jerk and the Duck⁄in⁄the⁄Wall. We did wheelies in the streets on our Sting⁄rays and tried to figure a way to get a girl to teach us something. We decided to call one up. We rode from the public library where we met every day and biked a few blocks over toward the apartment house where a "new" girl lived with her parents. She'd know dances from the part of town she came from, she'd be willing to teach us things. She'd want to be accepted. She'd want to make friends.

We biked over to a Laundromat around the corner from where we knew she lived, where we thought a pay phone might be. I was elected to make the call. We stopped by a booth. The phone was broken. The glass in the booth was all broken. The phone book's pages flapped in the wind from passing delivery trucks and automobiles and tanker trucks hauling gasoline around our city. A little gravel showered on my shoes. I had to do something.

I went into the little bungalow next to the phone booth, where I thought the Laundromat was. It was cool, dark inside. There was no sign on the front. I went through a short entry hallway, then turned into a large, darkened room.

There were round tables, and chairs, with people sitting inside. There was a long bar with stools. People sat on the stools. There was a mirror, shiny bottles along a shelf in front of the mirror, a stainless steel cash register, a few plants. All of the people were women. Some were in sweatshirts and some were in leather jackets. None of them wore dresses that I could see. They had haircuts like men—crew cuts and butch cuts, and hair slicked with pomade. A couple of them were in a booth by the side kissing each other. One would open her mouth, and I could see the gold fillings of her teeth sparkle a little with saliva in the soft light of a table lamp. Then it would be dark, her shining mouth eclipsed, swallowed by the black disk of another woman's mouth, the one who sat in her lap, who squirmed in it and fondled her partner's breasts under her loose shirt. I turned away.

I said something to the bartender, a heavyset woman wearing a garish aloha shirt. I might have asked for the *pay phone.* I might have asked for change. She ordered me out, saying I had to be *older,* I had to be *twenty-one.* I drifted out of the bar, stumbling back over the little chicane of darkness through the entryway, appearing in the bright, smoggy light and pneumatic rushing sounds of the large Los Angeles boulevard.

My friends awaited me. They were laughing, grinning. It was "a dyke bar!" they were saying. "A bar full of dykes!"

"What's a *dyke?*" I asked.

"A lezzie," someone said. "A *homo* woman!"

Two pranced and did the Funky Chicken in the dirt of the vacant lot where we stood next to the bar.

They hopped on their bikes, and I pursued. We went over to the new girl's apartment house without calling. We knocked on the door. She let us in. She had lots of records. Stacks of 45s. She taught us the Philly Dog, a cha-cha, the Hole-in-the-Wall. I got to *hold* her. I got to feel a slender teenage girl's flesh under a cotton blouse and summer shorts. I knew approval and I knew disapproval, but, to be human, I knew nothing of what I needed to know.

Fraternity

It was high school in Gardena. I was in classes mostly with Japanese American kids—*kotonks,* Mainland Japanese, their ethnic pet name originated, during the war, with derisive Hawaiian GIs who thought of the sound of a coconut being hit with a hammer. Sansei *kotonks* were sons and daughters of the Nisei *kotonks* who had been sent off to the concentration camps during World War II. School was tepid, boring. We wanted cars, we wanted clothes, we wanted everything whites and blacks wanted to know about sex but were afraid to tell us. We "bee-essed" with the black kids in the school parking lot full of coastal fog before classes. We beat the white kids in math, in science, in typing. We ran track and elected cheerleaders. We *ruled,* we said. We were dumb, teeming with attitude and prejudice.

Bored, I took a creative writing class with an "academically mixed" bunch of students. There were Chicanos, whites,

a black woman, and a troika of Japanese women who sat together on the other side of the room from me. They said nothing—*ever*—and wrote naturalistically correct *haiku*. Suddenly
among boisterous non-Japanese, I enjoyed the gabbing, the
bright foam of free talk that the teacher encouraged. An aging
man in baggy pants that he wore with suspenders, he an-
nounced he was retiring at the end of the year and that he
wanted no trouble, that he was going to read "Eeebee White"
during our hour of class every day, that we were welcome to
read whatever we wanted so long as we gave him a list ahead
of time, and that we could talk as much as we wanted so long
as we left him alone. We could read, we could write, we could
jive each other all class long. It was freedom. And I took advantage.

I sat next to a Chicano my age named Pacheco and
behind a white girl a class younger than me named Regina.
Behind us was a curly-headed white guy who played saxophone
in the marching band. He'd been in academic classes with me,
the only Caucasian among Japanese, a Korean, and a few Chinese. He was a joker, and I liked him, but usually stayed
away—we didn't fraternize much across the races, though our
school was supposed to be an experiment in integration.

Gardena H.S. wasn't so much a mix or blend as a mosaic. Along with a few whites and blacks, Japanese were in the
tough, college-prep, "advanced placement" scholastic track.
Most whites and blacks were in the regular curriculum of shop,
business skills, and a minimum of academic courses. The
"dumb Japs" were in there with them. And the Chicanos filled
up what were called the *remedial* classes, all taught imperiously
only in English, with no provision for language acquisition.

We were a student body of about three thousand, and we walked edgily around each other, swaggering when we could, sliding the steel taps on our big black shoes along the concrete outdoor walkways when we wanted to attract a little attention, making a jest of our strut, a music in the rhythm of our walking. Blacks were bused in from Compton; the whites, Japanese, and Chicanos came from around the town. Girls seemed to me an ethnic group of their own too, giggling and forming social clubs, sponsoring dances, teaching some of us the steps.

Crazes of dress moved through our populations—for Chicanos: woolen Pendletons over thin undershirts and a crucifix; big lowtop oxfords; khaki work trousers, starched and pressed; for the *bloods:* rayon and satin shirts in metallic "flyass" colors; pegged gabardine slacks; cheap moccasintoed shoes from downtown shops in L.A.; and for us *Buddhas:* highcollar Kensingtons of pastel cloths, A1 tapered "Racer" slacks, and the same moccasin shoes as the bloods, who were our brothers. It was crazy. And *inviolable.* Dress and social behavior were a code one did not break for fear of ostracism and reprisal. Bad dressers were ridiculed. Offending speakers were beaten, tripped walking into the john, and set upon by gangs. They *wailed* on you if you fucked up. A girl was nothing except pride, an ornament of some guy's crude power and expertise in negotiating the intricacies of this innercity semiotic of cultural display and hidden violence. I did not know girls.

I talked to Regina, saying "white girl" one time. She told me not to call her that, that she was *Portuguese* if anything, that I better *know* that white people were *always* something too. From vague memories of Hawai'i, I reached for the few words in Portuguese that I knew. I asked her about the sweet bread her mother baked, about heavy donuts fried in oil and rolled in sugar. I said *bon dea* for "good day" to her. I read the books she talked about—Steinbeck, Kesey, Salinger, and Baldwin. Her mother brought paperbacks home from the salon she worked in, putting up other women's hair—*rich* women's. We made up our reading list from books her mother knew. I wanted desperately to impress her, so I began to write poetry too, imitating some melancholy rock and country-and-western lyrics. She invited me to her house after school. It was on the way, so I walked her home. It became a practice.

Her father was a big, diabetic man from Texas. With his shirt off, he showed me how he shot himself with insulin, poking the needle under the hairy red skin on his stomach, working it over the bulge of fat around his belly. He laughed a lot and shared his beer. There were other guys over too—white guys from the football team, a Filipino, and one other Japanese guy who played left tackle. They were tough, raucous, and talked easily, excitedly. I stood alone in the front yard one day, holding a soft drink in my hand, the barbecue party going on around me. Regina and her mother were baking bread inside. No one knew exactly what was going on, and I was still trying to pretend all was casual.

I took photographs of her. We had a picnic on the coast by the lighthouse near Marineland, on the bluffs over the Pacific. It was foggy, mist upon us and the tall, droopy grasses in the field we walked through, but we made do. She wrapped herself in the blanket she'd brought for us to sit on. We were in the tall grasses of the headlands far from the coast road. She posed. I changed lenses, dropping film canisters, other things. She waved to me, unbuttoning the blouse she was wearing, her body full of a fragrance. The warm, yeasty scent of her skin smelled like bread under bronze silk.

We couldn't be seen together—not at the private, car-club-sponsored Japanese dances out in the Crenshaw District, not at the whites-dominated dances after school in the high school gym. Whites did not see Buddhas, and Buddhas did not see bloods. We were to stay with our own—*that* was the code—though we mixed some in the lunch line, in a few classes, on the football field, and in gym. We segregated our-selves.

Regina and I went to the Chicano dances in El Monte. Pacheco introduced us to them. Regina, tanned Portuguese, passed for Chicana, so long as she kept her mouth shut and her lashes long. Pacheco showed her what skirts to wear, his quick hands fluttering through the crinolines and taffetas in her closet at home. He advised me to grow a mustache and let my black hair go long in the back, to slick it down with pomade and to fluff it up in front, then seal it all in hair spray. I bought brown Pendletons and blue navy-surplus bell-bottoms. I bought hard, steel-toed shoes. We learned trots and tangos. We learned *cuecas* and polkas. We *passed, ese,* and had a good time for a couple of months.

One day, Regina got hurt. She was stopped by one of the football players at the beach. She was stepping onto a bus when he came up behind her and grabbed her arm. She tried to twist away, and the arm snapped. She crumpled. Everyone ran. She rode in a friend's car to the hospital that day and had the arm set. She didn't call me.

I heard about it after school the next day, crossing the street against the light. It was summer, and I was taking classes while Regina spent her days at the beach. I'd see her weekdays, stopping at her house on the way home. I was going to her when, just outside the gates of our school, a guy I knew taunted me with the news. He was Japanese, and it was strange to hear him say anything about Regina. I hadn't realized anyone from my crowd knew about us.

I wanted to run the rest of the way to her house. I crossed over a rise of bare earth, then down to a bedded railway—a strip line so that scrap steel and aluminum could be shipped from the switching stations and railyards downtown to steel and aeronautical factories near our school. Brown hummocks rose above eye level and masked the track of crossties, steel rails, and the long bed of gravel. I was set upon there by a troop of Japanese boys. A crowd of them encircled me, taunting, then a single gangly fellow I recognized from gym class executed most of the blows. They beat me, grinding my face in the gravel, shouting epithets like *inu* ("dog"), *cow-fucker,* and *paddy-lover.*

I've seen hand-sized reef fish, in a ritual of spawning, leave their singular lairs, gathering in smallish, excitable schools—a critical mass—and, electrified by their circling assembly, suddenly burst the cluster apart with sequences of soloing, males alternating, pouncing above the finning group, clouding the crystalline waters above the circle with a roil of milt.

All spring and summer, I'd been immune, unaware of the enmity of the crowd. I hadn't realized that, in society, humiliation is a force more powerful than love. Love does not exist in society, but only between two, or among a family. A kid from Hawai'i, I'd undergone no real initiation in shame or social victimization yet and maintained an arrogant season out of bounds, imagining I was exempt. It was humiliating to have been sent to Camp. The Japanese American community understood their public disgrace and lived modestly, with deep prohibitions. I was acting outside of this history. I could cross boundaries, I thought. But I was not yet initiated into the knowledge that we Japanese were *not* like anyone else, that we lived in a community of violent shame. I paid for my naïveté with a bashing I still feel today, with cuts that healed with scars I can still run my fingers along. I can still taste the blood, remember the split skin under the mustache on my upper lip, and feel the depth of an anger that must have been *historical, tribal,* arising from fears of dissolution and diaspora.

Separated societies police their own separations. I was hated one day, and with an intensity I could not have foreseen. I was lifted by my clothes, the hands of my schoolmates at the nape of my shirt collar and the back of the waistband of my trousers, and I was hurled against the scrawny trunk of a little jacaranda tree and beaten there, fists cracking against my arms as I tried to cover my face, thumping along my sides and back, booted feet flailing at my legs. I squirmed, crawled, cried out. And I wept. Out of fear and humiliation and a psychic wounding I understand only now. I was *hated.* I was high and needed lowering. My acts were canceled. Regina was canceled. Both by our own peoples, enacting parallel vengeances of their own, taking our bodies from us.

Our trystings were over, and, later that summer, Regina simply moved away. Her father was retiring, she said, and had found a nice trailer park up by Morro Bay. She wouldn't see me before she left. I had to surprise her at a Laundromat one Saturday. She gave me a paperback book. She laughed, made light of everything, but there was a complete *fear* of me that I felt from her, deeply, one I had not felt before—at least, it had never registered. *Race.* It is an exclusion, a punishment, imposed by the group. I've felt it often since. It is a fear of *fraternity.* A fraternity that is forbidden. I wept, but let her go.

The Legend

What I wanted, the city could not give me. I wanted *mercy.* I wanted the universe to bend down and kiss its own creation, like a parent does a child just after it's born, as if a tenderness were the pure expression of the world for itself. I wanted to believe that what was not given could be given, that were a man or a woman to cry out for solace, the world, for all of its steel plants and tire factories, for all of its liquor stores and razor wire—for all of that, it would still lay its soft wings of blessing upon you if you cried out in need.

From time to time, I'd recollect a story I'd heard during childhood, in Hawai'i, a legend about the creation of the universe. From an aunt baking *pan dulce* or a cousin flinging stones with me into waves along Hau'ula Beach, I'd heard that in order for the stars to turn and remain where they were, it took two special creatures who were parted lovers—a Weaver Maid to make the stars (Being) and a Herd Boy (Nonbeing) to keep them in their places. Weaver Maid and Herd Boy lived on opposite sides of the Milky Way, the band of stars that is our galaxy and which Asians see as a mighty river, the River of Heaven. The Herd Boy and the Weaver Maid are stars on its opposite banks, the one in a cluster around Antares, the other far away and down along the flow, in a spot near Aldebaran. All year, they long to be together.

They labor, dutifully fabricating the web and warp of Being, herding the star bands in an eternal solitude, both celibate, without love or companionship. Yet, for one night of the year, on an evening when the star sky is said to be clearest, the universe succumbs to an overwhelming pity for them. In the form of a flock of compassionate starlings or swallows in the Japanese or Chinese versions, in the folded and gigantic wing of Crow in the Tlingit and Haida versions of the North Coast Pacific Indians, the universe, *one turning*, responds by making a footbridge across the River of Heaven out of its own interlocking bodies, out of its own need to create mercy and requital in a night of love for the effortful sacrifices of two of its children. It is a vision of the afterlife, a promise that the world will provide for us a reward and a reason for our struggles. It is a parable about mercy and fulfillment, the response of the universe to the needs of the human heart.

But I was afraid of it in the poetry workshop. It seemed too fragile a truth, unintellectual, a child's fantasy. A *colonial* child's. I was writing lies. For seven weeks, I'd brought in my defenses against my own needs. I'd composed well-wrought studies in the rhetoric of cool, in the sophistry of jive. I wrote a monologue in the character of William Holden, lying facedown in a swimming pool, blood leaking from a hole in his neck where he'd been shot by the aging film star Gloria Swanson, angry at his having jilted her or told her the truth about her wrinkling face, drenched in mortality. It was a send-up of *Sunset Boulevard*, Hollywood's own self-conscious homage and satire about the early days of the industry. My poem ended with lines something like "You think this gigolo's life is easy?/Well, it ain't no picnic." I expected laughs, congratulations, and an elevation of stature within the workshop. What I got was silence. Then, our tall instructor spoke.

"I just *never* know *what* to say about your poems," he said, and shuffled pages, turning my poem to the bottom of the pile again, and we went on, no discussion necessary.

The next week, I brought in what I thought was a masterpiece. It was two or three full pages of poetry, in sections, about eighty lines or more, the story of Shakespeare's *Macbeth* done as a *samurai* movie. I'd read about Akira Kurosawa's version, a film in period costumes. He'd rewritten things so Macbeth was a medieval *samurai,* a subsidiary warrior chieftain, searching for power, seeking to change his destiny. I read about it in a book. I particularly liked imagining brawny and bearded Toshiro Mifune as Macbeth, on his "Throne of Blood," the English translation of the Japanese title. I wrote yet another dramatic monologue, in Mifune's voice, confessing to his life's errors the moment before he is assassinated by a rebelling troop of his own vassals, joining forces with the army of marching trees which have surrounded his fortress. I set the poem as a final soliloquy, the warrior speaking an interior monologue at the moment before being impaled by a darting flock of fletched arrows shot from the bows of his men. I made him appear as a kind of Japanese Saint Sebastian, only in leather and brass armor rather than naked, wearing a winged helmet rather than a crown of thorns. It was the wedding of imagination and kitsch.

Williams stared at me. He said simply, "What next? *Two Gentlemen of Ōsaka?*" And we went on. About my work, the workshop was silent again except for this damning judgment from our instructor, who did not use us easily.

The following week was brutal for me. I'd run through all the junk I could muster. I'd run out of fakes and verbal juking, exhausted my repertoire of rhetorical feints and darts. Cut off from defending, I could only fall back on my *experience*. So I wrote a straightforward narrative about a white woman crying on a bus that was traveling through Watts—the inner city of Los Angeles. She cries, and a young black man abandons the boom box he holds to his ear and walks up to her to ask if she's all right. She grabs him, grasping his soft hand with hers, holding his to her cheek, which is wet with tears, and pleads for him to stay with her, her body bobbing in a rhythm with the lurching and roll of the moving city bus. *Just stay with me until your next stop,* she pleads. The poem ends in a tableau of both of them bathed in the soft fluorescent light of the bus lamps, the black man bewildered but calmly holding the white woman's hand in his.

It was a poem about something I *hadn't* seen happen in Los Angeles, but that I wished could've happened. It was the story of the Weaver Maid and the Herd Boy, told in inner-city, contemporary terms. The poem emerged from my own wish to found an intimate village out of the chance, strangely merciful meeting of two people, one filled with need and one stumbling forward, impelled by his own mysterious compassion.

I brought the piece to the workshop the next week. It went through copying, was distributed to everyone ahead of time, made it up to scheduling, and would be read second or third during our session. I was filled with anticipation and resolve. I told myself that if Williams trashed *this one,* if he messed with me *this time,* why, I'd *kill* him. I went to the workshop, I read my poem, and then there was the customary long silence, filled by nothing except some nervous throat-clearing, the feeling of bodies and psyches frozen in tension. Then the caviling started up.

"Ohhhh, this is *so* sentimental," Michael from San Diego bellowed. "This is *so* much crap!"

"I *can't* believe this," a woman named Virginia started chanting. "A black guy and a *white* girl? Where did you come up with *this* story—*The Naked City*?"

"*The Twilight Zone*," Steve, a Lebanese, chimed in.

There were little, half-suppressed blasts of laughter from around the room. Guys were exchanging smiles with each other. A lot of the women simply stared into the carpeting, saying nothing, making no faces or eye contact. I was on my own again and it seemed I was really in for it this time. But Williams himself, who was normally the first, had yet to speak. He shuffled his stack of poems, and everyone quieted down.

"You're all wrong," Williams said. I clenched with fear against the attack I expected.

He pointed to my pages and tapped at them with a forefinger. Things were so silent, we could hear the pad of his digit against the barely flapping stack of Xerox bond.

"*This is the real thing.*"

I was stunned. His approval was nothing I expected. Williams gazed at me with large, lemur-like eyes. They suddenly seemed to me the kindest eyes I'd ever seen. He *fixed* me to my seat. My blood seemed to be made of sand.

"If you can write like *this*," Williams snapped, "I don't see why you waste your time writing *all that other shit*."

He tapped the top page again. I wanted to fall into his eyes, which looked as large as lagoons.

"What's *more*," he continued, bellowing, "I don't see why you're wasting *mine*!"

A long and difficult way, years long, had suddenly ended with that moment; with those words, Williams had fixed and inscribed a *standard* to my ambition, giving me a charge that, from that point on, became the center of my resolve. He'd recognized the poetry within me, telling me what *my* poetry was. He'd shared his judgment. It is the most valuable thing an artist has besides passion, besides experience. He would accept none of the false words I had been typing and handing in each week. From me, he held out for a truth—that there is a world of feeling and specificities among the vast and monolithic Other of race in America. When I gave it, he gave back. It was a blessing.

VOLCANOLOGY:
LAVA-WALKING

Lava-Walking

I WAS LAVA-WALKING on a fresh *pāhoehoe* flow that had skinned over. We also ran into an *'a'ā* flow which had cooled enough to traverse. I was with Rick Hazlett, a geologist from the University of Hawaii, and John Kjargaard, a videographer who was making an educational video on Kīlauea's lava formations. It was hot going over the flows. We encountered a long, uplifted ridge of tube-fed *pāhoehoe*, a hot and incandescent glacier moving slow as taffy, hardening up and stretching its pods and toes forward. Later, we went around the front end of an *'a'ā* flow, cresting at its front end like a line of surf coming into a beach. The *'a'ā* pussed and glowed red underneath a clinkered surface. We found a way to cross it, going over its back, riding along a layer of hardened rock only a few feet thick.

Hazlett and Kjargaard rolled down the sleeves of their shirts, and so did I. Hazlett had cautioned me to "bring lots of water—maybe two quarts," and Kjargaard had told me about long-sleeved shirts, which protected the skin on your arms from the heat of the lava. Levi's and whipcord pants were enough to shield your legs, boots protected the feet, and your face was gen-erally far enough away from the worst of the radiant energy that a beard or an upraised palm was enough to deflect the heat at its worst. But arms needed sleeves. I felt the baking reaching up elbows and wrists as I buttoned up the blue workshirt I wore. I felt the skin on my face tightening too, as it does standing over a barbecue when you poke at the coals.

The rock we walked on was brown-and-black 'a'ā hard-ened only days before, clinker swept along as the flow moved downslope toward the seacoast near Kalapana. I could see blue ocean a few miles away at one point, the ground shaped in a gradually declining slope toward islands and belts of green 'ōhi'a forest. Stripes and rivers of brownish 'a'ā slithered among wide swaths of metallic gray pāhoehoe, the different flows commin-gling, layering over, and sliding by each other so the land had a variegated appearance, each flow with a characteristic color and texture to it.

These flows were all easily dated within the last fifteen years or so from the Mauna Ulu, Pu'u 'Ō'ō, and Kūpaianaha eruptions. But I'd heard of one geologist who could date the flows on Mauna Loa by examining the carbon material under the frontal toes of the flowfronts, gathering burned traces of plant material and then carbon-dating them through a lab, map-ping out hundreds of flows down the big mountain over the last millennium. It was remarkable anyone could learn that much, I thought, mapping the age in the striations of rock on a mountain that closely.

At one point, we had to jump off the live flow, dipping down to a level of older, lichened-over *ʻaʻā* that was friable and broke easily like gypsum as we walked a few steps over it. Hazlett tapped my shoulder, gesturing for me to glance back. We were walking alongside a large *ʻōhiʻa* that had been downed, burned a bit by the flow, which must have stripped it of leaves and bark first, then ploughed on through, bringing it down so the log fell on its side next to the flow. I looked back, up toward Kjargaard, who was trailing us. He stood among smoking tree branches, little gnarls of white wood shaped like nerve bundles riding on top of the flow. Below him, where the moving rock had ground over the downed log, there was a red, vagina-shaped hole glowing with the fires of escaping gases from the spot where the butt end of the tree trunk had burned away and left the mark of its absence. If the flow had stopped right then, it might have become a tree mold lying horizontally to the ground. As it was, the *ʻaʻā* was going to grind on, consuming all with its slow collisions of making and unmaking.

Flowfront

The three of us stood beneath a line of old *pāhoehoe*, out of the scorching heat for a time, gazing about a hundred yards up-slope at the fractured and flowing face of the moving front bearing our way. The entire ridgeline seemed to be on the move, a brown wave of rock cresting almost imperceptibly, slumping downhill, bringing down a wide swath of the moun- tain about a hundred yards above us. It was brown-and-gray rock, but it was moving. I'd looked at it one moment, then turned away and gazed off into space, checking the clouds against a reference line on the ground, or looked downward over the roll of the land to the sea, and then turned back, tak- ing another glance at the mountain, perceiving its shift and curling over a terrace about a hundred yards upslope from me. It seemed that raging thousands, poised for hours on the ridge above, had suddenly been released to march slowly upon me in a delicate but relentless cascade. The fixed tree-soldiers of Birnam Wood were here transformed into their local disguises of clinkered rock. Judging by its distance and speed, I thought the red flowfront might be on us in about two hours if we stayed where we were.

We stood along the tops of a row of tumuli looking up- slope, setting our eyes on a point in the distance where the 'a'ā mounded up on itself, creating a wall about five feet high and sixty feet wide. Hazlett and Kjargaard were talking, bending to- ward each other, in twin profiles backlit against the flow, and I thought they could have been a pair of surfers waiting for a set to come in, studying the sliding break of a soft wave, ex- changing predictions, finishing some little piece of anecdote be- fore the big one rolled in. One was drawing down his line of sight, directing the other to some feature in the flow that seemed featureless to me, sharing some bit of experience, exciting him in the possibilities they saw.

When the wind kicked up, whipping upslope from the sea, billowing our opened shirts and cooling us, it fanned a

cloudline above us where the lava was boiling up a heavy load
of vapors that day. One of my companions pointed to the gathering head of graying cloud upwind and said that it was likely
a local, produced from the moisture of emissions escaping from
the lava lake. "See the little flash of electricals?" he said, pointing to a glint of lightning about two miles away. I marveled
that the world and its weather were formed so close at hand, so
instantly. I looked lower, toward the churn of brown rock moving toward me, and saw a coarse glow of red teeth. It was like
the willowing head on a surf of lavas billowing up and then
collapsing against the roughened incline of a shore. But for the
heat it brought, a baking like some gigantic, unapproachable
furnace, I could've watched it for hours.

When the wind shifted, the coils of its radiance flooded
over us and it felt as if I'd stepped inside some enormous sauna
hotter than anyone could stand. My skin prickled with sweat,
beading up, and I expected my shirt to become drenched, but
the heat's intensity evaporated any moisture almost instantly.
Underneath the blackened surface, the temperature was nearly
2000 degrees and close to eruptive intensity. I could see the
glow from the moving front, and the pile of rubble peeled
back for an instant to expose the glowing red taffy. When I
saw a red jet erupting out of some driblet close at hand, just
as I felt the scoriations of heat, I thought back to a time when
I once walked into a huge barnlike building in Los Angeles
and saw what furnaces and smelting did to solid matter, black
metal melted into the glowing, red-orange juices of a liquid
steel so hot I felt the kiss of incineration on my cheek even as
I stood within its light. A wind kicked up, and I had to lift
a hand in front of my face to protect it against the sudden rage
of heat.

Burning Kīpuka

At some point, just after crossing over the back of the moving flow on a long traverse, we emerged at the far edge of the flow where it was encountering a remnant of the 'ōhi'a forest it had been burning. Lavas droop downward in their moves to the sea, pillowing up, draining in slick red gutters of fast-moving streams, sliding along in the long tubes and flow systems down-hill. In moving, they can slip through a forest and burn it up almost entirely, ploughing through a five-hundred-year-old stand in a few days, encircling it, cinching it within the hot gray blobs of its embrace, cutting off whatever is alive from what it needs to keep living, and giving it only relentless heat.

A typical picture has a shallop of magenta *pāhoehoe* arriv-ing alongside a little isle of green, low-lying ferns with the sil-vered filaments of hundreds of scorched 'ōhi'a trees, stripped of their bark by a prior heat, lifted like garnishes of baby's breath above this *ikebana* just beginning to smoke and flame along about half of its length. The trees burn from the base of the trunks first, exploding and snapping off, flaming like Fourth of July sparklers stuck headfirst into the littered ground. The cone of Pu'u 'Ō'ō might be off on the rim of the horizon close at hand, fountaining with a little spout of red and a plume of white vapor graying as it lifts above the black and reticulated land of new lavas. The sky would be a little fish-eye panorama of blue above the lighter strip of blue that would be the ocean off the coast of Halepe, looking toward the old cliffline of the Hilina Pali. There might be a few outriggers of cumulus over the sea, rafting in on a steady onshore trade wind. This would give a sense of what a *kīpuka* is like, a "hole" or circle of remnant forest life, a green canoe drifting along on a black sea, just before it slips away into the renewing oblivion of a lava flow.

The *kīpuka* we encountered was slowly being scorched from underneath the flow first, the trunks of the remaining trees blackening and smoking inside the grove that was left. I could see little jack-o'-lamps of orange flames flickering on and flickering off in the dark world of the forest floor under the scorched canopy still partly alive. There were funny thudding noises like tiny thwocks of helicopter blades going off softly, seemingly underground. These were the methane explosions I'd been hearing about, when lava heats the ground and the buildup of organic matter there gives off its gas in little chambers just under the surface of the earth. These then explode, ignited by the heat in the advance line of the flow. They could be dangerous, and I was warned that if I heard any booms or popping sounds close by or saw trees shaking, it was probably a methane explosion ready to go off big, and I was to get moving as quickly as possible. Huge reservoirs of gas could build up under the root systems of the forest and, gone unburned for a while, could suddenly touch off, erupting explosively, tossing off a mixture of rock and wood in a cloud of naturally made shrapnel.

I stood out on a felled log about two feet in diameter and Hazlett snapped a picture. When I crept just a few more feet closer to the advancing edge of the flow, there was one slender log downed beside the one I stood upon. While the picture was being taken, the flow knocked down two or three more slender trees, crashing alongside the ones where I stood. I didn't move. It was too hot to jump off, I thought. The falling trees did not hit me, but in the picture, you can see them bending to the earth, leaning in their descent about ten feet behind me. There are shaky lines of white and gray ash—what used to be the trunks of other slender trees—running up the clinkery ground behind where I am standing. They look like the columns of ash that cigarettes might leave in a black tray. Little remnants of half-burned stumps lay about. In the photograph, I can see a puff of smoke rising from the butt end of a small tree on the farthest upslope edge of the kīpuka. I can hear a crackle and some vague popping, but I don't want to get out of there. I can feel something burning away from inside of me, and I don't need it.

SELF-HELP: AN ESSAY ON DESCENT FROM SPIRIT

I AM CHRONICALLY dispirited. I take from everything low in my life—the daily stupidities of the newspaper, the jealousies of friends and rivals, remorse over items of clothing forgotten in Mainland hotel rooms and Honolulu diners, anger over an old hurtful remark from one of the relatives—and I make out of them a fine focus that can last all the day long. Or else I indulge in that patented low-grade unhappiness of bewilderment and ennui that is the nearly constant state of one who is alienated from things. It is as if I were spread abroad like atmosphere itself, with no substance or engine of my own, but blown like the sulphuric clouds of gases from the volcano that drip acid from the sky, eating away at the car paint, congesting

the lungs and inflaming the soft tissue around the eyes, trigger-
ing asthma in children and bouts of intense spiritual suffoca-
tion in those with advanced degrees.

I've never understood how I fall into this. I get busy—
with chores or correspondence, with an ambitious project
months-long, with hosting literary events or going to them or
acting out my part as one of the interchangeable players, or with
tending to some minor ailment of the body—and suddenly, my
life is playing itself out on a level of the infernal. I am fuming
with discontent, prone to physical accident like cutting a finger
chopping vegetables in the kitchen, obsessed with personal tur-
moil, and spoiling for a bout of verbal contentiousness within
the dark house.

On a sunny day in Volcano, I walk the yard, picking up
withered, wind-broken fronds from the elegant tree ferns, and I
brood on the pettiness of the race, on my own arrogance and
pride. I look out from the picture window at the river of clouds
streaming over the tops of the Japanese cedar and the silver
limbs of the 'ōhi'a, and I'm thrown back into wretchedness. Indoors, I stare at the stack of sophisticated Mainland magazines
that come to us by slow boat through the post office, and they
have nothing for me but their fading glossiness and absurd ads
for Jamaican resorts and leaded-glass figurines shaped into animal dollops like soft ice cream. Cooking does nothing, and I
settle into weeks of unimaginative meals built around rice and
meat and a frozen vegetable. Or, I choose a book from my
home library and it cannot sustain me.

I decide to drive to Hilo and spend hours in the library,
finding every book I can from the latest East Indian postcolonial feminist to the most obscure book of Italian poetry in translation. I find Ueda Akinari's eighteenth-century supernatural

tales in the Japanese literature section, I find a book on native trees and shrubs in the Hawaiiana section, I find a history of things Japanese in Hawai'i, I find Robert Penn Warren's novels, and I find the latest book of enlightened mini-essays by Lewis Thomas. I throw the books into the trunk of the car, pick up a Pepsi at the Dairy Queen, and drive up the highway twenty-nine miles past the old plantation towns of Pana'ewa, Kea'au, Kurtistown, and Mountain View all the way back up to Volcano. I off-load the books and haul them in shifts upstairs to my study, stopping at the entryway, at the first landing below the stereo speakers and scroll painting of tigers, and at the balcony cluttered with boxes of toys. I line the books up against the back wall behind where I write. They gather dust and, on the book jackets, grow a dark, gray mold from the Volcano dampness that looks like a fine, wet ash. I am not distracted from unhappiness.

My father seemed thus to me, in a state of perpetual melancholy unmasked by intellectual thoughtfulness or academic projects. He could become paralyzed by his moods, the house falling to pieces, the lawn unmowed, cars spotted with the microdung of yellow, freeway-killed bugs. He shuffled and sleepwalked through our tract house dressed in nightclothes— pajamas, a robe and slippers—until noon seemingly every day of my childhood. He'd worked at physically punishing jobs as a younger man—highway construction in Hawai'i, fueling jet planes on a marine base, loading trucks at a warehouse. Then, when we moved to Los Angeles, he found a steady job troubleshooting on an assembly line in an electronics factory, checking electrical circuits and telemetry systems for helicopters—a job that, at first, was merely boring but that, eventually, like so many jobs in American industry, ended up degrading him.

From a childhood fever that weakened the tiny, friable bones in his ears, from neglecting to wear plugs while working a jackhammer, while pumping jet fuel while the planes revved their engines, he'd slowly become deafened. At first, he'd only missed the nuances and the tenor of conversations. Jokes escaped him, the progress of exchanges, the name of someone just introduced at a weekend poker party with neighbors and friends. He couldn't understand someone if their accent or regional dialect was different from what he was used to. We fell into the practice of speaking only the simplest pidgin with him at home. He was unable to make out huge pieces of conversation. Exchanges had to be reduced to the purest physical instructions. Friends gave up and drifted away. His social life ended. After a while, the relatives seemed to give up on him too. He couldn't follow what anyone was saying. He was cast aside from the social circle.

At work, after a few meaningless promotions, he started getting frozen out there too. He received only one raise in ten years. My mother complained and faulted him. His bosses cursed and yelled at him; fellow workers shunned him and made him the butt of their jokes. He couldn't know what they were saying, but he felt their rejection. He moved aside when they walked by, absently clicking their ballpoint pens, and fell into a lonely silence on the job. He fell to the fringes of workplace society, befriended by the Mexican and Asian immigrants who, like him, understood little of the talking but could feel the loathing. They made a borderlands of the lunchroom, the Coke machine, the drinking fountain.

Through the years, he'd been able to move up a little, switching from working graveyard shift to swing shift and then, finally, after the last promotion, to day shift. But the day-shift world became too complicated for him to manage. Its society made too many demands and his deafness hampered him badly. He didn't *want* to go out to dinner. To a party. To so-and-so's wedding. He didn't *want* to take my brother and me to the park or to Father and Sons' Day at the school. Partly for the increase in pay, but really in order to make things simpler, he finally switched back to swing shift. He moved from a world of discouragement, the daily expectations he could not fulfill, to a midnight world of quiet and some emptiness. Under the black milk of the sky, he drove home while rain pelted the roads and made a sheen on the asphalt that glittered with blue streetlight and red neon. He cherished these images and their accompanying silence. He made a corner of peace with his living.

Summers, home during daylight while the cool dichondra lawn he and my Kubota grandfather had planted years before dried and withered and then flowered into tall, vacant-lot weeds, he'd pore over the baseball box scores of the Sports page. He'd analyze the hot streaks and hitting slumps and relative health of the right-handed curveball pitchers versus a predominantly left-handed lineup of banjo hitters, predicting, quite accurately, shutouts at Wrigley Field in Chicago and laughers at Candlestick Park in San Francisco. In the fall, over breakfast at noon before leaving for work at three, he'd tune his radio into the race results at the track, going over his handicap and tip sheets, scripting out intricately figured ratios and odds for payoffs in the margins. His damaged hearing had an easy time receiving the rich, resonant baritone voices of the track announcers. Yet, he also preferred the withdrawal into another world, I think. He would use his life in pursuit of the abstract, in retreat from suffocating realities that made for pain and the death of delight in the act of the mind.

·   This was the pattern he'd discovered when he was a
teenager in McCully, spending his afternoons tending his collection of dwarf plants, *bonsai,* obsessing, trying to make of them
a world he could escape to. He was desperate to make art out
of his alienation. The *bonsai* would gather his unease and rest-
lessness, bundle what he felt to be abject and shopworn from
his life—the spiritless days of the public high school, the afternoons of shoe-shining along the chop suey stands on McCully
Street—into the deliberate lashings of gummy twine that resulted in a fruitless bole and the intricate and somewhat predictable twists in the gnarled limbs of a miniature tree. His
effort thus would make of bough and limb an order of beauty
powerful enough to hold the mind in contemplation and satisfy
the body's need for activity.

   I know my father's dwarf pines and plum trees offered a
repose for his mind. I've decided it was a way for him to work
out a need for order and beauty, that he was a botanical Wallace Stevens of Honolulu, working out a way to bring his mind
to its own perfection, working in the theater of miniature, in ornamental shrubbery and potted frangipani. With the plants, he
made his own rhythms, grafted a material beauty onto an orphaned teenager's life. It is the art of a *samurai* applied to peasant circumstances. Focus, precision, and discipline brought
together in a fragile, inexpensive beauty. It was a way to deal
with *angst.*

   It became a pattern he repeated, making himself over in
sequences of splendid diversions: as a teenager, in his collection
of plants, in baseball and other sports; when older, a flashy vet
returning from the war, he'd taught himself jitterbugging and
fox-trotting, fancy dress, and a way to oil his hair, shiny in any
light. Minus the broad-brimmed hat, he dressed like Miles

Davis in pictures I've seen of him with the Charlie Parker Band—*Zoot!* Gabardine jackets with padded shoulders, two-tone crepe shirts, roomy slacks with razor-sharp creases, and buckskin saddle shoes. Style, jack. USO. Ready for the dance. After the war and the fifties, he worked it out on horses, handicapping, studying racing forms and turfcraft sheets, picking winners and combinations.

When I was a child, when we were living in Los Angeles near the Shrine Auditorium and Felix Chevrolet—to me, magical palaces with their false architectural spires and cloth pennants flapping around a lot full of finned, nose-coned, gleaming automobiles—my father once took the family out on an evening drive.

We drove out on Olympic Boulevard for what seemed an eternity until we got to a monstrous edifice all of concrete and glass. Near its top, four stories or more above the amber street-lights, there were huge blocks of red neon letters that spelled CARNATION, a flower of extravagant softness like that of the trade winds I knew from *lei* sold at the airport and given with kisses. The brilliant colors of the word splashed through the rain-spattered window of our black Plymouth and I could see a candy-red light swim like a butterfly fish across the upturned face of my mother ahead in the front seat. There was a show-room of sorts on its ground floor—a glittering soda fountain busy with folks having fun. Yet, I sensed my parents' public stiffness, their withdrawal into a mild, unstated shame and the pain of not belonging.

We were among a mix of peoples, but most were *haoles*—in Hawaiian, a people without breath, without life—commonly applied by islanders to Mainland whites who owned the world we lived in and who were not welcoming of our boisterous plantation ways. We quieted ourselves as we entered, but I could not help being excited to be stepping into the higher, al⁄most deva⁄world of the Art Deco soda shop of green Formica tables, shining aluminum and stainless steel counter rims and stool columns, and the varicolored lights of its jukebox full of Elvis and the Platters. I chattered on in mixed pidgin and Mainland English, confused about what language to use. I wanted to play the jukebox, I wanted vanilla ice cream, I wanted a strawberry soda.

"I can play dah juke?" I said. "I can have vanilla cone?"

Then, reacting to the scowl on my mother's face, recalling the scoldings to "speak English—we're on the Mainland now," I shifted dialects even as I continued on in my childish ebullience.

"Can I have *some* ice cream?" I said, swerving the syntax, finding the magical inflection. "Can I play Platters on the juke⁄box?"

When my mother frowned again, I checked back over the sentence and found a rephrasing in my shallow repertoire.

"Can I play *the* Platters?" I corrected myself, acquiring an⁄other life, another culture.

The treats came, and I practiced a dialect I imitated from the evening news broadcasts of KNXT, from the jabbering of my classmates on the asphalt playgrounds of the L.A. City Schools. My father stayed silent.

On another day, a Saturday afternoon, instead of watch⁄ing sports or reading the paper or building a model airplane with me, he jingled his ring of house and car keys and an⁄nounced that he and I would be going for a drive to Santa Monica across town where he worked.

"Forget go playgroun'," he instructed. "We go book stoah tooday."

My mother was away, working overtime on her job as a clerk for the City of Los Angeles, and he had me home with him. My brother must've been with an aunt and cousins. I slept in the car nearly all the way there until we got to Sepulveda and a nearly endless lineup of plate-glass storefronts fading into the smog at both ends of the street.

There were shoe stores, drugstores, gun shops with black iron barring, and a music store full of cherry-red guitars and posters of Fabian. We went to a bookstall—a dusty shop full of paperbacks and magazines and bins of used comic books. There was a geared turnstile, a cash register, and a large brown radio console at the entrance where an unshaven man with a ginger stubble sat in a folding chair smoking a cigarette, reading the *Racing Form,* and absently twisting the radio's tuning dial.

"Hi, Al," he said to my father. "I'm tryna get the results from the Fifth at Santa Anita." He shortened my father's name, *familiarly,* as if he were a friend. In Hawai'i, people called my father *Albert.*

I could not believe not only that this old *haole* man *knew* my father, but that they'd spoken many times, that they had this interest in the horses together, that someone outside of the family had a feeling for my father and my father for him. There was a life here that was not of our little family huddled together in the two-bedroom apartment on Kingsley Drive. It felt like a *betrayal* to me, my father abandoning who he was, where he came from, leaving his own name in order to enter into commerce with the dusty new society of Los Angeles that sprung up around our family, a little island of Hawai'i. He was "Al" and not "Albert." He was a stranger to me.

"We got some new stuff in this past week, Al," the man said, knocking the long ash from his cigarette into a white-and-gold ashtray molded into the shape of a fish. "It's some of that hocus-pocus religion stuff you like, only *hardcover*."

My father pointed me to the bin of comic books—Archie and Veronica, Blackhawks, and the Atom—and rushed off, disappearing into the rear of the shop. He was gone a long time, but, after a while, the intensity of what had to have been a deep cultural fear seemed to fade as the man by the radio let me read any comic I wanted without rushing me to buy or to move along. I collected a stack of *Batman* and novelties like *The Fabulous Four*—the Hulk, Spiderman, the Rocket, and a voluptuous superwoman.

When I went searching for my father, I found him nose buried in *Tertium Organum*. He browsed in mystics—in Gurdjieff and Ouspensky, in Madame Blavatsky, in Yeats's *A Vision*. These names seemed to me more magical, more Hawaiian than anything else in our lives.

"What kine language dat?" I asked, counting and sounding the syllables in my head, trying to match them with my memory of Hawaiian.

Though he shushed me as if we were in the rare book room of a library, he answered, his accent dropping the fricative.

"One whole eart'," he said. "One whole creature azz de eart'."

My father wanted an answer. He wanted someone to explain his pain, to cure the absence of heart he felt every day in this life, to give him the solution for which gambling seemed only a substitute. Dressed in khaki trousers, open-toed Hawaiian wrap sandals, and a loose, Hawaiian-print rayon shirt, he pushed the raffia hat back from his brow and leaned against the dingy wall, holding the book in his hands as though it were a roll of bills. He looked to me like Poncie Ponce—the Hawaiian-born Filipino comedian on "Hawaiian Eye," the TV detective show set in Hollywood. He looked like a Honolulu cabdriver counting his tips for the day. But it was his incarnate soul that he thought upon, the wheel of a postcolonial's life sent to the industrial capital to find work. He was literate but dispossessed of a culture. Though he made a living, there was no center to this Mainland life that he could feel a part of. Not yet a religious man, he followed the horses season by season from Santa Anita to Hollywood Park and back again, but, creature of the Hawaiian earth, he had a hole in his life that money, excitement, and family could not fill. He liked reading in the occult. He liked Inspiration and Self-Help. He stared into books for what seemed hours until I tugged at the squared-off shirttail of his aloha shirt, impatient for home, a meal of Japanese noodles, and a television cartoon on the turquoise portable Zenith we had that could soften wax with its vacuum-tube heat.

He bought nothing for himself, but allowed me some war comics about a haunted Jeb Stuart tank in Europe during World War II. On the way home, I jabbered all the way from Sepulveda to Olympic. My father barely spoke, brooding, I imagine now, on the question of his proper place on the earth, perhaps deciding he may have found his and wondering if I might grow stronger in the glow of certainty he was only just then entering. The beautiful, for him, became an inconstant but habitable state of mind that had its inspiration in the gauzy lights we pursued at night across Los Angeles, or it came through memory—a row of dwarf trees and ornamental shrubs he'd tended as a teenager in Honolulu.

YUKIKO KATAYAMA, the woman from Kaua'i who was my father's mother, the woman who ran off and remarried when my father was six or so, performed a dance at her own eighty-fifth birthday party. A few of us from the Big Island flew over to Honolulu on Oʻahu, where it took place. I felt ambivalent. The woman was old. She really was my grandmother. My aunts were going and so were a few of my cousins—the gentler ones, the ones not so busy with work.

The party was held as a reception at one of the finest Japanese hotel-restaurants in Honolulu—one with a huge carp pond and *tatami* rooms. But we would have the banquet hall—a polished wooden floor, Japanese screens, rectangular tables, and a small stage up front. We ate thinly sliced raw fish, octopi and squid sculpted and filigreed to look like seaflowers, and flailed but living shrimps, morsels of gray-veined flesh still dancing on soft beds of vinegared rice. All was colorful and elegant in pattern, arranged on shining, varicolored porcelain trays.

Grandma Katayama sequestered herself backstage for almost the entire duration of the party. We saw a trio of her younger students perform—they were in their thirties, I guessed—then a quintet of her older students, who were in their fifties. Japanese music, churned out from a Sony cassette player backstage, was piped into the banquet hall through a sound system worthy of an underground shopping mall in Ōsaka. A generation ago, we would have heard scratches and pops and an old-time music that would have reminded me of splendors like plastic wisteria and dyed-paper lanterns at the O-Bon festival. Now, we heard a soft rattle and hum, and the music, though the same, seemed without scent, without spice, without that tidal flow of sexuality and fantasy that stiffened zeal and the inner organs. I waited.

I watched my aunts as they ate delicately with their chopsticks and spoke in mannerly ways with the guests at their side.

I watched my cousins, gesturing and smiling, minding children, snapping photographs and exchanging small gifts with
the family we were not part of, yet belonged to, as if we were
the dead that haunted an old burial site a new village had been
built upon. We came to show ourselves, to cast a benevolent,
living shadow behind the frail, guiltless body of our matriarch
who had fled from us and from the history we would make
without her. We came to absolve—her and ourselves. We
laughed and showed photographs of our children, our trips to
Japan and Disneyland, our houses and our cars. We came to
say things had worked out, that they were all right.

I thought of my father's grave, knowing it would be rude
to show the Polaroids of his headstone, to tell the story of his
life and his death. He'd have to be left out of the story here. He
was my own sadness, his woe thicker than the wallet of colorful plastic cards and photographs blooming inside the breast
pocket of my linen jacket.

Around the banquet table, a trilingual banter of Japanese
mixed with English and the local pidgin dialect caught me in
a wide, encircling net of sound, conversation like a shoal of
fishes thrashing, almost meaninglessly, in exhilaration. The net
gathered itself, and I heard a palpable quiet settle over us that
faded into applause.

My grandmother was dancing onto the stage, dressed in
rich brocades that trailed like a banner of clouds behind her.
She wore a thick wig and an ornate headdress too, her face
powdered white and her features lacquered in a classic red and
black. She posed and postured, dipping her shoulder and fluttering a golden fan, her head bobbing like a painted cork floating independently of her body. The music was live, a singer
plucking the buzzing strings of her *shamisen* at the left of the

stage, warbling a melancholy song I couldn't quite make out the words to.

I looked around the room. Everyone sat at rigid attention, their eyes taking in the old woman's dance. The long, heavy sleeves of her gown hung like sheets of rain trailing clouds at sea, and she vanished into the wings for a while so the singer could solo, quickening the pace, frailing at her three-stringed instrument like a banjo-picker at a midwestern state fair. I saw one of my cousins reach for a roll of *sushi*, gobble it, then wash it down with a jigger of tea.

My grandmother returned without the fan, but carrying a new, somewhat sporty prop. It was a kind of stylized hobo's stick with a small cedar bucket hooked onto its end with a gorgeously thick rope of interwoven bronze and black fibers. She did a skating rapper's step across the stage, back and forth, jouncing her head from side to side and holding momentary poses syncopated to the singer's *pizzicati* on the *shamisen*. I thought of how wealthy in time she must have been to work up such an act, to have devoted such delicate and thorough attention to an art of dress and gesture through part of childhood, a formal adolescent apprenticeship in Japan, and then the rude adulthood of life in the floating world of Honolulu's bar culture of the twenties. I wondered what happens to the heart in such circumstances, with so long a history. Her face betrayed no passion, only stylized flutterings of movement in her eyes, a downcast glance that symbolized modesty. Her youthful dancer's body, pale and unpowdered, had lain down with how many before she found the dark body of my grandfather? Three children came—my father, a sister, and a brother. My grandfather beat her and she ran off—*ha'alele hana*—and then lay down with the younger Katayama, a plantation *luna*—a man who beat men and not women—and she made two more sons, one an attorney and the other an investment broker who, according to the gossip among us cousins from another island, was said to have disappeared for a while, who then turned up drowned, his body locked in the trunk of a car that had to be dredged from Pearl Harbor.

Their kind children surrounded me, blank Japanese faces with no emotion for me, without knowledge they could share. I gave them courtesy and a feigned gentleness of mind. But I wanted death and a haunting, for flesh to turn vaporous as intermingled light and rain in the fogs of Volcano, for my grandmother to face me as pure spirit without the rot of time and incarnation between us.

She stamped her stockinged foot inside the elegant pad of a gold-and-white cloth slipper, and I noticed that her robes were more like elegant, billowing trousers gathered high in an *obi* sash around her chest and not skirtlike at all. She'd placed the bucket down at the front of the stage and slid away from the singer. The stick she'd carried it with, first over one shoulder, then over the other, providing for an ensemble of decorous shifting movements, she'd lain down at center stage, out of the path of the trailing, twin cloth wakes of her trousers. She produced a wooden dipper from the band of her *obi* and bent from the waist over the bucket, as if spooning water or sand into it. The singer sang a word or two I recognized—Ise, a place name, and then words for the reflection of a beautiful woman's face, sliding and breaking into ribbons on tidal waters.

This was the crux and climax of my grandmother's dance—*Matsukaze*—a wind in the pines, then a shining silver moon mirrored on the flat tidal waters of a Japanese seashore. She bobbed from the waist and made the motions of filling her

bucket with water again and again, perilously slowly. I saw the
scene suddenly, put together in staggered images from the dance
and scraps from the singing. She stood in water to her knees,
harvesting shrimp from the sea, scooping them into her bucket
and carrying them back to a rugged shore, again and again—
the tedious, mechanical work of a country beauty, far from the
capital. Startled, she sees the image of the moon on the waters
and recalls her lover of a year ago, an elegant and youthful
prince on tour surveying his lands. She glances back over her
shoulder, expecting the past and her lover to return, standing
on the shore behind her, but it is only the summer moon, rising over mountains and casting its light on the sea. Her mind
drifts into sadness at the recollection, and salt tears slide down
her face. She sees the moon in her bucket, the eternal face of
the universe, and, fallen into madness now, tries repeatedly to
scoop it out, weeping and imploring the moon to flee its habitation in the mirroring waters. It is her face, then, the dancer's,
that replaces the moon's, shining with tears and youth, luminous with madness and regret. When the dance ends, she
brings the spade of a flat hand to her brow like a broad knife
blade cutting across the blank space between her gaze and the
commingled reflections on the water, between the past and the
action of her mind.

A FRIEND who teaches at an urban university once sent me a
video he'd made of a poetry reading I gave to an audience of
his colleagues and students. I was amazed at my own ferocity,
my statements of passion for the lives of others. Inspired by the
audience—Filipinos, Samoans, H'mong, Vietnamese, and
Chicanos among whites and blacks—it seemed to me I caught
a complicated spirit and carried its history in my bones, in the

hunch of my shoulders, in the hugeness of my claims for the work of poetry. My body moved as it did when I was a teenager in Los Angeles, hunched against the cold in a thin jacket and waiting for a school bus to pick me up, jiving with black and Asian and Hispanic schoolmates. In every joke, with every heroic piece of "bee-ess" regarding conquest or survival, about triumph over whites or their culture, we signified and threatened each other, telling the rest of the world to steer clear of us. In the tape, my motions seemed dated and ghetto, lifted out of the sixties, full of the inner city. "So damn *street*," a student of mine once remarked critically, a Filipino from the Mission District in San Francisco—a barrio—and damn street himself. I was nothing like the standard image of a college professor. I was nothing like the intellectuals who had educated me. I was working-class—like Chicano rockabillies from East L.A. or the *chang-a-lang* bad boys that made up all the bands that played the clubs along Hotel Street in Chinatown Honolulu. There was no imperturbable chill about me. I fussed. I raged a little. A sacrifice to my passion, I was caustic and daunting on the screen, combative and elemental. Like raw earth, I boiled in my own moods, swollen in a petty defiance, telling myself I mimicked nothing.

NOW I KNOW that without love's pure passion or the kind of enlightenment the gentleness of meditative religion brings, emotions tend to prey on the fallen, delicate soul like the vultures that come to eat at the liver of Prometheus chained to a cliff. "I ache now without explanation," wrote the Peruvian genius César Vallejo. "My pain is so deep, that it never had a cause nor does it lack a cause now." His poem, which purports to speak of hope, in fact does not, but is a paean to existential *angst,* the pain without source, the feeling of being adrift, free of moorings and unpropelled. Vallejo's pain can't be dignified with religious overtones. His pain would be the same if he were Catholic, atheist, or Muhammadan. "I would still suffer it," he wrote. "Its cause is nothing; nothing could have stopped being its cause." It is a suffering without parentage, without specificity, not even tied to his personality. He envies the victims of tragedy and disaster—*they* have a source for their suffering. They can attribute sorrow to an act, of nature or of God or of man. His sorrow is as nothing itself. "I look at the hungry man's pain and see that his hunger is so far from my suffering, that if I were to fast unto death, at least a blade of grass would always sprout from my tomb. The same with the lover! How engendered his blood is, in contrast to mine without source or use!" It is a kind of perplexity, a frustration of the soul, a guilt without remorse or absolution. I recall one of the illustrations from an English edition of Vallejo's *Trilce,* that strange book full of neologisms, non sequiturs, and sentences with grammar so fractured and punctuation so bizarre that reading it seemed like reading transcripts of the reveries of a singing whale doped out on airplane glue. Large and dangerous and full of deep, mid-oceanic dives into consciousness. Sublime and incomprehensible. What struck me were the reproductions of the drawings a friend had done to accompany the text. There was one in particular, of Vallejo cupping the fractured triangle of his head in one hand, resting his chin on a curved palm. His fingers jutted like the tines of a pitchfork against his face and pressed up sharply against one inflated cheek. His expression was as if a surrealist train had rammed him on the forehead between the eyeballs and he was busy puzzling out Magritte the macabre engineer's motive. Perplexed. Pained. Why is there evil and why does it visit me? Worse yet, why can't I attribute this vague unease of my soul to an ancient, describable evil that emerges from deep within civilization?

Vallejo the poet is poised above an open notebook full of jottings. He is seated at a café table in some open European piazza. He stares blearily off into a nothingness beyond the reader's shoulder. He has written. "Today I suffer no matter what happens. Today I am simply in pain."

In Los Angeles, as a child and a teenager, I fell into an acquaintance with this mood too. No matter what I did or didn't do, the feeling would come upon me, seek me out like a bad friend. Watching television seemed to make it worse, episodes of "I Love Lucy" and "Batman" and "The Beverly Hillbillies" could not make me laugh or shake my heart into fear or love or excitement.

Lost, finding no way to weave Regina, my first and prohibited love, back into my life, I read for self-help. I searched the libraries and turned the paperback carousels at the supermarkets and drugstores looking for titles having something to do with me. I found *Catch-22* and *Little Big Man* in a downtown bookstall. I found Kafka and Joyce and Salinger in the school library. Their violence, mordancy, and sexual episodes fascinated me. They seemed to include more of the world and its nuances and oppressions big and small. Though not about me or any schoolmates I recognized, these books seemed more adequate to my reality than anything on television, in the composition lessons at school, or from the swaggering stories full of ghetto bullshit and bravado told by friends at gym class or during lunch. I was beginning to understand that the story I was looking for would not feature an old-style romantic adventurer, not a "hero" but a soul lost and without personal or cultural bearings.

At the Thrifty Drug on Redondo Beach Boulevard, at K & K Liquors on Western Avenue, at the Paperback Barn on Sepulveda, the carousels squeaked and spun, the brass wire holsters revolved, and I flipped through Bantams, Ballantines, Cardinals, and Dells until I grew to recognize the Black Cats, those "adult" books that were known as near-pornography at the time, except that they addressed some itch of my soul too. At a beachside bookstore I'd just discovered named the Either/ Or after the dichotomous philosopher's famous book, the owner—a middle-aged Bohemian woman—took pity on me, *caught* me, I'd thought at first, when she found me nose deep in an Evergreen book I picked up because I thought it was about trout-fishing.

"If you like this kind of thing, maybe you'll like these too," she said, leading me to the poetry room, a place I'd *never* ventured.

She showed me Rilke's *Letters to a Young Poet,* Kerouac's *Mexico City Blues,* Jeffers's narratives set in Big Sur, and Dylan Thomas's *Selected.* Thomas was full of celebrations of child-hood and Welsh seascapes that sang to me of my own waters of childhood in Hawai'i along the North Shore. I read for scenery, for explanations of my body and what was happening to it, and for those incredible arias of verbal splendor that made sense and beauty out of the overwhelming urban dullness that was smothering me.

As a teenager in Los Angeles, in the swerve of repetition that makes the lives of the past our lives also, I began to dis-cover that living needed its beguilements, something to take up the mind and give it focus. It needed something to desire, no matter how trivial or phantasmal. Once, bored with books too, I went driving north, up through the vehicular canal of suburbs, past the relentless string of L.A. strip malls, a golf course, whole city blocks of dilapidated factories, abandoned movie theaters, tracts of stuccoed three-bedroom homes, and clutches of old-fashioned storefronts bristling with iron caging. I drove on through zones of urban sprawl named Torrance, Carson, Lawndale, Hawthorne, and Inglewood. I stopped at a drive-in, and my eye caught a sign above a glassed-in storefront across the street. TROPICAL FISH, it said on a simple white board painted with black lettering unbelievably plain for what it advertised. It was a hobbyist's refuge with scores of burbling tanks filled with colorful neon tetras, Jack Dempseys, black and yellow angelfish, silver archerfish, and miniature clowns. I spent an afternoon wandering in its dazzle of colors, enthralled with those darts and wings of beauty, feeling the coral growing back in my blood, the salt resolving itself in my own inner seas. For an hour or more, I fell into a powerful dreaminess that made the heart still from wanting. And, for those moments, drugged by the orphic purposelessness of creation, I desired nothing.

When I first came back to Volcano, I sensed it could become a beguilement that would be lifelong. There was enough beauty and mystery to capture my mind and all of its energy for torture and pain and transform it into something like love—a love for natural beauty, an attachment to a local habitation, an inheritance of a name, my own family's name. There was enough to try to find out—of family drama, of regional and natural history—to engage heart and intellect for a lifetime. Who could be bored? Even a poet would have insurance against ennui.

I like to think of the story I heard a Kiowa tell once. A famous writer, he was speaking to a huge crowd of non-Kiowa at a public ceremony on the Mainland. He said that when he was a child growing up on his grandfather's ranch near the reservation in Oklahoma, he'd come upon a box of huge animal bones under the rafters of the barn across from the house. He asked his grandmother what they were. "They are the bones of a great horse," his grandmother told him. "A horse of great strength that helped the Kiowa people." Legends grew around the horse. The horse led the way on a long pilgrimage to the source of all souls. And led the way *back*. It was a magical horse. These bones in the barn were his. The boy was to notice how large they all were, how huge the jaw, how massive the teeth and eye sockets. He went to the barn nearly every day, making the bones part of the circuit of his daily play.

One day, the boy went to the barn and the bones were gone. The boy felt sick inside. The bones had become part of his routine, a focus for his regimen of games and travel through what had become an *imaginative* world as well as an authentic landscape for his entire being. What happened? he asked his grandmother. She told him someone had stolen the bones. Why? No one knew for sure, but perhaps for greed, to exhibit in a traveling show, or, most strangely, for nothing at all. It could have been purposeful—to deprive the Kiowa of a glory, stealing the monument to a former time, an old way of life, an order of imagination. Who could know? The horse's bones had tied the child to the landscape and to stories of his Kiowa people. And it tied the people to the very grand story of their annual migrations up through the land corridor from Oklahoma to North Dakota, to the expanded universe of the entirety of the Great Plains itself. To heaven. With the bones gone, it would be harder to tell the story that gave them happiness and a pride in the land they used to know, harder to join the child to the

barnyard that was part of the plains, part of the Kiowa. With
the bones gone, who could remember now if they were part of
anything?

The bones, a story, tied the present to the past, the self to
a landscape, gave the mind a place to go with its thoughts, its
need to belong to something beyond time and the personal. It
gave the Kiowa myth and the lost boy his place in it.

What I need from stories and my own returning to Volcano is this same kind of thing—a way to belong and a place
to belong to. A way to belong that, at once, ties me to human
culture and to a living earth that is itself without culture or care
for human life. *Pele.* In other civilizations the priests and
necromancers provided this, the early poets and storytellers
weaving orbs of myth and human history. I suppose I could
stand us doing this again, though I wouldn't want to legislate
it. My perpetual unease, though, is that I try to live without it,
puzzled and completely contemporary.

Cynthia says we are each in charge of our own happiness,
that, like the Hopi, it is our duty every day to make a bit of
peace that we can inhabit and thus engage the world. My wife
is existential that way, was raised so, lives so. She takes the
morning paper and has a knack for finding the funny in an
otherwise saccharine story, the true inspiration in an otherwise
ludicrous one.

"Listen to this," she'd say some Sunday back in Volcano,
sipping Kona coffee, and proceed to quote the lead from a story
about a local fireman who was building his house out of the
old timbers and beams of the Honomu Hongwanji—one of the
Buddhist temples built for a plantation camp in the canefields
back at the beginning of the century—bought at auction years
ago. "It says he bid on the boards back in 1978! The guy was

already planning to build his house out of them way back then! And he didn't even own land! How about *that* for *faith!*" she says, drawing her lesson from it and her spirit for the day.

A heathen and not a Hopi, not Kiowa, I have no such talent for daily parable, for a complete trust in the communal building of certainty and optimism, for participation. I take myself out. My heart is at constant war with things. I read in Kierkegaard, in *Fear and Trembling,* that misery and alienation is a necessary and useful phase toward the building of a modern inner subjectivity. Like the "abandonment neurotic" that Martinican intellectual Frantz Fanon describes in *Black Skin, White Masks,* I am ever fearful of being cast out or left behind. I live with these pains constantly and tell myself that this incessant brooding on things is useful, that I am giving to a poetry, to a life that is part of a familial constant, a kind of psychological karma working itself toward becoming part of the beauty my father made tending his collection of plants, part of the austere, carnal loveliness my grandmother made building her repertoire of narrative dances.

ON THE MAINLAND, I've been talking to two other poets whenever I can. They are Asians too, and when we meet, I try to see if they are at all like me. One is completely aggressive in his dissatisfactions, in his inner drive, and the feeling about him is that he is one who is on a spiritual quest. He admires the thief Genet—passion is all and without compromise. He is a criminal for passion. He is of the air, a pure transience like wind. "I can remember weeping at the sight of pure light falling through a pepper tree, splashing into the little cups of leaves," he says. "I was five, Garrett, weeping for light! There is no time!" The other poet is like water—a perfect reflection of the actions others take, and yet, in itself, its own tidal force. Dressed in sensuous fabrics—the flamboyant pastel of a washed silk shirt over white cotton trousers—he speaks to a crowd of uni' versity students and, brave before any topics of sexuality or alienation, articulates their individual and consensual uncon' scious, putting formative, politicized language to the barest inklings of individual worry or desire. "In my twenties," he says, "because I didn't realize I had no idea *who* I was, because of the Camps and the refusal of the Nisei to talk about them, I engaged in all kinds of practices—*rampant sexual promiscuity*— in order to *feel* something, in order *to be* a self." Shocked, his audiences begin thinking.

Privately, we chatter on about how we've trained ourselves to live in contradictions and dissatisfactions. In loneliness. In alienation. And it is not so much race that determines us and our characters as it is our *cultures* and our having been sundered from them at birth. We live in the confusion of having grown up within great worlds that turned and boiled and streamed past all the steady rocks of culture along a route of dispersal like storm clouds climbing up through the rain forest over the vol' cano. Our beginnings were a volatile secret shielded from us by our parents and the societies they tried to choose and conform to and which we rejected perhaps more than they rejected us. We rebelled and instead pursued the vanishings of former times which we suspected of a grandeur that would illumine what we felt to be a paucity in the lives we were given. For Wind, be' ginning was in the spiritual passion and great learning of a min' isterial father, an American cleric fallen from the elite of Mao's own circle. For Water, it was the Japanese American commu' nity before the social and psychological cataclysm of the Camps—the supposition that there had been a rich enclave so' ciety, full of ebullient disclosures and sexual thirsts, growing out of the joy of being present in this new, un-Asian world. I talk with them and it's suddenly not so lonely for me, and I allow myself to measure my thoughts against theirs, to gauge sensibility and examine conscience in a way I don't always do with others. What this clarifies, what their friendship helps me to define, is my obsession *without* race, *without* the anxiousness of feeling diaspora and marginality. I feel bound all of a sudden, like raw earth to itself, wound around my own origin in a bath of first things.

WHEN I WAS FOUR, or perhaps younger, before the languages diverged, I saw a performance of *katarimono*, the recitative of Japanese ballad singers, who were themselves called *tayu*, or "master narrators." It was in Kahuku, in the plantation town on the North Shore of Oʻahu where my parents went with me after they'd left Volcano. I remember that all the adults used to gather in a movie theater on Saturday nights. My father would drive us over from Walkerville, the little cluster of plantation *luna* shacks just beside the main village, and we'd watch a movie with the others. One night, there was no movie. The auditorium was filled with only Japanese people rather than the mix of Filipinos, Chinese, Hawaiians, and Portuguese I was used to. They were dressed in *yukata*, in cotton, summer robes as if on their way to the bath. Yet, I could smell how clean everyone was already. When the social hubbub quieted down, a man in a formal *hakama*, a stiff, almost military gown of intricately sewn and shaped heavy cloth, undecorated in a dark, subdued color, stepped in front of the audience. He held a fan. His face was set. He wore black Japanese socks with white soles—*tabi*. He cinched the fan into the belt around his robe and sat with his legs folded under him. He bowed, touching his head to the mat spread on the wooden floor. He bowed again, touching his head to a bound, hand-stitched text he held against his head. He cleared his throat. He grasped his fan, snatching it out of his waistband, snapping it open, unfolding it, exposing a flash of brilliant golden color with the design of a pine tree on it. He furled it shut, using a decorous, feminine motion. He placed it closed on the mat in front of him. He began chanting. He began speaking. He told a story I could not understand. He was speaking in Japanese, rhythmically, chant-ing the story, speaking gutturally, then in falsetto, then whis-pering, almost singing, weeping, spitting, growling out his country romance. People were laughing, laughing in unison, brought together by the chanter, the storyteller. Then they were silent for a long time. A woman wept, then others, moaning quietly, keening. The men dropped their heads, shading their eyes with their hands. The storyteller picked up his fan. He un-furled it. The audience gasped, together as one, then began to applaud. A woman, her back bent, walking like a pigeon, shuffled up to the front and tossed some coins into a clattering wooden box. Then more came, men and women. My father gave me some coins, silver disks with eagles on them, and I walked up there too. I saw the singer up close, still sitting, his head bent forward in a formal bow, bending to each kindness, each coin tossed. I walked from the theater, holding my mother's hand, my father's hand, and I could still hear a woman sobbing, a man laughing, a group of relatives chatter-ing with excitement. *Erai tayu da neh!* they were saying, "What a great singer!" What a great teller of tales.

KUBOTA

F OR ALL THAT I had *not* been told about my family, there was yet one story that seemed to me always to have been told—a part of my upbringing, a telling that made it clear that I did come from some sort of emotional lineage, at least on my mother's side of things.

On December 8, 1941, the day after the Japanese attack on Pearl Harbor in Hawai'i, my maternal grandfather had barri- caded himself with his family—my grandmother, my teenage mother, her two sisters and two brothers—inside of his home in Lā'ie, a sugar plantation village on O'ahu's North Shore. This was my mother's father, a man most villagers called by his last name—Kubota. It could mean either "Wayside Field" or else

"Broken Dreams," depending on which ideograms he used. Kubota ran Lā'ie's general store, and the previous night, after a long day of bad news on the radio, some locals had come by, pounded on the front door, and made threats. One was said to have brandished a machete. They were angry and shocked, as was the whole nation, in the aftermath of the surprise attack. Kubota was one of the few Japanese Americans in the village and president of the local Japanese-language school. He had become a target for their rage and suspicion. A wise man, he locked all his doors and windows and did not open his store the next day, but stayed closed and waited for news from some official.

He was a Kibei, a Japanese American born in Hawai'i (a U.S. territory then, so he was thus a citizen) but who was subsequently sent back by his father for formal education in Hiroshima, Japan—their home province. *Kibei* is written with two ideograms in Japanese—one is the word for "return" and the other is the word for "rice." Poetically, it means one who returns from America, known as "the Land of Rice" in Japanese (by contrast, Chinese immigrants called their new home "Mountain of Gold").

Kubota was graduated from a Japanese high school and then came back to Hawai'i as a teenager. He spoke English—and a Hawaiian creole version of it at that—with a Japanese accent. But he was well liked and good at numbers, scrupulous and hardworking like so many immigrants and children of immigrants. Castle and Cooke, a grower's company that ran the sugarcane business along the North Shore, first hired him as a stock boy and then appointed him to run one of its company stores. He did well, had the trust of management and labor—not an easy accomplishment in any day—married, had children, and had begun to exert himself in community affairs and excel in his own recreations. He put together a Japanese community organization that backed a Japanese-language school for children and sponsored teachers from Japan. Kubota boarded many of them, in succession, in his own home. This made dinners a silent affair for his talkative, Hawaiian-bred children, as their stern *sensei,* or "teacher," was nearly always at table and their own abilities in the Japanese language were as delinquent as their attendance. While Kubota and the *sensei* rattled on about things Japanese, speaking Japanese, his children hurried through their suppers and tried to run off early to listen to the radio shows.

After dinner, while the *sensei* graded exams seated in a wicker chair in the spare room and his wife and children gathered around the radio in the front parlor, Kubota sat on the screened porch outside, reading the local Japanese newspapers. He finished reading about the same time that he finished the tea he drank for his digestion—a habit he'd acquired in Japan— and then he'd get out his fishing gear and spread it out on the plank floors. The wraps on his rods needed to be redone, the gears in his reels needed oil, and, once through with those tasks, he'd painstakingly wind on hundreds of yards of new line. Fishing was his hobby and his passion. He spent weekends camping along the North Shore beaches with his children, setting up umbrella tents, packing a rice pot and *hibachi* along for meals. And he caught fish. *Ulua* mostly, the huge surf-feeding fish known as the jack crevalle on the Mainland, but he'd go after almost anything in its season. In Kawela, a plantation-owned bay nearby, he fished for mullet with a throw-net, stalking the bottom-hugging, gray-backed schools as they gathered at the stream mouths and in the freshwater springs. In an outrigger out beyond the reef, he'd try for *aku*—the skipjack tuna prized for steaks and, sliced raw and mixed with fresh seaweed and cut onions, for *sashimi* salad. In Kahaluʻu and Kaʻaʻawa and on an offshore rock locals called Goat Island, he loved to go torching, stringing lanterns on bamboo poles stuck in the sand to attract *kūmū,* the red goatfish, as they schooled at night just inside the reef. But in Lāʻie on Laniloa Point near Kahuku, the north-ernmost tip of Oʻahu, he cast twelve- and fourteen-foot surf rods for the huge varicolored and fast-swimming *ulua* as they pursued schools of squid and baitfish just beyond the biggest breakers and past the low sand flats wadable from the shore to nearly a half mile out. At sunset, against the western light, he looked as if he were walking on water as he came back, fish and rods slung over his shoulders, stepping along the rock and coral path just inches under the surface of a running tide.

When it was torching season, in December or January, he'd drive out the afternoon before and stay with old friends, the Tanakas or Yoshikawas, shopkeepers like him who ran stores near the fishing grounds. They'd have been preparing for weeks, selecting and cutting their bamboo poles, cleaning the hurricane lanterns, tearing up burlap sacks for the cloths they'd soak with kerosene and tie onto sticks they'd poke into the soft sand of the shallows. Once lit, touched off with a Zippo lighter, these would be the torches they'd use as beacons to at-tract the schooling fish. In another time, they might have made up a dozen paper lanterns of the kind mostly used for decorat-ing the summer folk dances outdoors on the grounds of the Buddhist church during O-Bon, the Festival for the Dead. But now, wealthy and modern and efficient killers of fish, Tanaka and Kubota used rag torches and Colemans and cast rods with tips made of Tonkin bamboo and butts of American-spun fiberglass. After just one good night, they might bring back a prize bounty of a dozen burlap bags filled with scores of bloody, rigid fish delicious to eat and even better to give away as gifts to friends, family, and special customers.

It was a Monday night, the day after Pearl Harbor, and there was a rattling knock at the front door. Two FBI agents presented themselves, showed identification, and took my grandfather in for questioning in Honolulu. No one knew what had happened or what was wrong. But there was a roundup going on of all those in the Japanese American community sus⁄ pected of sympathizing with the enemy and worse. My grand⁄ father was suspected of espionage, of communicating with offshore Japanese submarines launched from the attack fleet days before war began. Torpedo planes and escort fighters, dec⁄ orated with the insignia of the rising sun, had taken an ap⁄ proach route from northwest of Oʻahu directly across Kahuku Point and on toward Pearl. They had strafed an auxiliary air station near the fishing grounds my grandfather loved and de⁄ stroyed a small gun battery there, killing three men. Kubota was known to have sponsored and harbored Japanese nationals in his own home. He had a radio. He had wholesale access to firearms. Circumstances and an undertone of racial resentment had combined with wartime hysteria in the aftermath of the tragic naval battle to cast suspicion on the loyalties of my grand⁄ father and all other Japanese Americans. The FBI reached out and pulled hundreds of them in for questioning in dragnets cast throughout the West Coast and Hawaiʻi.

My grandfather was lucky, he was let go after only a few days. But others were not as fortunate. Hundreds, from small communities in Washington, California, Oregon, and Hawaiʻi, were rounded up and, after what appeared to be routine ques⁄ tioning, shipped off under Justice Department orders to hold⁄ ing centers in Leupp on the Navajo Indian Reservation in

Arizona, in Fort Missoula in Montana, and on Sand Island in
Honolulu Harbor. There were other special camps on Maui in
Haʻikū and on Hawaiʻi—the Big Island—in my own home
village of Volcano.

Many of these men—it was exclusively the Japanese
American men suspected of ties to Japan who were initially
rounded up—did not see their families again for over four years.
Under a suspension of due process that was only after-the-fact
ruled as warranted by military necessity, they were, if only tem-
porarily, "disappeared" in Justice Department prison camps
scattered in particularly desolate areas of the United States designated as militarily "safe." These were grim forerunners of the
assembly centers and concentration camps for the 120,000
Japanese American evacuees that were to come later.

I am Kubota's eldest grandchild, and I remember him as
a lonely, habitually silent old man who lived with us in our
home near Los Angeles for most of my childhood and adolescence. It was the fifties, and my parents had emigrated from
Hawaiʻi to the Mainland in the hope of a better life away from
the old sugar plantation. They had left Volcano after losing the
store and property, settling in Kahuku. In a few years, when I
was five, my father came to study electronics at a trade school in
Los Angeles. After a year of this, he got a regular job and was
able to send for us, and we were a family again, living in apart-
ments around midtown. Then, after some success, my parents
were able to buy a suburban home and had sent for my maternal grandparents and taken them in too. And it was my grandparents who did the work of the household while my mother
and father worked at their salaried city jobs. My grandmother
cooked and sewed, washed our clothes, and knitted in the front
room under the light of a huge lamp with a bright, three-way

bulb. Kubota raised a flower garden, read up on soils and grasses in gardening books, and planted a zoysia lawn in front and a dichondra one in back. He planted a small patch near the rear block wall with green onions, eggplant, white Japanese radishes, and cucumber. While he hoed and spaded the loam-less, clayey earth of Los Angeles, he sang particularly plangent songs in Japanese about plum blossoms and bamboo groves.

Sometime in the mid-sixties, after a dinner during which, as always, he had been silent while he worked away at a meal of fish and rice spiced with drabs of Chinese mustard and cat-sup thinned with soy sauce, Kubota took his own dishes to the kitchen sink and washed them up. He took a clean jelly jar out of the cupboard—the glass was thick and its shape squatty like an old-fashioned. He reached around to the hutch below, where he kept his bourbon. He made himself a drink and retired to the living room, where I was expected to join him for "talk story"—the Hawaiian idiom for chewing the fat.

I was a teenager and, though I was bored listening to sto-ries I'd heard often enough before at holiday dinners, I was dutiful. I took my spot on the couch next to Kubota and heard him out. Usually, he'd tell me about his schooling in Japan, where he learned *judo* along with mathematics and literature. He'd learned the *soroban* there—the abacus which was the orig-inal pocket calculator of the Far East—and that, along with his strong, *jūdō*-trained back, got him his first job in Hawai'i. This was the moral. "Study *ha-ahd*," he'd say with pidgin emphasis. "Learn read good. Learn speak da kine *good* English." The mes-sage is the familiar one taught to any children of immigrants—succeed through education. And imitation.

But this time, Kubota reached down into his past and told me a different story. I was thirteen by then, and I suppose he

thought me ready for it. He told me about Pearl Harbor, how
the planes flew in wing after wing of formations over his old
house in Lā'ie in Hawai'i, and how, the next day, after Roosevelt had made his famous "Day of Infamy" speech about the
treachery of the Japanese, the FBI agents had come to his door
and taken him in, hauled him off to Honolulu for questioning
and held him without charge. I thought he was lying. I thought
he was making up a kind of horror story to shock me and give
his moral that much more starch. But it was true. I asked
around. I brought it up during history class in junior high
school and my teacher, a Jew, after silencing me and taking me
aside to the back of the room, told me that it was indeed so. I
asked my mother and she said it was true. I asked my schoolmates, who laughed and ridiculed me for being so ignorant. We
lived in a Japanese American community and the parents of
most of my classmates were the Nisei who had been interned
as teenagers all through the war. But there was a strange silence
around all of this. There was a hush, as if one were invoking
the ill powers of the dead. No one cared to speak about the
evacuation and relocation for very long. It wasn't in our history
books, though we were studying World War II at the time. It
wasn't in the family albums of the people I knew and whom
I'd visit while spending weekends with friends. And it wasn't
anything that the family talked about or allowed me to keep
bringing up either. I was given the facts, told sternly and point-
edly that "it was war" and that "nothing could be done."
Shikata ga nai is the phrase in Japanese, a kind of resolute and
determinist pronouncement on how to deal with inexplicable
tragedy. I was to know it but not to dwell on it. Japanese
Americans were busy trying to forget it ever happened and were
having a hard enough time building their new lives after

"Camp." It was as if we had no history for four years and the relocation was something unspeakable.

But Kubota would not let it go. In session after session, for months it seemed, he pounded away at his story. He wanted to tell me the names of the FBI agents. He went over their questions and his responses again and again. He'd tell me how one would try to act friendly toward him, offering him cigarettes while the other, who hounded him with accusations and threats, left the interrogation room. *Good cop/bad cop,* I thought to myself, already superficially streetwise from having heard the stories black classmates told of the Watts riots and from having watched too many episodes of "Dragnet" and "The Mod Squad." But Kubota was not interested in my experiences. I was not made yet and he was determined that his stories be part of my making. He spoke quietly at first, mildly, but once he was into his narrative and after his drink was down, his voice would rise and quaver with resentment and he'd make his accusations. He gave his testimony to me and I held it at first cautiously in my conscience as if it were an heirloom too delicate to expose to strangers and anyone outside of the world Kubota made with his words. "I give you story now," he once said. "And you learn speak good, eh?" It was my job, as the disciple of his preaching I had then become, Ananda to his Buddha, to reassure him with a promise. "You learn speak good like the Dillingham," he'd say another time, referring to the wealthy scion of the grower family who had once run, unsuccessfully, for one of Hawai'i's first senatorial seats. Or he'd then invoke a magical name, the name of one of his heroes, a man he thought particularly exemplary and righteous. "Learn speak dah good Ingrish like *Mistah Inouye,*" Kubota shouted. "He *lick* dah Dillingham even in debate. I saw on *terrebision* my

self." He was remembering the debates before the first senatorial election just before Hawai'i was admitted to the Union as
its fiftieth state. "You *tell* story," Kubota would end. And I
had my injunction.

The town we settled in after the move from Hawai'i is
called Gardena, the independently incorporated city south of
Los Angeles and north of San Pedro Harbor. At its northern
limit, it borders on Watts and Compton—black towns. To the
southwest are Torrance and Redondo Beach—white towns. To
the rest of L.A., Gardena is primarily famous for having
legalized five-card-draw poker after the war. On Vermont Boulevard, its eastern border, there is a dingy little Vegas-like strip of
card clubs with huge parking lots and flickering neon signs that
spell out THE RAINBOW and THE HORSESHOE in timed sequences of varicolored lights. The town is only secondarily famous as the largest community of Japanese Americans in the
United States outside of Honolulu, Hawai'i. When I was in
high school there, it seemed to me that every Sansei kid I knew
wanted to be a doctor, an engineer, or a pharmacist. Our fathers
were gardeners or electricians or nurserymen or ran small businesses catering to other Japanese Americans. Our mothers
worked in civil service for the city or as cashiers for Thrifty
Drug. What the kids wanted was a good job, good pay, a fine
home, and no troubles. No one wanted to mess with the law—
from either side—and no one wanted to mess with language or
art. They all talked about getting into the right clubs so that they
could go to the right schools. There was a certain kind of same-
ness, an intensely enforced system of conformity.

We did well in chemistry and in math, no one who was
Japanese but me spoke in English class or in History unless
called upon, and no one talked about World War II. The day

after Robert Kennedy was assassinated after winning the Cali'
fornia Democratic primary, we worked on calculus and elected
class coordinators for the prom, featuring the 5th Dimension.
We avoided grief. We avoided government. We avoided strong
feelings and dangers of any kind. Once punished, we tried to
maintain a concerted emotional and social discipline and would
not willingly seek to fall out of the narrow margin of protective
favor again.

But when I was thirteen, in junior high, I'd not under'
stood why it was so difficult for my classmates, those who were
themselves Japanese American, to talk about the relocation.
They had cringed too when I tried to bring it up during our
discussions of World War II. I was Hawaiian-born. They were
Mainland-born. Their parents had been in Camp, had been the
ones to suffer the complicated experience of having to distance
themselves from their own history and all things Japanese in
order to make their way back and into the American social and
economic mainstream. It was out of this sense of shame and a
fear of stigma I was only beginning to understand that the Nisei
had silenced themselves. And for their children, among whom
I grew up, they wanted no heritage, no culture, no contact with
a defiled history. I recall the silence very well. The Japanese
American children around me were burdened in a way I was
not. Their injunction was silence. Mine was to speak.

Away at college, in another protected world and in its
own way as magical to me as the Hawai'i of my childhood, I
dreamed about my grandfather. I would be tired from studying
languages, practicing German conjugations or scripting an
army's worth of Chinese ideograms on a single sheet of paper,
and Kubota would come to me as I drifted off into sleep. Or,
I would be walking across the newly mown ball field in back

of my dormitory, cutting through a streetside phalanx of ancient eucalyptus trees on my way to visit friends off-campus, and I would think of him, his anger, and his sadness.

I don't know myself what makes someone feel that kind of need to have a story they've lived through be deposited somewhere, but I can guess. I think about *The Iliad, The Odyssey,* the *History of the Peloponnesian War* of Thucydides, and a myriad of other books I've studied. A character, almost a *topos* he occurs so often, is frequently the witness who gives personal testimony about an event the rest of his community cannot even imagine. The Sibyl is such a character. And Philomela, the maid whose tongue is cut out so that she will not tell that she has been raped by her own brother-in-law, the king of Thrace. There are the dime novels, the epic blockbusters Hollywood makes into miniseries, and then there are the plain, relentless stories of witnesses who have suffered through horrors major and minor that have marked and changed their lives. I haven't myself talked to Holocaust victims, but I've read their survival stories and their stories of witness and been revolted and moved by them. My father-in-law tells me his war stories again and again and I listen. A Mennonite who set aside the strictures of his own church in order to serve, he was a marine codeman in the Pacific during World War II, in the Signal Corps on Guadalcanal, Morotai, and Bougainville. He was part of the island-hopping maneuver MacArthur had devised to win the war in the Pacific. He saw friends killed when bombs exploded not ten yards away. When he was with the 298th Signal Corps attached to the Thirteenth Air Force, he saw plane after plane come in and crash, just short of the runway, killing their crews, setting the jungle ablaze with oil and gas fires. Emergency wagons would scramble, bouncing over newly bulldozed land men

had used just the afternoon before for a football game. Every
time we go fishing together, whether it's in a McKenzie boat
drifting for salmon in Tillamook Bay or taking a lunch break
from wading the riffles of a stream in the Cascades, my father-
in-law tells me about what happened to him and the young men
in his unit. One was a Jewish boy from Brooklyn. One was a
foul-mouthed kid from Kansas. They died. And he *has* to tell
me. And I *have* to listen. It's a ritual payment the young owe
their elders who have survived. The evacuation and relocation
is something like that.

Kubota, my grandfather, grew sick of life in Los Angeles and, without my grandmother, went home to Hawai'i before I graduated from high school. He wanted to be near the
sea again. He missed his foods and his "talk story" sessions
with the old-timers and the neighbors. He wrote me a few
times, sent celebration money for my graduation. Once I was
in college, my grandmother rejoined him there. Within only a
few years, he fell ill with Alzheimer's disease and became
strangely diminished in mind for some time before he died.

At the house he'd built on Kamehameha Highway in
Hau'ula, a seacoast village just down the road from Lā'ie where
he had his store, he'd wander out from the garage or greenhouse
where he'd set up a workbench, and trudge down to the beach
or up toward the line of pines he'd planted while employed by
the Work Projects Administration during the thirties. Kubota
thought he was going fishing. Or he thought he was back at
work for Roosevelt planting pines as a wind- or soilbreak on the
windward flank of the Ko'olau Mountains, emerald monoliths
rising out of sea and canefields from Waialua to Kāne'ohe.
When I visited, my grandmother would send me down to the
beach to fetch him. Or I'd run down Kam Highway a quarter

mile or so and find him hiding in the canefield by the roadside, counting stalks, measuring circumferences in the claw of his thumb and forefinger. The look on his face was confused or concentrated—I didn't know which. But I guessed he was going fishing again. I'd grab him and walk him back to his house on the highway. My grandmother would shut him in a room.

Within a few years, Kubota had a stroke and survived it, then he had another one and was completely debilitated. The family decided to put him in a nursing home in Kahuku, just set back from the highway, within a mile or so of Kahuku Point and the Tanaka Store where he'd had his first job as a stock boy. He lived there three years, and I visited him once with my aunt. He was like a potato that had been worn down by cooking. Everything on him—his eyes, his teeth, his legs and torso— seemed like it had been sloughed away. What he had been was mostly gone now and I was looking at the nub of a man. In a wheelchair, he grasped my hands and tugged on them—violently. His hands were still thick, and, I believed, strong enough to lift me out of my own seat into his lap. He murmured something in Japanese—he'd long ago ceased to speak any English. My aunt and I cried a little, and we left him.

I remember walking out on the black asphalt of the parking lot of the nursing home. It was heat-cracked and eroded already, and grass had veined itself into the interstices. There were coconut trees around, a canefield I could see across the street, and the ocean I knew was pitching a surf just beyond it. The green Ko'olaus came up behind us. Somewhere nearby, alongside the beach, there was an abandoned airfield in the middle of the canes. As a child, I'd come upon it while playing one day, and my friends and I kept returning to it, day after day, playing war or sprinting games or coming to fly kites. I recognize it even now when I see it on TV—it's used as a site for action scenes in the detective shows Hollywood always sets in the Islands: a helicopter chasing the hero racing away in a Ferrari, or gun dealers making a clandestine rendezvous on the abandoned runway. It was the old airfield strafed by Japanese planes the day the major flight attacked Pearl Harbor. It was the airfield the FBI thought my grandfather had targeted in his night-fishing and signaling with the long surf poles he'd stuck in the sandy bays near Kahuku Point.

Kubota died a short while after I visited him, but not, I thought, without giving me a final message. I was on the Main-land, in California studying for Ph.D. exams, when my grand-mother called me with the news. It was a relief. He'd suffered from his debilitation a long time and I was grateful he'd gone. I went home for the funeral and gave the eulogy. My grand-mother and I took his ashes home in a small, heavy metal box wrapped in a black *furoshiki*—a large silk scarf. She showed me the name the priest had given to him on his death, scripted with a calligraphy brush on a long, narrow talent of plain wood. Buddhist commoners, at death, are given priestly names, re-ceived symbolically into the clergy. The idea is that, in their next life, one of scholarship and leisure, they might meditate and attain the enlightenment the religion is aimed at. *Shaku Shūchi,* the ideograms read. It was Kubota's Buddhist name, in-corporating characters from his family and given names. It meant "Shining Wisdom of the Law." He died on Pearl Har-bor Day, December 7, 1983.

After years, after I'd finally come back to live in Volcano again, only once did I dream of Kubota, my grandfather. It was the same night I'd heard that H.R. 442, the redress bill for Japanese Americans, had been signed into law. In my dream that night, Kubota was torching, and he sang a Japanese song, a querulous and wavery folk ballad, as he hung paper lanterns on bamboo poles stuck into the sand in the shallow water of the lagoon behind the reef near Kahuku Point. Then he was at a worktable, smoking a hand-rolled cigarette, letting it dangle from his lips, Bogart style, as he drew, daintily and skillfully, with a narrow trim brush, ideogram after ideogram on a score of paper lanterns he had hung in a dark shed to dry. He had painted a talismanic mantra onto each lantern, the ideogram for the word "red" in Japanese, a bit of art blended with some superstition, a piece of sympathetic magic appealing to the magenta coloring on the rough skins of the schooling, night-feeding fish he wanted to attract to his baited hooks. He strung them from pole to pole in the dream then, hiking up his khaki worker's pants so his white ankles showed, and wading through the shimmering black waters of the sand flats and then the reef. "The moon is leaving, leaving," he sang in Japanese. "Take me deeper in the savage sea." He turned and crouched like an ice-racer then, leaning forward so that his unshaven face almost touched the light film of water. I could see the light stubble of beard like a fine gray ash covering the lower half of his face. I could see his gold-rimmed spectacles. He held a small wooden boat in his cupped hands and placed it lightly on the sea and pushed it away. One of his lanterns was on it and, written in small, neat rows like a sutra scroll, it had been decorated with the silvery names of all our dead.

VOLCANOLOGY:
DEEP MYSTERY

I TREKKED OUT with Ken Hon, a USGS geologist who took me out to the shield of Kūpaianaha sometime during my first year back in Volcano. It is the latest of a succession of lava shields built by Kīlauea's eruptive activity. We carried packs, a heavy tripod, and some kind of tough measuring instrument with dials and knobs to monitor the newly forming magnetic field of the lava flow out there as it developed orientation and a characteristic pattern in relation to magnetic north. I went as an observer, mainly interested in getting a look at the shield itself, perhaps gazing over the lip of the crater rim into the lava lake of Kūpaianaha. For this I walked miles across gray and brown lavas, passing over terrain that looked like landfill clogged with a brown refuse the texture of drying dog food, crunching over shelly *pāhoehoe* and falling through up to my calves, crossing the brittle remnants of small lava pools which had ended in large and hardened paddies shaped like the crowns of gigantic jellyfish flopped onto a black sand beach.

We hiked across a large lava plain, cutting in at the edge of a burned piece of the forest, scrambling over pileups of burned and fallen *'ōhi'a,* dropping down to a magnificent view that stretched out for miles over nothing but a black field of new lavas. Looking upslope toward Mauna Loa far in the distance, the only other features on the land were a low-lying spatter rampart topped with green tree ferns and the pyramid-shaped cone of Pu'u 'Ō'ō smoking with a trail of vapor on the near horizon. The shield was the rim of land between them, the upwelling around a lava lake that had built up the level of the land with successive layers of overflow. There was a crater filled with a lake of lava that I couldn't see from where I stood. After almost fifty different eruptive episodes starting from 1983, a lava lake had formed in 1986 near the vent site about thirteen miles east of Halema'uma'u. The eruption had become continuous, and the lake came to be surrounded by a dome of new lavas swelling over the site. Things had begun with a brief but spectacular fissure eruption that ran along ground cracks between Nāpau Crater and an old lava cone named Kalalua. Fissure eruptions shot from within the spreading crevices on the forest floor, at first singeing and then burning down the trees, ferns, and brush around it, building up a desertlike clearing full of gray cinderfall. After that, high-fountaining eruptions at Pu'u 'Ō'ō came, burning down larger stands of *'ōhi'a,* showering the ground with new, black cinder rock that smoked with the heat and vapor of escaping gases. Fire-fountaining would give way to inactivity, and then the cycle would start again, repeating itself in that pattern for three and a half years until this all gave way to the lava lake.

Underneath the vent site, a single vertical pipe fed all erup-tions. It was a conduit fifty feet in diameter filling with magma before fountaining episodes, then expelling, then dropping in level for a few weeks until it filled again just before another eruption.

We had been away on the Mainland, and during that time, eruptions had thrown up a spatter cone eight hundred feet high. It was a dark, conical mountain, its sides sulphur-stained and unstable, its open center steaming with hot, vol-canic vapor. Scientists and photographers had hiked out to it, taken measurements, written observations, and collected gas samples from the clouds escaping from the cone. At night, a red luminescence visible for miles around rose up from under its plume. Hawaiian elders tapped to name it had called the cone Puʻu ʻŌʻō, which meant hill of the ʻōʻō bird, an extinct honeycreeper of the rain forest. One photographer took him-self and a partner out there and stood, for some hours, on one of the rock ledges near its rim. He planned to shoot upward toward the lip of the cone where his partner perched himself on a pile of cinders crumbling under his feet. They waited past nightfall and captured on film a luminous radiance ris-ing upward from lavas snaking around in a little pool of lavas below. It was a burning cloud of methane gas, almost all blues but rimmed with a tinge of red-yellow at its outer edges, a kind of rising Niagara of fire levitating out of the cone. In the photo, his partner's silhouette looked like a rendering of god from the *Bhagavadgita,* Vishnu arrived out of fire in an even greater wheel of fire, piping a song of worlds to come. He stood just this side of its burning edge, the deep purple film of light only inches away. Inside its flow, a meter or two from his eyebrows, a column of flame burned at a temperature of more than 900 degrees. He would have vaporized like a moth had he stood a few feet closer.

Tourists and locals fell in love with what they could see even from as far as the highway, miles from the blossom itself. They would stop at the wooden fence of a grassy turnout along Volcano Highway across from the Hirano Store at Glenwood and gawk for a few minutes, snapping photos of the steaming hill, a black piece from inside of the earth thrown up against the long gray edge of the island. A few cattle grazed in the grasslands of the foreground, and the country rolled away under the emerald patches of *kīpukas,* little remnant islands of the forest thick with ferns in the distance. Whenever I'd stop to look or steal a glance speeding along the road, the cone looked to me like a warrior's helmet, medieval Japanese, and its ribbon of vapor and smoke seemed its feudal banner of identity. The land was a new joint in a global tectonics, a node of earth adding to itself like the stand of yellow bamboo that sprouted up new shoots beside the highway at Glenwood. The cattle were a bucolic eighteenthcentury Anglocentric touch, and the deepfocus, panoramic view I saw shaped a syncretic pastoral, more stark than any Luminist's, that hung in a mental gallery I was just beginning to fill.

In 1986, the pipe underlying the vent ruptured, and lavas broke out at the base of the cone, cracking the ground as it formed a new route to eruption. There were fissure outbreaks, lots of spattering, and then activity came to a site completely new about two miles farther down the East Rift Zone from Pu'u 'Ō'ō. There, lava spilled and eddied out with no spectacular fountaining, eventually forming a little, perched lava pond, a small lake of orange light bordered by a low rim of slathered, solidified lava that held it in—kind of a lava-cream pie in its crackled gray crust. But this gave way too—to an even larger lake, like the one inside of Halema'uma'u that Mark Twain saw during the previous century. Hawaiians named the new landform Kūpaianaha, meaning "mysterious" or "extraordinary."

In aerial photographs, the lake looked like a huge gray kidney lying on its side, swirled with a hardening froth, pumping itself full and draining lava to the sea through a long tube at its expulsion end. It had the shape of a gigantic razor clam funneling lava-sand through its neck, which was long and thick and shaped like a horse's penis. At low ebb, seen from a helicopter spindling in the air above the lava column tucked far down the steep and craggy walls of its embankments, the pond seemed a brilliant red fungus puffed to fill the fluted hollow of a decaying log in the Oregon woods. But, no matter what analogy I floundered for, they all took growth and fecundity as traits. Its image attracted comparisons to the biological world and to the sublime horrors of the body at first violated and then understood. There was *kapu* involved, breaking taboo. Standing over the swirling lake, I remembered a poem, written by a contemporary, that told of Italian Renaissance painter Luca Signorelli seeking the body's pure internal light, carving into the cadaver of his own dead son.

I stood at the lip of the lava shield, just outside of a fissure line that ran in a jagged loop around the rim. Ken Hon waved his arm—*hard*.

"Stand back of that line," he said casually. "In case it cracks off."

I nodded, then moved back obediently, feeling more con‑ trite than fearful. There was a quaking presence in the land. Kūpaianaha was the manifestation of something that grew from much deeper within the earth, from within the boiling core of the planet itself. I thought of it as a long‑stemmed flower, an orange chanterelle blooming from inside a cache of newly hardened lavas, its neck reaching down two miles or more, through a ribbonlike system of piping, to another gi‑ gantic bulb of magma that was still another unseen blossom surrounded in new earth. This was the magma chamber that served as the reservoir for all the current eruptive activity. It was the "root" source of Kīlauea's splendor, a rhizome of man‑ tle material far out of reach to anything except seismic instru‑ ments. It was so hot—about 2000 degrees Fahrenheit—that there were those who were thinking of ways to make use of it to heat and power hotels and airports not yet built. It seemed to them a source of wealth and worth the scheming, but, to me, it was rich enough as mystery, a sublimity chambered into the earth and made visible as a violent, arterial light under the hardening surface of the lava lake I saw into.

A thick, reptilian cloud of smoke, as if from ten thou‑ sand firecrackers, rose from the pit below. Under its long shadow, I could see glassy gray mounds and black hummocks of new lava shimmering in the light, acidic rain that fell upon them. There was a thick, thrashing sound—like that of a high winter surf—emanating from the rocky amphitheater below that mingled with the velocities of wind dervishing around. There were mushroomed crags and cracked rock all around me. The ground was treacherous, newsprung earth, damp and

fungal, stained yellow and white on the near bank, magma separated into its components of lava and gas. I took in bites of
air that was damp and sulphurous, hurting my lungs as I
breathed. I felt a strange, internal whispering that seemed to
enter my body from a source deep in the huge, minelike pit
gouged into the rock I was looking at, a fuming canyon that
dropped away about a hundred feet below the surface where I
was standing. A curl of fear swirled up and cuffed my ankles.
I chattered notes into a handheld tape recorder. Abyssal gray
tiers of rock fell away from the rotting walls of the crater. There
was the flat, tearing surface of a dirty two acres or so—a lake
of primal matter—churning and leaping in seams and red eddies, boiling up in occasional incandescent domes of fire. At
a loss for feeling so much awe, I quoted the modernist poet
Wallace Stevens.

"Tigers in red weather," I said into the Sony recorder. "A
drunken sailor catches tigers in red weather."

I stood on the shore of pure creation. Like my child
Alexander begging for more raisins or soup for his rice, banging
his spoon on the dining table, I wanted to say something else.

The lake boiled and skinned over, dividing the shields
of its hardening surface into the huge slats and scales of a
sleeping, metaphysical dragon. It made itself more and more
and more. It boiled again, lavishing the air with a pustule of
orange, a dome of emerging gas flecked with small crusts of
black rock that just the moment before had been part of the
skinned surface of the lake. A hundred feet above, a full acre
away, I heard a muffled implosion, a far-off sound dissyn-
chronous with the bursting. It was a thing of delay like the
shearing thundercrack that, during a storm, reaches your living room seconds after a splash of lightning floods the picture

COLONIAL

Faith

VOLCANO CAME to be a kind of faith to me after a while. We came and went so many times, but it became the place I *wanted* to come back to, to which I believed I *could* return. I needed it like an identity, a way to mark myself. "I was born in Volcano . . ." began the morning chant in my head, like "I am a Jew" or "My parents came from Ennis, county Clare," to others. Like a pilgrim bowing toward Mecca, I wanted a prayer to be the anchor of my own presence to myself and in a renewable relation to something much greater. So, Volcano— its rain forest, villagers, and calderas—came to mean a preserve of identity and consciousness to me, a thing almost like a faith. I'd meet strangers and say, "I am from Volcano," and feel my soul bow toward a memory of Mauna Loa rising above a skirt of clouds, bruised at the base with rain.

And yet this was all so silly. How can one derive a sense of self from something as lately invited into one's life as Volcano was for me? I was born there, but left it after only eight months. It was a mystery to me, and one for which I had no special curiosity until I was past thirty. Though my anxiety demanded that identity have its source in the unchanging—a place and attendant culture somehow "fixed" in the scheme of things, a thing easily characterized and identifiable—my thoughts ran otherwise, saying I belonged nowhere, that a shopping mall in Missouri or a trout stream in Oregon or a Hilo movie theater could explain me as well as the lava eddying out of the lake at the vent of Kūpaianaha. My father, after all, was buried in a cemetery in San Pedro, overlooking Los Angeles Harbor in California.

If you stood at his marker and gazed toward the water, a steel suspension bridge between the mainland and the naval shipyard at Terminal Island was usually visible through ocean vapors and the constant smog. His grave was near the curb of the road that wound through the hillside plots, and the mottling shade of a stand of eucalyptus trees swept his headstone at dusk. Nothing on it said he was a "local boy," that he raised *bonsai* on Wiliwili Street and shined shoes on McCully Street in Honolulu, that he was a son of Hawai'i who never came home.

The day of his funeral, a saxophone player from my brother's old blues band played "Amazing Grace" at the graveside while mourners tossed loose, single blossoms into the grave. My brother and I threw in the flower *lei* his sisters sent from Hawai'i. A cousin I hadn't seen since our childhood, an engi-

neer with three children and a Japanese wife—he lived three
miles from my parents' house and we'd seen him not once in
the five years he lived there—pressed a twenty-dollar bill into
my hand when I extended it for him to take. It threw me for a
loop and it was only the shock of the entire event that prevented
me from becoming incensed. The wind blew hard that day,
pressing the dark gabardine clothes against our bodies, whipping hair out of its oil-held shapes, and I tried to let its currents
carry my anger and give it no place to rest.

Years later, at a funeral in Kea'au for Shiotani-sensei, Volcano's old Japanese-language schoolteacher, I realized that my
cousin's gesture was only the crude execution of the Japanese
custom at mourning to give koden—cash in an envelope marked
with your name—at a booth manned by family friends or the
kumiai, a Buddhist funeral association. It was a way to pay for
expenses, to show respect and solidarity, to give a gift and to
share in the burden a little. In Hawai'i, in Japan, the practice
made sense and was ritualized to the point where people followed it without much fanfare, without awkwardness, with certainty and a kind of comfort that supported the flutterings of the
heart. You gave Kazu an envelope in a booth outside the Hongwanji temple. He bowed to you and you bowed back. An assistant—Yamamoto-san—opened the envelope immediately,
pulling the check from it or fanning out the bills if it was in
cash, saying your name and the dollar amount out loud, quietly but enough so Kazu could hear and record the information
in a ledger for the bereaved so that they could thank you with
a printed card sent through the mails much later. It all made
sense, it had dignity and sweep, and it had a cultural buoyancy
that I craved. My estranged cousin pressing the crisp bill into
my palm was delivering a relict—some faint, marginalized rep-

etition of all of this which had its real life, its fullest expression, back home in Hawai'i. At my father's funeral, though all of a genuine grief and honoring was there, there were only these lit, tle and ragged ways of finding symbols and completed processes, and the sadness had no way of entering my mind as anything more than the sincere white noise of modern loss, a consolational fumbling toward ceremony in diaspora. I felt shame, embarrassed for everyone, and I thought of Hawai'i. Boyishly, I said I would live out my grief by going back, as if to retrieve some honor. I wanted to look upon life, upon death, and pass both of them by with less blinkering of the eyes. I came to Volcano.

Colonial

In a preface to one of his nonfiction books, the Caribbean au, thor V. S. Naipaul writes that he travels (to India, to Iran, to the American South, etc.) because "it became the substitute for the mature social experience—the deepening knowledge of a society," which he was deprived of by his background and by the nature of his experience. He started out as a colonial, trav, eling in a world still ruled by "colonial ideas," he says, uncer, tain of himself and undefined and yet bound up in the attitudes of a tightly circumscribed world which dictated how its citizens were supposed to behave, putting limits on the imagination and what roles in society the colonial self could play. On a jour, nalist's assignment in Surinam, when the official (like him, In, dian by blood) showing him around remarked that Naipaul was the first of them to come on a mission usually reserved for the Dutch, Naipaul became a *post*colonial—one absented from the blindered repose of an innocent belonging to a conquered place and a people. A stolen child.

Not continuing to live *within* that world, he fell apart from it without really ever going back. And yet, he found no alternative society to be part of away from it. He doesn't say it, but I conclude that he must have decided against allowing himself to completely assimilate into English culture as well, though he has often been accused of joining it. He refused to wear what Martinican essayist Frantz Fanon describes as that "white, psychological mask" over the dark skin on his own face so as to interpose something racially and politically neutral between it and that of the mystified, lettered, and nearly completely Eurocentric society which might have accepted him in London.

I project my own experience in America onto Naipaul's in England. On the Mainland, amidst the tweedy faculty, I cannot bring myself to translate my colonized and tropical beginnings into conversations at cocktail receptions after the visitor's lecture nor will I give accountings for my own proficiency in the language. I am not jolly. I do not fulfill expectations. Needless to say, I challenge this world of pipe-smoking scholars to refuse me too, and I, like Naipaul, excluded from the easily available alternatives, had no easy maturing into a complete social experience, no "deepening knowledge of society" except to continually hanker for one, recalling the invitations of my relatives in Hawai'i and the sublime beckonings of the volcano and the rain forest that would have, had I not acted on them, dwindled into nostalgia and become faint through time.

Instead, Volcano welcomed me, whatever I was, and I became, along with Cynthia, Alex, and Hudson, our baby who

was born there, something *added* to its society, part of a ge-
nealogical story that, for over thirty years, was interrupted and
then was taken up again an entire generation later. Volcano became for me what I had not finished getting from them. The
village was thus a living form of heaven, an afterlife that I
stepped into and took lessons from. Its villagers were to me all
prophets and angels. And I a traveler in their paradise.

Ebesu's

We had come to Volcano again for another year, and I wanted
to buy Cynthia a flower *lei*. She had just given birth to our second son, Hudson Hideo, named after our maternal grandfathers.
I went to Ebesu's, the old florist shop in Hilo on Keawe Street,
the ancient main street of the old, pre-*tsunami* downtown. My
aunt had mentioned Ebesu's a couple of times as the place where
one went to get flowers. I'd noticed it when I was shopping—
it was a huge concrete, garage-like space completely open to the
street. To close up shop, the workers simply pulled down a huge
slatted metal door and locked it shut as if it were a hangar. To
open, they rolled it back. It was always crammed with aproned
flower-ladies, plump Japanese women wearing reading glasses,
working over long tables cluttered with bundles of bright flowers and intricate fronds of choice greenery. They held their hands
together, twining needle and thread through stem and corolla of
luscious flowers like the fragrant plumeria, a ray of creamy petals
turning to yellow; white carnations like tiny bouquets of cool
crinoline skin; succulent vanda orchids that made a heavy pur-

ple sash as if the delicate flesh of a hundred lips and ears had been strung together in a splashy cummerbund.

I drove to town and parked on the street in front of the store, paid the meter, and walked into the bustling shop. I stopped a youngish clerk in jeans and a T-shirt, her legs en- capsulated in a pair of long black fisherman's boots. I told her I wanted to buy a *lei* for my wife.

"What kind of *lei*?" she asked.

"I don't know," I said. "Something special."

"All *lei* are special," she said smartly. "What's the oc- casion?"

I hadn't counted on this level of complexity. I'd expected some kind of choosing ceremony, perhaps a simple sequencing of preferences, but not anything having to do with suiting gar- land to occasion. I hesitated a moment, then replied slowly so I wouldn't stammer.

"She's just given birth to our second child," I said. "A boy," I added, wondering if that might influence anything, per- haps the color or style of *lei*.

The clerk looked at me strangely, in the way I came to re- alize meant that I'd foundered in my attempts to pass as a local. She was recalculating my identity. I noticed her eyes were some- what close together, almost crossed. They divulged no emotion, no thoughts. It was a look I often got from Japanese, particu- larly women, both in Hawai'i and on the Mainland. If their eyes weren't averted, they'd peer at me, stare a little, their eyes twin dark pools of mystery. The clerk turned away then, asking the older ladies for help with me. With me she could do nothing.

"Clara," the clerk shouted, walking away. "Will you help him, please? He wants to buy a *lei* for his wife who's just given birth!"

I heard a chorus of giggles from the women standing over the tables that surrounded me. A small woman with gray hair came away from one of the refrigerator cases and walked up to me. She stepped daintily with the short, pigeon-like gait I recognized as classic for the graceful and petite Japanese shop clerk.

"What's diss about a *lei* for your wife giving birt'?" she asked.

"My wife and I," I began, stammering, "our second, a boy . . ." I felt suddenly helpless. I knew that I'd made a very basic error, and I felt a shallow wave of panic washing through me. The chorus of old ladies tittered again. They were amused, but I felt ridicule.

"We don't usually buy *lei* at the birt' of a child, yeah?" said the small woman, smiling. I sensed kindness and felt relieved.

"Well, my aunt said to come here if I needed something for special occasions, yeah?" I said, slipping into pidgin, introducing the family tie.

"Your aunt is who?"

"Charlotte Goya," I said firmly, as one might have used the name of the President of the United States.

"Ohhh . . . Charlotte *Goya!*" the woman exclaimed, completely softened at last. "You dah nephew from dah Mainland, yeah? You dah one come back live Volcano, yeah? Ohhh . . . yeah, yeah. Charlotte your auntie. Charlotte Goya his auntie! He dah one come back from Mainland!"

The ladies threading *lei* ceased their tittering at me and began a chorus of *ohhs* and *ahhhs* and *yeah-yeahs,* interspersed with frequent nods and glances back and forth between each other. "He dah one," they murmured, and "Oh, dah Mainland nephew ass why." It was as if I had initially upset and put on guard a hive of assiduous bees, and then sent, finally, the right pheromone through. They rushed to pass it among one another, becoming quiet and receptive at last. I felt more relaxed myself.

"Well, if you like get your wife one *lei,* we get you one *lei!*" the small woman said. She was enthusiastic now, and I sensed her ease was inspired by condescension. All through my childhood, moving back and forth between Los Angeles and Hawai'i, I fought with other Japanese constantly over my iden-tity. And now, here again as an adult, I was still involved in combat with it again. What was I if neither *kotonk*—the deroga-tory, island-chauvinist term for a Mainland Japanese Ameri-can—nor "local boy"—the parental familiar for all favorite sons of Hawai'i? Was there anything else?

"Your grandfather, Torau Hongo, was quite a ladies' man, you know," the woman said, peering over her reading glasses at me, dropping my *lei* into a plastic bag. She dipped a hand into a plastic bucket of water and shook it over the flowers, then folded over the top and handed the bag to me, neat as you please, as if finishing off a kind of minuet for hands and flowers. It was a small, finicky performance, part of Hawai'i, part of the sign that you were among clever, courte-ous Japanese.

I heard the chorus of titters start up again. I sensed all the ladies glancing back and forth between each other, passing the pheromone along again.

"Yess," she said. "He had lots of wives and was well known at the teahouses!"

She turned away and back to her work then, marching alongside one of the tables covered in bundles of roses wrapped in plasticine, rows of spotted dendrobium orchid sprays drooping out of leaking buckets, lobster claws of heliconia ascending out of its rubbery stem like scarlet Buddhist saints in an ancient temple's frieze, ribbons and bows and potted miniature pines arranged like an orchestra on the far end. She reached out and scooped up a bundle of purple vanda *lei* and boosted them up to the crook of her arm so that it looked as if she'd dressed herself, like a Japanese courtesan, in a garment of trailing brocade, a heavy purple sleeve decorated in flowers. Still walking in the short, mincing steps of a bird, she crossed the entire length of Ebesu's cement/floor store behind the now silent chorus of old weaver maidens again making busy with their bountiful work.

Newspaper

Pennies mattered to us. We needed coupons from the local news/paper to save. We called the circulation office and got home de/livery started. The next day, a small, battered Japanese pickup truck drove by in the afternoon and dropped off a raincoat/yellow plastic box with the paper's logo stenciled onto its side. With the forest so quiet most of the time, the engine noise and the shifting of gears from the road in front of the house were sounds we all noticed right away. It was our delivery man, mak/ing the first, anonymous call of what was a constant small di/mension, a portal, of our daily life in Volcano.

I went out into the misty afternoon to the driveway, re/trieved the box from the ground, pulled out the rolled news/paper, and found a little slip with a mimeographed note on it. The greeting was from our carrier, a man with a Hawaiian first name and a Portuguese last name. I recalled a thick brown arm in a white T-shirt leaning out of the driver's-side window, flipping the box out onto the lava drive. I glanced up the road, wondering if I'd been his first or his last stop along our lane. I saw how my neighbor had nailed his drop box onto the utility pole at the entrance to his drive. Mine had nothing as available as that. There was a large lava rock with a green thatch of mosses. There were two steel posts so the drive could be chained off. There were two ʻōhiʻa saplings growing quite closely together, their trunks about the thick-ness of Alexander's stumpy legs. I jammed the plastic box be-tween them and it held.

Over the next few weeks, our carrier came every day at about the same time. Sometimes he'd bring a child along, some-times his wife or girlfriend. He'd be at the wheel, cruise his truck up to the box, and then a skinny brown boy or a teenage girl in shorts and a tank top would jump out with the paper and shove it in, trying not to glance up the drive into the house where we would be, Alexander playing on the rug of the liv-ing room, Hudson gurgling on his mat on the floor, while Cynthia was on the sofa reading a book. I'd be washing dishes or busy with some silliness talking on the telephone.

Frequently, the delivery might be our only contact with anyone all day long, and we began to look forward to it as an excitement, the retrieval an errand of delight. I'd see the old pickup drive up, and I'd dash out to get the news, as much to get some blood moving and some words from the outside world to get me going and out of my own dreaminess.

Alexander, by then a preschooler and accustomed to Mainland day care, was suddenly lonely without any other com-pany in Volcano, and he began to want to come out with me, insisting on dressing in his slicker, putting on sandals, and ask-ing me to open an umbrella, making a little theater out of the daily chore. If I was upstairs, reading or writing, when the paper came, Cynthia would take it as her opportunity and get to the paper first, reading it through, full of news and opinions about it before I'd even had my chance. She'd announce the baseball scores during dinner, cut out supermarket coupons, and circle stories she thought amusing. The arrival of the news-paper became a kind of ritual and its simple retrieval became an act that began to gather its own small tributes of competi-tion. Eventually, we found that it could even mean stepping into minor bits of myth as well.

Cynthia liked the beauty contest photographs, the obitu-aries, and the birthday and anniversary announcements. There was always a beauty contest of some kind, it seemed, and each time there was a winner, the paper would publish her portrait and often pose her with a court of the runners-up as well. Their names would be a mix of languages and nations—Maile Rosario Kauahikaua, Stephanie Haunani Yamashiro, Evelyn Marie Cachapero, and so on. If there was a feature or an in-terview, the winner would explain her background—"I was born in Hamakua and went to public school in Pāpaʻikou. My high school was St. Joseph's in Hilo. My mother is Puerto Rican–Filipina, my father is Hawaiian-Portuguese-English-Welsh-Scottish."

In the obituaries, the articles frequently attested to how beloved the deceased were by publishing their nicknames. While I sliced fish for dinner or washed rice, Cynthia would tell me about the vital statistics of Benjamin "Shorty" Pehana, eighty-one; Emma "Aunty Divine" Ah-fook Lee, ninety-two; Kojiro "Lefty" Imamura, seventy-eight; Kawika "Cruiser"

Esteves, sixty⁄two; and Harold "Errol Flynn" Kanakaole
Bridges. Their names would have come from their social lives,
from a time in high school, from fellow workers or bowling
pals, rarely from a church group. It made a loving familiarity
at death, and softened what would have been the kind of cold
and dry information that could make the dying nearly anony⁄
mous. I imagined gangs of drinking pals, dressed in catsup⁄red
or mustard⁄yellow rayon bowling shirts, their nicknames em⁄
broidered in a humble script over the top of a left shirt pocket—
"Sunday Punch," "Flash Gordon," "Itchy," "Kangaroo," and
"Queen Victoria." I imagined the deceased, laid out in an open
coffin at the funeral, trussed in a dark suit or a cocktail dress
by the mortuary, one eye closed in a wink to the weeping gang
of mourners.

"Hey, no cry," the endearments seemed to say. "My name
stay living yet." And people lived so long here, Cynthia noticed.

"Look at the ages of these people!" she'd marvel.

We wondered why it was. Was the myth about Hawai'i
being a paradise true? Here were working people frequently liv⁄
ing into their nineties. We theorized about reduced stress, about
the diet ("fish and *poi*," I joked, quoting a *hapa haole lū'au* song),
about the lack of well⁄demarcated temperate seasons all tending
to lengthen lives chronologically.

"You think maybe living all your life in one place might
help?" I asked.

"Staying where your friends are," Cynthia said, "with
family around. Yes—that would've helped me with Alex."

She was thinking about her hard time out in the Midwest,
nursing and caring for a newborn with no family around.

"But you ain't dead," I joked. "We no can count you for
statistics until time⁄of⁄decease." I shifted into my Hawaiian ac⁄

cent, trying to sound like a local bureaucrat speaking officiously in pidgin.

I thought of my father, living most of his life in L.A. with no close friends, speaking, in essence, a different language than most of the people around him. Being secure as part of things would tend to keep you happier, I thought. Village life. A name your friends would give you. A large family to share in your name. In itself an afterlife.

Trooper

One day, I noticed that our carrier had changed. The battered brown Toyota pickup with its growling engine was replaced with a shiny-new bronze Isuzu Trooper—a four-wheel-drive, middle-class family vehicle. For about a week, the new Isuzu Trooper came by, stopped, and a child would lean out of the cab with the paper and shove it into my yellow box. I noticed that a slender woman with long dark hair was driving, and that there were two or three children along with her distributed among the bench seats. I guessed their ages as ten and younger. They'd come by, go off to my neighbors, continue down to the end of the street, then turn around at the dead end and drive back out to the paved road. The vehicle seemed all full of gentle, curious eyes whenever it drove by. My thought was it was a pretty nice car for newspaper deliveries.

Once, I went out to fetch the paper when the Trooper had just made its turnaround and was bounding back toward me on the dozed lava road heading back off our little forest lane to the paved road. I waved at the woman driving, and she slowed down and stopped. I expected her to. People in the country do that. They talk to each other. They'd drive up beside a neighbor raking his driveway of dead *hāpu'u* limbs and stop to chew the fat a little. Or a Ranchero would wave at a Subaru going in the other direction and they'd both stop dead in the middle of the road, pulled up alongside of each other just so the drivers could talk, both of them leaning out of their windows.

The woman who drove up in the Trooper was dark-skinned with a long, thin face—part Hawaiian, I guessed—with deep, almost black circles under her eyes, which were pouchy, like she'd been crying. In my memory now, the kids jouncing in the seats around her seemed the same—with dark, pouchy eyes.

We spoke a brief moment, exchanging pleasantries. She explained how she'd just taken over the route. When the conversation paused to close, I was about to turn away and walk back to the house when she suddenly said something that startled me.

"You're the poet, aren't you?" she said. "I saw your name on the circulation list."

I nodded, not knowing what to say. It seemed so odd to hear a stranger announce my identity, speaking it out loud in the forest that way. I remember the rest of what she said was like a monologue.

"I read your poem about the Japanese graveyard in a magazine last year. It helped me. I could tell you knew about things, about sadness, and that you could feel it in the land. It just rises up, doesn't it? My daughter got sick with leukemia last year and we had to fight for over six months. She was sick until the end. She died last summer and I just couldn't snap out of it. It felt like we had *all* died. I even say it like that— *We* died last year—you know? Then I read your poem and it helped me. To know that people could live with sadness. And I took this paper route in Volcano just to get out of the house. It brings in a little money, but the main thing is it gets me out. My husband thought it was a good idea. I just couldn't re-cover staying inside with all my feelings. We don't live in the village, but up by the summit near the golf course, and I needed an excuse to get out. So we took this job for after school, the kids and I together. Then I saw your name on my delivery list and I just couldn't believe it. I remembered your picture in the magazine and I waited for my chance to get a look at you. You must have seen us peeking out from the car, looking around the trees. My kids were just trying to help me, seeing if it was you. And it is. You *are* the poet. And you're on my route. I don't want to interrupt you too long. I just wanted to see you and to tell you."

She said goodbye and then drove off. I stumbled back to the house and told Cynthia about what had happened.

"This place gives something to you every day, doesn't it?" she said, just as if we were standing over the volcano, taking in a vista.

I thought of my early lessons in poetry. I began to be-lieve that words could join me to people and not sunder me from them.

At the kitchen table, I unfolded the paper and began to read, for a long while having to start the simplest of stories—a lead about state health care or the eruption flowfront in Kala-pana—again and again, comprehending nothing that was printed on the page.

Derelicts

Driving the highway back and forth to Hilo and the super⁄
market in Keaʻau, Cynthia and I started noticing some regu⁄
lars along the roadside. Day after day, it seemed, we would
round a bend in the road near Mountain View or be coming
down a straightaway chute of high moguls near Glenwood, and
we'd catch sight of one of them traipsing on the cinder path be⁄
side a high stand of bamboo or silhouetted against a powder⁄
blue sky, the pyramid of Puʻu ʻŌʻō steaming in the distance
behind them. We assumed, I imagined, that they were home⁄
less, that they were on their own individual quests.

The first was a big, beefy blond man who went barefoot
and wore long, billowy camouflage pants and psychedelic tank
tops. I called him "Hulk Hogan." He was over six feet tall,
and seemed always to be brooding on something, walking like
a Sasquatch through the crossroads at Keaʻau Junction, his
hands and arms hanging straight from his shoulders, uncoor⁄
dinated with the movement of his walking. I'd spot him sitting
on the benches by the camera and video store of the little shop⁄
ping complex there, rocking on his haunches, his eyes glazed.
Sometimes a few local boys would be gathered around him,
tanned Hawaiian and mixed⁄blood surfer⁄boys smoking ciga⁄
rettes, laughing quietly, flicking their butts a long ways out onto
the asphalt of the parking lot, posturing like popcorn pimps in
a Scorsese movie.

Hippies on welfare came by too, stopping briefly at his
station after gathering small bags of groceries from the market.

The hippies always had such blank and haggard looks—*like speed freaks from the Filmore,* I said to myself, thinking of the Haight in San Francisco twenty years before. After seeing him like this a few times, I steered as clear of him as I could. I didn't know for certain if there were hard drugs on the Big Island, but his aura gave off an urban feeling of despair that I felt I could place only after I started trying to imagine him surrounded by derelict housing projects and twenty-four-hour liquor stores rather than by acres of abandoned sugarcane fields. He made his own sense, hanging out the ruined shingle of his business, and I stopped paying attention except to avoid him.

There was also a transvestite hitchhiker we called "Old Weird Harold." He was a thin, reedlike man with a freckled face who wore a blond wig done up in a sixties flip, cotton jersey skirts, and single-piece sweater dresses even in the hottest weather. He sometimes hitchhiked done up in gloves, high heels, and a purse. He never wore a *muʻumuʻu* that I recall. And I never saw anyone stop to pick him up. I know he wore a wig because I came upon him once as he was getting up from his makeshift bed outdoors by the roadside in Volcano, a lair in the long grasses with cardboard boxes as his mattress and a blue plastic tarp as his roof. I drove through a road slot in the forest, cutting through back roads to Volcano Highway, and there he was. His wig was off, and I could see his dirty blondish hair was in a military crew cut, that he was perhaps a teenager who had run away from home or else a serviceman on leave. He was so thin. He wore a white T-shirt with a V neck over BVD briefs. The skin on his bare legs and arms was the color of a pale moth's wings. He was stepping into a gray skirt, looking up at me behind mirror sunglasses as I drove by. There was a fan of a fern bough behind him where something yellow drooped down. It was the wig, perched for the night on the *hāpuʻu*. As he stepped into the circle of his skirt, at just the moment before he pulled it up over his waist without curve, I could see that his oblong head bobbed from his frail neck the way an afghan hound's does as it runs, chasing some fleet thing in the brush before it.

But I was inspired whenever I saw one derelict in particular. He would *walk* Volcano Highway. I'd spot him gaitering up toward the summit, passing him going the other way on one of my errands to Hilo. When I'd return back up the mountain later that afternoon, he'd be a few miles farther upslope, still walking, having gone from Pūʻāinakō a mile from the sea up to Keaʻau or even Mountain View, about sixteen miles from it. I don't think he was hitchhiking because he always kept up such a brisk pace, moving heelandtoe in that halfway hobbled step like one of those Olympic competitors. He might have been striking simply because of his height—he was over six feet and extraordinarily thin. But his features were Southeast Asian—high cheekbones, an oval head, and a thin jaw. And his skin was dark—the color of muddy harbor water. He was AfroAsian, perhaps a love child of the war in Vietnam, son of an American GI and a Saigon whore. Physically unusual even in Hawaiʻi, he walked as if compelled rather than transfixed, eyes purposeful. I could see him gasping for breath as he moved along through the hot, monoxide air beside the thickest Hilo traffic. He would lean into the side of Kīlauea, mounting his charge up to the summit around Kurtistown, pumping thin, spindly arms. The hollows around his eyes were sunken, full of deep shadows and mystery. I imagined he was on some religious quest. I thought of the Japanese soldier in a novel called *The Burmese Harp* who, hav/ ing killed and seen hundreds more killed in the war in South/ east Asia, abandons his infantry unit to wear the robes of the local Buddhist monks. He takes up the harp, strumming and plucking a few notes while he chants sutras, hoping to heal the wounds on his conscience, to make up for the grossest of human violations.

Plantation Boy

A friend I made after coming to Volcano is an astronomer up on the NASA Infrared Telescope on Mauna Kea. He's an astrophysicist who studies comets, tracking them through com/ plex mathematical calculations that come spewing out of the massive computer attached to the telescope. From Honolulu, where he's part of the Institute for Astronomy attached to the university, he goes up to Mauna Kea about once a month, carrying his laptop computer and a small suitcase, calling me every once in a while, asking me if I want to get up there, thirteen/thousand/plus feet into one of the clearest night skies in the world.

"No heat shimmer, no city lights to distort viewing," he says.

He's a local boy, Japanese American and third/generation, born near Wailuku, Maui, in a plantation camp. He went to SUNY Stony Brook and had a postdoctorate at Arizona for his advanced training, but we were schoolmates and slight ac/

quaintances at the same college. He was a math-science whiz living in the foreign-language dormitory. We spoke maybe twice, at a reception after a symphony concert, two Japanese Americans from Hawai'i in exile away at school, keeping a distance from the enclave subculture that was mutual between us.

In Hawai'i, though, we found each other again. We began to talk and compare lives, sharing what we had. We'd both come through a strained apprenticeship to become what we were, both university professors in esoteric fields. Yet we tried to keep something of the past close by.

We met often for lunch at an old Japanese restaurant down in Hilo. He'd have just flown in from Honolulu and have a few hours to kill before his shuttle took him up to the summit where the telescopes were. When he'd call, I nearly always told him I'd make the drive down from Volcano.

"Meet me at the *koi* pond," he'd say, mentioning the one spot of beauty in the old place. "I'll be feeding binary numbers to the fish."

It was a rueful joke. He often complained that, though he got into his profession "to see the stars," it wasn't often that he could look into the raw night sky at its river of lights, at the luminescence of creation he craved to feel more a part of.

"I'm inside all the time, staring at numbers on a computer printout," he told me. "Funny. To see stars, I gotta walk outside the building, get a pass, and stalk around in the cold."

He is a thin, small-boned, and quiet man with a square face and black curling hair. He wears glasses and light cotton clothes. There is about him a powerful air of gentleness and the serenity that comes with thoughtful detachment and being outside of things, away from the fracas and the comfort of society. His skin is pale and unlined. Though over forty, he is often mistaken by whites for someone only twenty-five. He told me once that he goes back to Maui *all the time.*

"I take the plane over, and I go back," he said. "I rent a car at the airport and drive from there to Spreckelsville—to the old sugar plantation camp near Wailuku on the north side of the island. From Spreckelsville I go up the hill to where the Japanese camp used to be, just barracks and shacks, walking up the sugarcane roads past all the old homes that are left. I have to count streets all the time—one, two, ch'ree, yeah?" he says, slipping into pidgin for a moment. "Just to find the one we used to live on.

"It's all gone now," he said, continuing. "All the plantation shacks, all the rows of houses. Just foundation stones left and little pieces of broken gate and fencing. I got to cut ch'rough overgrown cane, all gone wild and tasseling, bushwhack my way almost, just to get back to where our house used to be. I count my way there, slipping and stumbling through the canefield, and I wait for night to fall."

His face smooths as he speaks, falling into the telling. His voice softens even more than usual, a little harp strummed by aeolian breezes.

"When the stars come out," he said, "then I feel all right. I can remember when I was a kid, staring up at the sky, hearing the cane whispering, the wind coming in from off the sea, and the whole universe staring down at me while I'm staring up, my face a moon looking at the moon. I remember *why,* and I feel good. If no one in my life can, at least I *myself* can say I'm a Maui boy and I come from a plantation camp."

My friend crosses a universe in his studies, and yet he feels his boyhood soul constantly calling him back to humble beginnings.

29 Miles, Volcano Highway

On my birth certificate, issued by the Territory of Hawaii, on the line for "Place of Birth," it says "29 Miles, Volcano High-way"—the road distance from the oceanfront in Hilo up to the Hongo Store near Kīlauea caldera itself. "29 Miles" was the mile marker for the old village before it had a name. It was the address of the old United States Post Office that was located *inside* of the Hongo Store from 1929 until 1968. When I was a child, I looked at my certificate once—a small black sheet on tacky photo-paper—assigned to do so by my first- or second-grade teacher, and wondered why it didn't say "Hilo, Hawaii"—the big town where the hospital was, where I'd always been told I was born. When I asked my mother about it, she told me it was just our postal address in Volcano in those days, that it only meant "Address of Parents" and that I was, indeed, *born* in Hilo like she always said.

"That's just the way they addressed everything," she said another time I asked. I was in my mid-twenties, in graduate school, writing a poem that recalled a photograph of the Hongo Store. "Twenty-nine Miles, Volcano Highway, was our address, and that's how everything was listed—for tax purposes. For voter registration, for the mail, for *everything*. So that's why it says you were born there. It's just an address—a *country* address."

During the first year I came to live back in Volcano, I met Dallas Jackson, a geophysicist at the Volcano Observatory who was something of an amateur historian and a collector of local lore. We were seated around the kitchen table of his guesthouse—part of a sugarcane baron's summer home that he'd bought—talking about the history of the village. He told me that it may indeed have been called "29 Miles" at one time— referring to the distance between the Hongo Store and Hilo— that the old mile marker was just a few yards down from the gas pumps of the old store.

When my uncle drove me by the place that first time I was taken there, he turned to me as we passed in front of my grand/ father's store on Volcano Road. He said, "*There* the place," nodding, dipping his head in that soft, familiar way of the lo/ cals. "That's where you wass born, yeah?" He pointed to the store, and before I could register perplexity, my aunt shushed him—a little harshly I remember—saying, "He *was not*! He was born in Hilo Hospital, Richard."

Muscatel

After Hudson, our second son, was born, my mother came from Los Angeles to visit and I found an opportunity to ask her about my name. She was sitting on the couch, reading a magazine, doing some embroidery, and I ambushed her with my question.

My father had told me once, when I was about eighteen and back home from college for Easter or Thanksgiving, that I'd been named after a bottle of wine.

"In Hongo Store where you was born," he said, stretch/ ing it out in his thick pidgin, "hottest/selling item next to white rice was diss t'ing call 'Garrett's Muscatel.' And me I like the name so I geeve 'em, eh?"

Eighteen years old, I laughed, as much at the trick of being thwarted as for any bluntness or humor from my father. "What chu laughing for?" he said to me then. He pretended to bristle in indignation. "Better than Italian Swiss Colony!"

I told this story to a teacher of mine once, an Irish American from Los Angeles, puzzled and obsessed as I was about the essential character of our similarly complicated and divided pasts. His father was a film star, born in Connemara amidst bogs and peat-cutters, but he, the son, had been raised in Malibu among the palms and horses and swizzle sticks, then gone on to Princeton for buffing and lacquering. Yet his name and blood were Irish. In school, he found Yeats and Joyce and Flann O'Brien, and he was teaching them to me then. Satirist that he had become, he laughed too.

"That's *perfect!*" he said. "You've got to write that."

"But how?" I asked, a little angered.

"Why, just like that," he said, still laughing. "It tells the whole story right there."

"*What* story?" I said, asking myself the same thing. It was a mystery to me. There was nothing there but a joke and my father's Hawaiian irony, a knack for comic deflation. It mocked me. How could a story like that explain anything?

"There *was* a wine by that name," my mother said, finally admitting to it another half-life later. I was thirty-six now, a poet and college professor, and a father myself. I felt I deserved answers.

"In the back of the store, on the shelves, there was a box labeled like that—'Garrett's Muscatel' or something or other—

but I didn't want to name you after a bottle of *wine,* for gosh sakes. But I read it again in one of my novels. You know— one of those romances you don't like. I rummaged it from a rack in the store too. We had comic books and westerns and stuff like that. Murder mysteries. For a dime or a quarter or something. All on one big wooden rack in the front. In Vol- cano there was never anybody to talk to, and the rain was al- ways falling, and we didn't have TV, so there was nothing to do but read. And everybody read, even the farmers would come in from the lettuce fields after work, rubber boots and muddy hands, buying bread, rice, and a softcover book. So me, I found this romance about the South and Reconstruction after the Civil War. And there was a man named Garrett in it, so I fi- nally agreed."

And so it was true. I was named for a drink, confirmed by an example from a paperback romance.

Searchers

Volcano is full of searchers, odd ducks, misfits, dreamers, and derelicts. My neighbors are scientists attached to the Hawaiian Volcano Observatory of the United States Geological Survey: a Ph.D. in petrology from Johns Hopkins who plays an elec- tric cello; a part-Hawaiian geophysicist who sings Brahms and Haydn in the Easter and Christmas programs at the Hilo Pres- byterian Church; a reformed yahoo from Colorado who mea- sures electromagnetic fields by day and reads Tom Robbins novels by night; a saint from Missoula who lives with twenty-

nine cats and lava-walks and lava-talks and can hear the argu-
ments her neighbors have at night through the echo chamber of
a lava tube that runs in the space between their homes. Or, they
are a waiter, a part-time mechanic, a playwright, a potter, a car-
penter, or a flower salesperson for an orchid farm on Volcano
Highway. They are a weekending civilian scuba diver for a secret, porpoise-training naval unit. They are a violin virtuoso
from the Upper East Side in New York, trained by Raphael
Bronstein, who somehow managed to ruin a concert career that
covered two Western continents and one Asian archipelago.
One fellow, a transplant from San Francisco who found as-
trology in the Haight-Ashbury during the sixties, runs the production line for chocolate macadamia nuts. A woman counsels
clients at a weight-loss diet center in Hilo, leads aerobics at the
Volcano Community Center on Tuesday nights, and, in the
summer, teaches creative dramatics to local schoolchildren on
vacation. The Carsons down my street have turned their house
and outbuildings into a going bed-and-breakfast business, con-
verting an old WW II Quonset hut from the military camp that
they found on their property into an overnight cottage. Michael
Gates, a Seneca Indian from upstate New York, is a fireman
with Hawaii Volcanoes National Park and one of my hiking
partners. Everybody is here because they've got something
they're looking for or something they found here. Everybody
looks at the snow on Mauna Kea after a rainstorm on a cold
winter night, driving down the center of Wright Road going
north just to see it better. Everyone stops once in a while over
in Glenwood at the turnout across from Hirano Store just to
see the steam coming out of Pu'u 'Ō'ō or the red glow of the
lava pond lighting the belly of a low-lying cloud at night.
Everybody.

F a l l e n H ā p u ' u

One summer, I was alone and living in the Rodrigueses' house, trying to learn the forest. I'd spent two months there, then I had to leave yet once more. I was getting ready to drive to Hilo Airport for the return trip to the Mainland. Some days before, I'd noticed, backing my car out of the driveway on some errand (the dump, the post office, a milk run), that there was always one yellowing, mottled bough hanging a little lower than before, drooping over the car as I pulled out, brushing the rear window, sweeping over the roof, and streaking my windshield. I ignored it. I drove on, dismissing any thoughts or worries that might have risen to consciousness. I needed supplies. I wanted my mail. Trash needed dumping. I hurried on. I was preparing for a trip to the Mainland, and I needed to get ready.

The next day, a frond hung so low that I thought I might need to cut it, saw it off as we do when a *hāpu'u* bough dies on the tree.

And then, during the stormy night before I was to leave for my trip, the *hāpu'u* leaning over my driveway toppled all the way over, completely blocking me in. It was a huge brown column of fiber soaked with over a ton of water, its voluptuous fronds, still lush and alive, radiating upward from the trunk like feathery green surfboards stuck in beach sand. I was frustrated and I cursed the air.

I put on a plastic slicker and went outside. There was a morning drizzle. Why didn't I realize what had been happening? There was a hobbyhorse in the garage. With that and some two-by-fours I might have made a kind of trestle for it, propping it up in the way I remember my Kubota grandfather used to do for the Japanese pines and maples he wrapped and trained in our yard on the Mainland.

But I'd done nothing and the tree fell. *It doesn't want you to leave,* I thought. I walked around it, stepping over the wet, earth-smudged boughs. I thought of a pod of whales beached years ago on the Oregon coast, inflated the significance, and dismissed the recollection. I thought, maybe I could get a grip under some of the strongest branches, thick as the fiberglass poles for vaulting, and *lift,* resurrecting the entire tree, pushing it slowly upright with stiff hands like a circus roustabout lift-walking a pole to the Big Top. *And then what?* How would it stay upright? I thought I'd just push it out of the way and deal with it later. The *hāpu'u* would live anyway.

I pictured harbor fishermen, standing in surf and teamed together in a circle, dragging in a harvest of shorefish in a big, kelp-green net they were pulling toward shore. That would be how I'd resurrect my fallen *hāpu'u*—hooking my hands in a kinesthetic duet underneath the soaked trunk, leaning backward and lifting it, inexorably, with a team of others, as if I were taking up my own station in a sea pond and the downed tree were the span of netting that I pulled, writhing with heavy red fish. But when I waded into the bundles of limbs and tucked my hands under the beardlike flesh of its trunk and tried to lift, I could feel the dense immensity of its full weight barely bending to my force, resisting, rubbing the wet duff of its glistening bronze hairs onto my blue rain slicker and pant legs. The trunk bounced a bit, then sank back onto the mossy earth. It felt like I was trying to lift a rain barrel with a pair of barbecue tongs. *Don't leave.* I needed a plan.

I decided to cut. I ran like a child on an errand across the road to my neighbors, Wally and Jeff, who worked as handy‑men around the village. I roused them out of a Sunday sleep. They were in down bags, stretched out on the new floor they were building. I told them what had happened.

Jeff said, "Dah foress say, *No go,* eh, Garrett!" And he laughed at his joke, crawling out of his sleeping bag, pulling on his Levi's, hopping from foot to foot. The forest light streamed in through the plastic sheeting that made up the south wall of the house they were still building. Jeff grabbed a pack of Pall Malls, flipped one out, and jammed it into his mouth, shivering a little in the chill of the morning without his shirt on. He looked around for matches and his boots.

Wally, out of bed already, was putting some coffee on. He said, "Pele saying, *No leave,* eh Hongo?" They agreed to help me.

I got a rusted saw out of the garage, Jeff got a machete and a saw from his tool kit, and we began to hack away. A transparent, coppery gel seeped out of each frond as we slashed them off and tossed them aside from the trunk. I was ap‑palled. *Tree blood,* I thought to myself. I sliced and envisioned the *hāpuʻu,* imagining it still had its foliage, churning a gelati‑nous plasma up from the trunk that was dripping from the severed stalks. I tried to be tough, to harden myself against what I was doing. Wally was working too, piling the ampu‑tated boughs into a shallow mound under an *ʻōhiʻa* across the driveway.

He said, "No worry, Garrett," gesturing to the pile of slash. "I take care for you and ch'row away after."

He hummed as he worked, smiling, catching my eye once or twice, repeating his Pele joke a couple of times. *No go!* the merriness in his eyes was saying, laughing with Jeff and me.

We worked fast. The *hāpu'u* limbs came away easily, like cut-ting celery with a paring knife. I'd be able to get out.

In less than half an hour, I was hanging the rusting saw back on its nail in the garage and saying goodbye to my two neighbors, shaking their roughened hands, drinking in the spark of fondness from their eyes, their *aloha*. After a moment's goodbye we didn't try to hold for long; I jumped into my car and backed out of the driveway, cleared of its obstacle but lit-tered now with soft green debris. I drove it under my tires.

Quickly, I got out onto the lava road that took me past the grid of paved roads through the undeveloped subdivision and out onto the highway. Glancing back as I drove away, I saw the checkerboard of green life and blank clear-cuts that was the forest, houses and cottages and patches of blemished trees mottled in sunlight, abloom with the red crests of *lehua,* the few skeletal sentinels of dieback *'ōhi'a* like finger bones reaching through to the leached sky. I made my plane, flew to Honolulu and on to the Mainland to keep my appointments. I didn't know it then, but it would be more than two years before my life would let me get back to Volcano again.

"But," Wally might say, "not ch'ore *own* life, Hongo. *Pele* life."

MENDOCINO ROSE

THERE IS a blossoming vine that I love. It threads up the bole and through the crown of an 'ōhi'a tree beside Volcano Highway near Kīlauea Summit just about a hundred yards downslope from the entrance to Hawaii Volcanoes National Park. In bloom, it looks as if a *lei* of pink carnations has been wound through the soft green, medallioned leaves of 'ōhi'a, through its streaky, silver-and-black limbs. It is beautiful in the rain, it is lovely on sunny days, and it shines to me in fog. I drive by it, and I feel comforted. I think of a few things.

The vine is a variety of wood rose, Latin name *Rosa california*, an introduced species from California that flourishes along the North Coast wine country there, a kind of mild and

benevolent kudzu-like briar overgrowing abandoned barns, gar-
nishing the oaks and, gone wild, cascading in thorny cataracts
of dark vine and boils of pink-and-red blooms down the Pacific cliffsides beside Highway One. It grows all through the
Mendocino coast up through Crescent City and the mouth of
the Smith River near there. It especially thrives in the dampest
places, the rain forests, the spongy wood rot of abandoned
shacks that have soaked up a season's worth of precipitation,
the islands and sandbars in and beside a river's green lagoon.

Some years ago, a few months after my father died, Cynthia and I took a trip from Los Angeles north through Big Sur,
crossed the Golden Gate Bridge at San Francisco, and drove
up slowly through the Mendocino coast. We were on our way
to Oregon, where she is from and where we planned to live that
summer. I was between jobs. I'd just finished a year's teaching
down in Southern California and I'd signed a contract for a
new job in Missouri. But we needed a place to spend the summer. Cynthia was pregnant and our baby was expected just before school was to start, so we wanted to be near a hospital
where we had coverage. It turned out that two of our options
were the plantation village in Kahuku, Hawai'i, on the North
Shore of O'ahu where I'd lived as a child, or else Eugene, Oregon. Though I didn't realize it then, I had a deep inner hankering to go back to Hawai'i, but I had no close family ties left
in Kahuku. We decided to go to Eugene because Cynthia felt
more confident about being pregnant with her family around.
We drove up in June after school was out.

Mendocino, strangely enough, a midpoint on our coastal
trip north, was the beginning of my wanting to go back to
Hawai'i. Driving up its switchbacks, braking on the wet highway and in the dips and the S curves, feeling the seacoast cliffs

just meters beside us and the headlands plunging to short
rocky benches below, I kept getting the feeling I was back on
the Big Island where I was born, the volcano country that I
had visited only a couple of years before. The land had a similar sense to it—Mendocino is wet like Hawai'i is, its primary
weather seemed to be a thick fog rushing in from the sea uphill over cliffs and headlands that were like the sheer rims of
craters when the earth suddenly drops a hundred yards away
from itself. And the hillside lands roll as they do in Hawai'i,
gaining dramatic altitudes, seductive and powerful as a pod of
breeching whales. On both coasts, you can see a long ways,
gazing out under cloud cover banked low over the Pacific to
a gray nothing on the horizon that could signify the rest of the
world.

On our drive, I'd seen flowers braceleted along the eaves
of an old farmhouse or wood shed like a string of tiny Japanese
lanterns strung in preparation for a festival. Gentle garlands, they
reminded me of Hawai'i. We'd admire their beauty as we drove
by—a kind of strength and persistence of growth that seemed a
frailty for all its perseverance. The vines covered everything and
softened their shapes. An old shack became a kind of flowering
haystack beside the road. A wooden fence, smothered by the
vines and flowers, seemed like the frothing face of a wave.

I was listening to a tape on the car stereo, playing it to the
end, finding the right song and playing it again and again. It
was a ballad sung by my favorite tenor, a Hawaiian folk artist
named Gabby Pahinui, a man who'd begun as a jazz guitarist
and entertainment singer at the Royal Hawaiian Hotel in the
thirties and forties. Eventually, he dropped out of the tourist
scene and started playing his own kind of music, old Hawaiian
songs and original compositions, singing first a rusty kind of

falsetto, then a gritty and clogged baritone, to ballads and *hulas* and even an old chant sometimes. To most everything, he accompanied himself on the twelve-string guitar. Around his lead, he grouped a string bass, the ukulele, then other guitars to play rhythm or a Hawaiian steel background and lead. Old friends played with him, his grown sons played with him. And he became a local legend, a leader in the return to Hawaiian folk music, a symbol of authenticity. He gave his concerts in Waimea Canyon with the natural white curtain of a waterfall behind him and once on Rabbit Island on Oʻahu's windward coast with seagulls screeching overhead. He gave his concerts in the *country*. And Gabby was deep. He found old ballads and tunes written by descendants of Kamehameha and put them into new arrangements. Everything had Hawaiian lyrics and he rarely sang in English. Skidding from the crest of a yodeling falsetto to the gravel bar of his baritone, he praised places known for great fishing and beautiful flowers, beaches with a gentle, curling surf. The songs had titles like "Mokihana" (a gentle, fragrant flower), "Aloha ka Manini" (Hail to the Angelfish), and "Wai Huʻihuʻi o Keaniani" (The Heart-Stopping Waters of Keaniani).

My favorite song is his version of "Ipo Lei Manu," a late-nineteenth-century lament written by Victorian-era Queen Kapiolani in sadness for the unexpected death of her husband King David Kalākaua, who'd become ill in London while on a world tour. The song is about the dying of a loved one who is far away from home, in a kind of exile, bereft of kinsmen and the spirit of the islands.

In Mendocino, listening to it as we drove through that countryside, I took it to be the dirge for my own father and I wished I had known enough to have sung it or had it sung at his funeral. I couldn't understand much, but I picked out a few syllable sounds I recognized from childhood, a few words and phrases—*lei* for "garland," *manu* for "bird," *ha'ina ka puana, ehyah* for "alas, sing it again, this song of my heart." But it was the *style* of saying things, singing them, that moved me most. The way Pahinui let his falsetto drift off into an elongated diminuendo at the end of a verse, how he shifted the syllabic emphasis around despite the beat, as though he were singing the blues, only not the blues. The sweetness of the harmonies, the lavish lingering over vowel sounds, the chopping canoe-paddle-stroke rhythms, and the picking style like the sweep of a hand in *hula*-dancing or rain falling through the gentle upslope of a windward canyon all felt familiar to me. And the song's poem was about a man's death far from his home. Death without return. And no beloved around you. I was hearing a song of profound sorrow and its connections to my father were power-ful. When I realized what the man was singing, true grieving rose up in me like a swelling breaker and I dove under it. I looked off from the black asphalt road winding ahead to the roses blooming around me as though they were a music too. I looked off over the cliffs across the Pacific.

It was a fleeting but powerful premonition of change. The song and the rose opened me again to something I'd had when my father and Kubota grandfather were alive. It was not only a place but a resolve of purpose, I suppose, a feeling of con-nection not so much to any particular place, though that helps, but to the world of *feeling* and openness to it, that exchange be-tween the human and whatever might be the rest—the infinite, say, or the natural world of pure spirit that the nineteenth-century romantic philosophers defined as sublime. Whatever it is that is greater than the self but that, nevertheless, empowers the self, overwhelms and inspirits the self. "And who, if I cried, would hear me among the angelic orders?" wrote Rilke, skeptically, in his *Duino Elegies.* "Even if, suddenly, one of them were to grip me to his heart, I'd vanish in his overwhelming presence." Beauty is nothing but the start of a terror we can hardly bear, he concluded, a scorn so serene it could kill us. It is the Buddhist's *vajra,* the lightning bolt of pure, cosmic perception, a grieving that leads to eternity.

Later, having stopped for the day in a seacoast village, I saw the flowers again. They were in bushes in a vacant field across from our hotel room. I walked over there, jumping a wooden fence, scuffed out over the clumps of wild grasses, and stood up next to the vines, grabbing up a blossom or floret, and twisted it gently in my hands, holding pure beauty for a second, like touching the gentlest skin of a lover till the soft hairs rise and you turn blue inside. I felt the breezes kick around me, lifting up my hair, curling around the back of my neck, and then I gave it up, dropped the small fluffs of color from my hand, and looked around, surveying the coastal pines, the fog shoving down the hillside, the half-moon harbor choked with a fleet of sporty and derelict yachts below me. Whatever had flickered alive for a moment would have died by then, and I walked back through the blooming field, dove through the fence, and strutted across the paved street to the hotel lobby again, trying to forget the roses and putting my mind to whatever was ahead—the drive, dinner, or a phone call. I got busy inside where, only an instant before, as briefly as a match flare, I'd been revealed to myself.

What I felt, holding a rose in my hand, feeling the droplets of condensed fog whiskering down my face, recalling Pahinui's lament, was an inkling—a sense of a borderlands between two geographic immensities. I was at the rim where the

Pacific plate was diving under America, pressuring the rock above it, melting down in a slow behemoth's roll, dissolving into the mantle and folding up the surface of the earth above it, sending up, through an intermittent series of dikes, vertical shards of basaltic monoliths to the surface, shearing off the edge of the continent. We get Morro Rock this way, Cape Perpetua and the spectacular cliffs of the Oregon and Northern California coasts. Up on dry land there, you get a feeling you're standing on the edge of a ripping nowhere, witness to the birth of beauty that is born from dying—a part of the earth viciously dissolving into another, shards of the planet sliding away from the main mass in little drifts of *bonsai*-islands necklaced with surf. You get a similar feeling standing on the shore as huge, mid-ocean waves cannonade against a seacliff on the Big Island of Hawai'i. There, the land rises from deep within the planet itself amidst thousands of miles of nothing but open sea.

The inkling engendered a kind of emotional rhyme in my own sensibilities. Built from powerful upthrusts of planetary motion, Hawai'i an island emerging from a thermal plume bursting up from the mantle through the middle of the Pacific plate, Mendocino rising from the immensely slow collision between that plate and the American continent, itself an island. They are both purgatorial lands surrounded by vast seas. Mysterious islands. Places for the renewal of incarnation. And I took, from the craggy distances and pitching deeps I saw in both, from the deep and flowering upwellings of material cosmos within them, images and symbols for the regeneration of spirit within myself.

AFTER I FINALLY returned to Volcano to live, after my first winter there and its genuine chilliness, the months of dampness and learning to get used to it, a mountain spring came slowly uphill from the Pacific like a cloud of blossoming and gentle breezes. I started seeing that there was a variety of colorful birds—the guides gave me elegant names like ʻelepaio and ʻiʻiwi—hopping through the ʻōhiʻa outside our windows. I took drives around and began to notice that, on the roadside by the park entrance and distributed within it along the circle drive around Kīlauea Crater, there were three ʻōhiʻa trees with a scanty wood rose vine threading through them, all abloom. Little pink puffballs like popcorn carnations, like the revival of love. The first time I spotted one, the one just outside the park entrance, I hit the brakes and skidded until the car fishtailed a little—like Mendocino's, the pavement in Volcano is *constantly* wet and slick. I rubbernecked like a cruising teenage swain in a battered Buick spotting an old girlfriend at the beach. Love made even more beautiful by a switch in time and surroundings. Busting through the tufts of fog around Kīlauea, I'd crossed past death and into the world of the next life.

Dante, in the *Commedia,* talks to us about the function of earthly love and compares it, not unfavorably, to the light of God—itself the true stream of love given to us as grace. He says that earthly love, his love for Beatrice, the beautiful teenage girl he met once standing in the punch-bowl line at a party, was only a means to guide his conscience on its path toward the under-standing and appreciation of divine love. Maybe the perception of beauty and indulging our need for it, accepting that we are weak in the knees and the soul for the soft petals of a wild rose and its muted fragrance carried on the spring wind, is actually *real good* for us and gives us something like a taste for the eter-nal that is within us and emanating from all of the earth, a feel-ing of strength and order and empowerment *without* our quite being able to put our grasping fingers on it. Something elusive, *beyond* the mind. But it's in the loins, *a priori,* in the twists and angularities of the mind as it vines itself in an entanglement with creation, in the singularity of passion's impure flowering. *That* is what I felt about the rose, *ehya.* I was *led* by the rose to my feelings about returning, *ha'ina,* a child united with its cord of birth, *perned in a gyre,* a beam of love from the eternal to the noth-ing we are.

Volcanology: Curtain of Fire

One night, under a midsummer half-moon, I took a long hike across the broad black caldera of Kīlauea from Volcano House on the crater rim to Halema'uma'u, the old firepit of the volcano where a lava lake had boiled for over a hundred years from 1823 to 1924. I wanted to see earth-shimmer on the black lavas, to see moonlight pooling in the crevices of fu-maroles spouting their vaporous ghosts. I wanted to feel what-ever there was from starlight glistening over new skin on the earth.

At dusk, I made a quick descent through stumpy 'ōhi'a and the fern forest against the north rim of the crater. *Kāhili* gingers bloomed by the trailside. Their thick yellow scepters radiated out of the deep greenery I passed through. When the evening wind came up the trail, I saw fingers of mist stirring through every friable green thing. After a while, I could see that a soft rain was splashing on the upturned face of the dark, vol-canic sea ahead of me. Clouds breezed through the cool arms of the ginger flowers, *origami* cranes alighting like bundles of white flames on the fleshy leaves of the forest.

In less than an hour, it was past nightfall and I stood on a fissure line ripped open from the caldera floor, the spatter rampart of an eruption that had sent a curtain of fire fountaining along its entire length for nearly a full day in 1982. There had been a long red wall of volcanic blossoming, sheets and spinnakers of incandescence. The lavas had thrown themselves up from a boil of old rock, sending new gouts and slashes up through a slit in the earth nearly two hundred yards long. On one side of the split were low hummocks and hogbacks slumping inward toward the long crack in the earth. But, on the other, there were huge, cowling crests like ocean waves just about to crash onto the black shore of the caldera. Standing next to them, I felt those lifting shapes were as immense and powerful as any set of waves I'd surfed, only thicker and completely substantial.

I scrambled up beside a huge lip of purple and gray seven feet high. There were ocherish reds streaked with white under its concave side. In moonlight, the gray-buff and reddened lava looked like the nippled line of skin upraised on the mound of a woman. I imagined the way the earth had opened itself—the flap of molten matter, partly congealed, the covering tufts of spatter shaped into a single part thrown upward with the surge of sudden fountaining, coolish rock curling against the heightening spume, the long ridge along the fissure gradually shaping itself into a chain of lips boiling with earth's passion. It seemed to me that I stood on the body of a woman, and the glistening lavas were her hills and thighs.

I wanted to kiss and to lie down. I wanted to taste weariness and feel an infinite ache. I curled myself inside one gigantic lip and gave in to the smell of its sulphurous climate.

A blue night dropped upon Kīlauea. Around me was the whirling, nocturnal depth. I felt burning and cold all at once, encircled by a curtain of fire that coiled away in shrouds of sleepy mist. I surrendered to the earth, body of a woman.

Self-Help: Envoi

Volcano is *not* the Volcano of the past, not Macondo, Hawaiʻi, as it was for my grandfather. Yet, I live in it. The postmaster and the other old-timers see it in me, me in it. I am *of* that history, born at the end of that period, a plantation boy on the rim of the volcano. Sharing coffee on the porch of the Upper Store, the old Okamura Store at the corner of old Volcano Highway and Haunani Road that was once a warehouse, then an *onsen* of gamblers and *geisha* during World War II, Kazu speaks to me and, through me, he speaks to my father, my grandfather, and we both speak with the history in our talk, the former web of relations, the old village in the clouds of air between us, in the sharp vapors of our minds. The ghosts are there. And I speak to them, my voice dropping, head about to bow. The sign over the quick-stop market still says HONGO STORE, and the ghosts wrap themselves in fogs around the gas pumps and haunt the scruffy stand of bamboo behind the rusting water tank. I buy wheat bread, milk, rent a martial arts video at five o'clock on a Friday, and the people nod, knowing who I am, whose grandson, whose son. My every step is ceremonial, a performance for those not born of this village to witness and comment upon.

On the wooden bench in front of my grandfather's store, under an abbreviated eave that does not shelter me from the vagrant mists of the forest, I talk story about the village past, going over the sequences of farm plots along Haunani Road, along 'I'iwi. Kazu explains that the Japanese community planned and built their own golf course up here back in the thirties, laid it out and cut through all the 'ōhi'a, bulldozed the hāpu'u, crushed over all the lava tumuli, and filled in some big lava tube that everyone said ran all the way down from Mauna Loa under the village, behind Hongo Store, and down along old Volcano Road. *Yeah, yeah,* he says, and *Ass right, ass right,* providing the oral assent, the *amens,* to his own stories once he gets rolling. Who is there to confirm veracity anymore? No one but old bachelor Goya-san left from all of the farmers who used to live here and work this ground. All the sons and daughters have moved away, and there is only me, half *kotonk,* as Kazu says, *wit' one haole wife.* The last days, so far as those Nisei can see. It is a new world, and what fools these strangers be.

When I speak to Tom Wright, scientist-in-charge of the Volcano Observatory at the crater rim, I speak to a grandson of Frank Lloyd Wright. We share references and an orientation to the culture that built Taliesin, the Guggenheim Museum, and the green-marbled Imperial Hotel. He plays cello in the string quartet with my wife. They do Mozart, Vivaldi, Haydn. I've cast him in a play I'm writing for the Kīlauea Theater, our troupe of community players. He poses with an 'ō'ō stick for publicity stills I'm shooting, then again for the "CBS Evening News" with Dan Rather, framing himself against a backdrop of Kaimū Black Sand Beach overrun with fresh lavas, streaming through coconut palms near the shore and steaming into the sea. For our friendship, for Hawai'i, I transform him into a *kahuna* of volcanology, Kīlauea's Gandalf the White presiding over the latest volcanic inundation—a Ceremony of Pele. We care for her, and hush our voices. She makes the earth and its vapors.

I'm at lunch at Kilauea Military Camp, in the cafeteria with Christina Heliker, another geologist. She tells me about seismic swarms under Kīlauea and the inflation of the shield. She tells me about a new outbreak along the flowfront, spewing a geyser of lava that they're already calling "the Firehose" into the sea. Down in ʻŌhiʻa Estates, a few streets below us, where the tree line is a little lower, I have dinner with Patrick Edie, a man whose job is quality control and supervision of a chocolate macadamia nut candy factory. A native of San Francisco, he tells me he knew about a past life as a Hawaiian priestess near Kona, that he *had* to come to Volcano, *had* to live near natural beauty and the spiritual powers of earth creating itself in order to feel in harmony with his past. He tells me that the conjunction of Jupiter and Mars before the lunar eclipse foretells an epochal change in the workings of our world, that we'll have a chance to make things better. Sitting in his living room, surrounded by his visionary paintings of dreamscapes, tarot symbols, and the geometries of planetary movement scripted out over lavish portraits of Hawaiʻi's flowers, I know he'll be an elemental part of giving us that chance. I run into Pam Frierson at the post office. A writer herself, she schools me in ecofeminism and hips me to the Environmental Literature program at UC Davis. At the post office, I do a session of Mainland-style, white male power-talk with my down-the-street neighbor, Joe Halbig, a geologist from Southern Illinois who teaches at the local branch of the University of Hawaii. We discuss academic politics, real estate deals, and volcanic hazards, saying "shit" and "damn," referring all the while to Mainland

sports teams. I talk Lakers and work in a mention of my ab﹣
horrence of the L.A. football "Lambs." He likes Kansas City,
the Chiefs and the Royals. Across the street, Wally Nagy, a
part﹣Hawaiian from Maui, and next door, Gerald Gacayan, a
Filipino from the C. Brewer plantation town of Pāhala down
the Ka‘ū side of Kīlauea, both speak a pidgin with me and I
with them. "Ahh," Wally is fond of saying, "I wake up t'ink﹣
ing—dere dah poet and dah violinis' togeddah." Six feet and
about 240 pounds, he holds his large, bearish hands together
and tilts his body a little sideways when he tells me this, swarm﹣
ing himself into a full﹣torso smile. Down at the other end of the
road, the Carsons, the couple who run a bed﹣and﹣breakfast,
give me the latest village political gossip—the lowdown on the
golf course residents' current efforts to put in a chain Speedy
Mart on the highway, etc. "We live in the bush," Tommy Car﹣
son says self﹣disparagingly. "Away from the big, bad world."
For them, I am local, a native son, and yet I am global, a prodi﹣
gal one.

No matter that I try, with all material emphasis and psy﹣
chic earnestness, to be almost *solely* of this village, I am yet out﹣
side of it, going farther. Like the ingenuous, sincere diplomat
from a small, postcolonial country sent to the capital for an ed﹣
ucation, sent to outposts on assignments, I am returned home
for a brief reward, then sent elsewhere again. Away on the
Mainland, I attempt to carry home with me in photographs,
dress, and a few trinkets. But, *auwē*, too often, for my "mind
of winter" and back home in Volcano, it is the Mainland out﹣
posts that I carry with me most of all. I rise early, and, before
7 a.m. and getting the boys off to the schoolbus that takes them
down the mountain to an old plantation school, I've already
spoken to New York on the phone, to academics on the Main﹣

land. I award, I edit, I make final changes for a book review. I'm busy with literary worldliness, bloated with bifurcation and entanglements.

But what the capital has given me is a way *not* to live in a local's identity. I don't have to live in the past, as the past was lived. I don't have a laborer's job, don't have to worry about the soil or the water supply or the availability of seed at a subsidized price. I'm not locked in to the opinion of the community here, not enclosed and defined by its gossip, not subject to all of its mores. Yet, full of nostalgia and retrospect, I catch myself wanting to be. I feel a bit ashamed that I, a man, can make *sushi* the way they made it in Kahuku Village a generation ago and two entire islands away, and I won't be howled down for it at Volcano's Saturday Market or at the Fourth of July fair. What will be noticed and with amusement, by the old-timers I care about, by the leftover parliament of Japanese matrons still sprinkled through the village, is that a *man* made the *sushi,* and not his wife or mother, or his daugh-ters. Or it will have been made by his *haole* wife. I see that if the ethnic past is to be transmitted, it will be through this un-gendered and interracial jumble like the dark core of vinegared vegetables and pink shrimp powder at the center of a roll of sweetened rice. Like a *haole,* I am free to speak whatever's on my mind—no one can beat me, fire me, or cast me out with ridicule and shunning. I belong nowhere, I tell myself. And, *I belong in Volcano.*

I cast off the peasant sandals, the plantation raincoat of thatched *ti* leaves and *pili* rushes. Telephoning the Mainland, jabbering in literary talk, I'm filling orders like my storekeeper grandfathers, buying and selling, wholesale and retail portions of my own writing life. My mind is back on the plantation, rac-

ing like a child through the dirt streets in the evening, hearing
the rice pots banging and swilling in the kitchens, hearing the
itinerant food vendor's call—a mixture of Chinese, Hawaiian,
and English—truly *chop suey:*

> *Mana pua! Pepeiao! Fresh kūlolo!*
> *Come quick, you gettem.*
> *Mo bettah fo' eat den poi!*
> *Mo bettah den poi wit shew-gah!*

I HAVE DECIDED that chronic dispiritedness is the result of
being *blocked* from who you are, from *knowing* who you are. It
separates you from feeling, fosters the modern kind of detachment that not only separates you from woe, which you may
have a knowledge of and experience with, but from joy as well,
which you may not know. If you have been part of something
hard to accept, if you feel socially stigmatized or psychologically
haunted by an aberrational past, then a certain kind of detachment may protect you. This is the solution the Nisei generation
came up with. They *detached* themselves from a previous, im-
migrant identity; they *detached* themselves from a defiled history;
they *detached* themselves from white Americans; and they *detached*
themselves from their children, the Sansei who would grow up
middle-class, with a better command of English, with no internal shame about their identities, about the dishonor of the relocation. It was thus with my family. My father *detached* himself
from whatever shame he might have felt for his upbringing and
the people he sprang from, those who had abandoned him. He
lived a life of serene, self-enclosed detachment, so much so that,
without the evidence of his bookish trinkets, without my wit-
nessing those few and almost anomalous events of his reflective

and pleasurable indulgences, it would have been impossible to figure out what he cared for.

And I grew up *detached* too—from a family history, from a feeling of a kind of *personal* and a kind of *tribal* stake in the world. I came from no culture, from no history, growing up with the barest minimum of a family story. My father kept me out of it. What I learned, others told me. My mother's people were plantation workers who left the fields after one generation. My Kubota grandfather was sent back to Hiroshima for a good Japanese education so that, when he came back to Hawai'i, he could attain the position of storekeeper and *not* have to work the fields. The karma of indenture was thus broken. My mother and her sisters then grew up and left the plantation town, left Hawai'i, and left history behind. My father seemed to be without history altogether, a deafened Oedipus who walked back into his home village only to be cast out within a year of returning. He shambled to his Colonus on the Mainland and schooled himself to live in the eternal perplexity and psychic insulation of smallish pleasures.

But what happens, I think, is that the next generation begins to *miss* something without knowing quite what it is. We *fear* something. Without the larger family, without root in time and place, without the oracle bones of ancestry, we rage.

Wind, an Asian born in Southeast Asia but raised here in the Rust Belt of the U.S., tells me that he gets *panic attacks* once in a while. He'll be in a supermarket, he says, over the frozen foods or the dairy section, or picking out fruits or judging the tomatoes, and, suddenly, he'll look up and notice that all the faces around him are *Caucasians*. And he'll feel his stomach curdle, the hamstrings in his legs go out, and all the sinew in his arms combust against his bones. He'll crumple up inside of his jacket, pull at his hair a little, bow his head, trying to hide his face under the collar of his coat, and then have to find his way through the aisles past the checkout, through the automatic, pneumatic, doors to the parking lot, where he'll search frantically for his car and dive in behind the wheel, holding it, panicking, feeling the uncontrollable confusion, the fear of being *found,* the fear of being *lost,* the revulsion of being *nothing* to this world, a no one without place, without people, without history. *I am an Asian,* his soul is screaming. *I was born in a foreign city that smoked with death and terrorism. Bodies lay on the streets. The sun rained down like bullets through leaves on a ginkgo tree. I am exhausted. You cannot feel kindly toward me. You cannot soothe me with radio, with good fruit, with fresh meat and fish. You must loathe me as I loathe myself. I am alone and this world does not want me.*

My attacks are less dramatic. I merely feel worthless. Or lost. Dispirited. I drive along a road and, suddenly, woe and melancholy overcome me. Or, feeling isolated in a faculty meeting, sensing that I am the only voice supporting some cause, I realize I am without that governing story of a familial past everyone else has tucked like a pillow under their comforted hearts. I realize everyone else around me is white, and I feel their scorn, imagining a tacit caucus locking me out. I give in to rage and embarrass myself. I make a scene and excoriate whomever I take to be the worst lackey of domination over the wretched. I feel shame. I lose respect. They *have* who they are. I have nothing. I am detached from all legitimacy. I own no body of culture, no accomplishment of generations. I am here on *sufferance.* A token. An emblem of a distance. I am *more* than twentynine miles from the Hongo Store, a ways from origin, vaporous and far from home, removed from earth and the volcano.

I'VE HEARD IT SAID that children who suffer abuse carry
that abuse with them always and to the point where they are
given to repeat the crime in their own lives, on children of
their own. It is an Aeschylean cycle that these children cannot then themselves parent. Societies thus collapse. A family
line is dissolved in its own emotional dissolution. If Mrs.
Katayama, Yukiko Kiriu, my grandmother the dancer, left
any legacy behind, it is the one of detachment, of abandonment, of things let go. Sent away from her own childhood,
she could bury feeling for her own children, escape to the
other man, not my grandfather, across Honolulu all her life
long, never seeing my father and his siblings again until they
were past grown. It is a powerful ease with an emotional absence that can create that much denial. My Uncle Bobby inherited it. For years, he lived in the same town as my father,
yet, something like Nathaniel Hawthorne's Wakefield, who
moved across the street from his own wife and children, spy-
ing on them for years without revealing himself, Bobby never
made contact with my father once in all that time. I'm not certain there was feuding but think instead that it was merely the
long ceremony of detachment that kept them away from each
other, neither knowing how to belong to the other again with
their childhoods in Hawai'i so far away. My father never
spoke ill of Bobby, nor did his brother berate him when we
met. He spoke to me with a kindness as if the family had only
gathered the week before, in Kona or Vegas or somewhere,
and we could take up conversing as if we'd had the secure
repetition of family stories tying us to each other every holiday
for decades, ancestral ghosts wrapped in approval over the
steaming meals of our predictable reunions.

My father too lived a curious drama of detachment all his life, never developing friendships, never communicating with his sisters in Hawai'i, and, to me, never revealing that he knew his mother was alive, never mentioning the name of the foster mother who raised him. He swaddled himself in melancholy, in loneliness, his deafness a wry, poetic, and crudely physical rendering of what was already the just sentence of isolation his aspect and psychology had already dictated. He lived in a dreamy world of his own, escaping to peace with box scores and handicap sheets. Yet, later in life, he turned to me, giving his blessing, a car, letters and sports clippings faithfully sent wherever I lived, a new shirt, even *The Complete Dream Songs* of John Berryman once when his book club offered it, when I was nineteen and curious to become a poet. He gave, managed it without having been given to. That surely is the wrinkle of compassionate irony he worked into our inheritance.

The abandonments began with Yukiko Kiriu sent off to walk through a canefield in Kaua'i, that seven-year-old who would be a dancer, banished by her own family. If that abandonment is answered by this current living in Kīlauea's rain forest, in Alexander's baby meals of Cheerios and mashed tropical fruit, in the pitching of a green sea of sugarcane behind the day care at the Kurtistown Jodo Mission where Hudson is playing, in Cynthia's humming a Bach chaconne as she does chores in the kitchen or walks across a lava driveway to retrieve the daily paper, and in my cautious steps, brushing through club moss and bamboo orchid back into the fogs of Volcano, then it will have taken the better part of four generations to have been absolved.

I HAVE BEEN casting myself out. I've let something go— a border. Cynthia, in her optimistic way, says I've become a "citizen of the world," but that's not it—it is as if my identity did not exist before I came to Volcano, before I stuck to *one* place in my mind and heart and tried to build an identity from there. I leave the diaspora, stepping off the plane at Lyman Field in Hilo, and the blast of warm, subtropical air caresses me like a kiss. I tramp onto the wooden walkway steps, and I see the lower foothills of Mauna Loa rising to thick banks of clouds. I see the dotted stubble of macadamia nut trees far in the distance, feel the roll of the land as it rises away from the passion trees on the plain near the airport and upward, over the lowest flows, through old caneland and the little neighborhoods of Hilo up through the beginnings of the lower rain forest, and I feel the soul in me fall to its knees almost every time.

I recall the story of the Hawaiian youth, sent away by his *ali'i* parents for an education in New England, returning home in a Yankee schooner, who, impatient for reunion, overcome with passion and the flooding emotion of homesickness relieved, strips off his Western clothing—the coat, the collar, the bow tie, the ruffled shirt, his large-buckled shoes—and dives off the deck and into the waters of Lāna'i Harbor, stroking furiously for hundreds of yards just to meet the canoes, full of divers and paddlers who all are relatives, pulling himself over a gunwale, kissing everyone, bowing, weeping into his hands with joy at his own return.

When I first saw the scene, a rendering from a Hollywood movie developed from a commercial writer's novel, I absorbed it uncritically, as merely a story. When I read it in the book, years later, after college, during graduate school, I felt obliged to be scornful. This was a *haole* writer's version, I thought, *romanticized,* completely inauthentic and sentimentalized. Yet, the man who wrote it had lived in the South Pacific longer than

I. He knew stories that held the living of a variety of peoples in them.

Years later, I was returning to Hawai'i to spend a week with biologists from Fish and Wildlife, in an observation station about ten thousand feet up in the national forest on Mauna Kea. I stepped off the plane, and when the full blast of the island's erotic and natal wind hit me, when I caught sight of Mauna Loa's purple slopes disappearing into clouds, a sob of gratitude filled my chest and choked my throat. I wept and felt like falling to my knees in daedal mimicry of my soul's Icarus. I had luggage to retrieve, and I did so, but, I tell you, my heart gave itself over to the roiling cloud of feeling of that moment. I think I gave up detachment. What radiates as knowledge from that time is that there is a beauty in belonging to this earth and to its past, even one locked in mystery and prohibition, unstoried, that exceeds all the passion you can claim for it. The nineteenth-century Hawaiian returning from Harvard knew it. A *haole* novelist knows it. Every singer of every mountain of magnificence in every land knows it. I wish you knowing. I wish you a land.

ACKNOWLEDGMENTS

This book was written largely in solitude—away from community. Yet, communities did sustain me. In Hilo, it was important to have been welcomed by Charlotte and Richard Goya, and Lily and Ben Inouye. In Volcano, I was helped and encouraged by Sue and Rob McGovern, Tommy and Brenda Carson, Richard Hazlett, Tom Wright, James Kauahikaua, Alan Tokunaga, Jane Takahashi, Kazu Okamoto, Thane Pratt, Christina Heliker, Paul Higashino, Jim Jacobi, Jack Jeffrey, Dieter Mueller-Dombois, Lani Stemmermann, Dina Kageler, Robert Notkoff, Robert Stone, William Mull, Michelle Fulton, Fay Hovey, and Wayne Kekuewa. In Honolulu, Leon Edel and Marjorie Sinclair, John Griffin, and Susan Yim extended aloha to me. In Eugene, Myles Brand, Norman K. Wessells, T. R. Hummer, Corrinne Hales, Tracy Daugherty, Chang-rae Lee, Shelly Withrow, and Inez Petersen helped keep faith alive. Mark Jarman and Edward Hirsch phoned me wherever I roamed.

Though Volcano was its own retreat, I also found writerly refuge in other places as well. My thanks to the Bellagio Study Center, the MacDowell Colony, Villa Montalvo, and Yaddo for residencies; to Leonard Michaels for the use of his cabin.

Very real support came by way of grants and fellowships. A Guggenheim Fellowship made a return sojourn to Volcano possible. On two occasions, research grants from the University of Oregon released me from teaching.

Abigail Thomas and Sonny Mehta believed in my project when it was only an idea. Sarah Burnes, Lynn Freed, Christina Heliker, Edward Hirsch, Philip Levine, Sonny Mehta, and Charles Wright read various drafts and provided useful advice. At a critical stage, Cynthia Thiessen gave me the organizing principles that helped shape the book's final structure. Roy Kamada helped check the Hawaiian spellings. I am grateful to all of them.

I owe the life that is the book to Cynthia Thiessen.